Verbal Learning

Verbal Learning

JOHN JUNG

York University
Toronto

Holt, Rinehart and Winston, Inc.

New York   Chicago
San Francisco   Atlanta   Dallas
Montreal   Toronto   London

To My Parents

Copyright © 1968 by Holt, Rinehart and Winston, Inc.
All rights reserved
Library of Congress Catalog Card Number: 68-28178

03–065400–9

Printed in the United States of America

01234 22 9876543

Preface

erbal learning research dates from the earliest years of experimental psychology, beginning with the classic studies on memory by Ebbinghaus in 1885. Since then, the area has continued to be actively studied, so much so in fact that the *Journal of Verbal Learning and Verbal Behavior* was recently established (1962) to aid in publishing current research. Although our knowledge about verbal learning has rapidly increased, there has been no integration of the theory and empirical findings available since a 1952 work by McGeoch and Irion.

The goal of the present book is to provide an overview of the problems, methods, theoretical formulations, and experimental evidence in contemporary verbal learning research. I have attempted to present selected material that is representative of the different central issues in the field rather than to provide comprehensive reviews of the research literature available on various topics.

The content and level of presentation are directed to the advanced undergraduate student who has little or no background in the psychology of learning. The text would be most suitable for use in a course on human learning, or for courses on the general area of learning if combined with a text emphasizing animal learning. It may also be used in courses concerned with such cognitive processes as thinking and problem solving.

Mrs. Sonya Weber Ward, an undergraduate, read the entire manuscript from the viewpoint of a student being introduced to verbal learning. Her careful reading and intelligent questioning were invaluable in pointing out sections that, although clear to me, might be hazy to students.

I wish to thank Professor Rod Wong of the University of British Columbia, Vancouver, who read parts of the manuscript and provided useful criticism. I am especially indebted to Professor Geoffrey Keppel, of the Institute of Human Learning, University of California, Berkeley, for his constructive comments on the entire manuscript and for his kind encouragement.

Finally, I must acknowledge the influence of Professor Benton J. Underwood of Northwestern University, who introduced me to the field of verbal learning. As is true of his other students, I have been impressed not only by his outstanding research and scholarship, but also by his skill and enthusiasm as a teacher.

J. J.

Toronto
August 1968

Contents

Verbal Learning

CHAPTER 1

The Nature
of Learning

T he topic of learning occupies a central position in the field of psychology today. Most aspects of human behavior are affected or modified by the influence of this process. At birth, the human organism is capable of few behavioral processes other than eating and crying. As its experiences increase over time, perceptual discriminations and recognitions are formed. Pleasant and unpleasant associations are acquired with objects, events, and persons in its environment. On a more complex level, the developing child learns to talk, think, and solve problems. By adulthood, the human has learned a vast repertoire of habits and associations which determine and influence virtually all his behavior. It is no wonder that psychologists have devoted so much time and effort to studying learning.

American psychology, since its beginnings in the late nineteenth century, has been highly pragmatic in orientation. Its emphasis on the study of learning recognizes that learning removes limitations of capabilities and enlarges the repertoire of behavior. At the turn of the century, the spirit and optimism of a developing young nation were agreeable to a concern with the nature of learning.

Perhaps another influence which focused attention upon learning at that time was Darwin's theory of evolution, which had been proposed some years earlier. Although it deals with physical modifications of entire species through mechanistic interactions with the environment, evolution is somewhat analogous to the process of learning, which can be viewed as the means by which an individual organism adapts behaviorally to changes in its environment. Change in one aspect or another of the organism occurs through interactions with the environment in both evolution and learning.

Conceptions regarding the nature of learning have been strongly affected by the philosophical views of the British empiricists. These philosophers proposed that all mental experience is directly obtained by means of the senses. They rejected the views held by such men as Kant that the nature and contents of mind were innately determined. Instead, each sensory event was supposed to produce an "idea" in the mind of the experiencing organism. The laws which governed the mosaic of mental composition formed by these sensory impressions were called the *laws of association.* Such laws, which include contrast, similarity, and contiguity of associations in time and space, date from Aristotle. In the eighteenth century they were again advanced by associationistic philosophers such as Locke, Berkeley, and Hume.

Eventually psychology developed as a scientific discipline without introspective and philosophical affiliations. But even then, the associationistic influence could still be discerned in the theoretical formulations of experimental psychology. It influenced thinking in the study not only of sensation and perception but also of higher mental processes such as memory. Although memory is not considered a higher mental process today, in the late 1800s it was the most complex psychological process investigated by experimental means.

Experimental
Approaches

In contrast to philosophical speculation regarding the nature of mind, Ebbinghaus (1885) undertook an objective evaluation of the conditions affecting memory. Using himself as his subject, he memorized literally hundreds of lists of nonsense syllables on which he later tested himself for retention. Ebbinghaus chose nonsense syllables because he thought meaningful words and connected discourse already contained too many associations. He was interested in how associations were formed initially and assumed that nonsense syllables, which are three-letter sequences usually containing a vowel between two consonants, had no inherent associations. The subsequent invalidation of his assumption is not incompatible with his general aim, which was to examine the formation and retention of simple verbal habits rather than to study learning in more complex naturalistic settings. It was hoped that, with experimental methods, the factors which affected the rate and amount of learning and retention could be determined. For example, contrast, similarity, and contiguity—the factors of classical associationism—could be manipulated in experimental tests to ascertain their influence on learning and memory.

Following the lead of Ebbinghaus, other investigators studied learning. The experimental attack on the nature of learning has since been made in a variety of situations and tasks with both animals and humans as subjects. Many of the conclusions obtained with one class of subjects are equally applicable to the other class. However, it is obvious that humans possess higher mental abilities than other organisms. Furthermore, verbal and linguistic abilities are found only in humans, and types of learning tasks discussed in this book involve verbal skills exclusively.

While the types of verbal abilities involved in the tasks considered here are complex when a phylogenetic comparison is made, they are relatively simple by comparison with other human abilities. The term "verbal learning" probably elicits associations with language and meaning and creates confusion about its scope. However, the majority of the research in contemporary verbal learning deals with simple forms of learning. Let us make a distinction between verbal learning and verbal behavior.

Verbal learning deals with the acquisition, retention, and transfer of associations of verbal units formed under controlled laboratory situations. An attempt is made to study "raw" learning under controlled conditions so that the effects of different variables can be assessed. Increasing evidence shows that "raw" learning is difficult to observe since past verbal learning, such as of language habits, may interact with the acquisition and retention of experimental verbal tasks. We may still employ simple laboratory tasks as learning material in order to assess the effects of different variables, but we should no longer ignore the context of pre-experimental habits in which laboratory verbal learning occurs. The major concern in the study of *verbal behavior,* on the other hand, is to examine characteristics of the emission or performance of already learned verbal associations. The line between verbal learning and verbal behavior is arbitrary and not always clear-cut. It roughly corresponds to the distinction made between learning and performance in other learning situations. *Learning* emphasizes the acquisition or formation of associations, whereas *behavior* refers to overt performance of acquired habits.

As mentioned earlier, the analysis of verbal learning in the laboratory deals with simpler aspects of learning than those found in natural situations involving verbal habits. It parallels the approach of the physical sciences in which complex phenomena are tackled by studying segments or parts in controlled but artificial situations. The assumption is made that an understanding of complex phenomena will become possible only through controlled study of their smaller and simpler aspects.

In the case of human learning in natural situations, such as in the classroom, on the athletic field, and in the office, too many uncontrolled variables make it difficult, if not impossible, to identify the factors which affect learning. For example, in school the students of one teacher are noticed to do better on standard tests than those of another. Why is this the case? If we knew the answer, we could take measures to improve the learning of all students. One hypothesis might be that one teacher uses a superior method of teaching. If this were the case, we could determine the nature of that method and make it available to other teachers. However, suppose the students assigned to one teacher just happened to be of higher intelligence than those assigned to the other. This factor alone would produce differences in test scores.

Suppose that the teaching methods of the two teachers actually were different and that the classes were of equal intelligence. What aspects of the two teaching methods are critical and which are irrelevant for better learning? One teacher might give more homework while the other might give more class quizzes. The teachers undoubtedly differ in their organization and selection of material, style of lecture presentation, rapport with the students, and so on. Which one, or combination, of these factors causes the difference in test scores? It is even conceivable that none of the noticed differences between the two teachers is responsible for the differences in scores but that some other unrecognized factor is operating.

This example should serve to illustrate some of the difficulties one faces in drawing conclusions about the factors responsible for observed effects in uncontrolled situations. Experimental methods are needed to determine the causes of observed effects. A laboratory investigation starts with naturalistic observations such as the one described above. Suppose an investigator notes that teachers who give homework have classes which learn better than those which are not given homework. He might hypothesize that the amount of homework determines the amount of learning. In order to rule out alternative factors, a controlled experiment might be performed with two classes which are composed of randomly assigned students. Two comparable teachers are randomly assigned to the classes. On a random basis, one of the classes is selected to be assigned homework and the other not to receive homework. Because the only systematic difference between the two classes is whether or not they receive homework assignments, it is now legitimate to attribute any reliable differences in learning to the variable, homework or no homework. If no differences in learning are evident, we may tentatively discard the homework hypothesis and seek other hypotheses on which to test different factors under controlled conditions.

Our example is oversimplified in order to contrast the types of conclusions that may be reached by natural and by controlled observation. In the example there may be many factors, other than homework, which would affect learning. While it is obvious that experiments are needed to reach conclusions about causal relationships, it is equally obvious that experimentation is only a beginning.

We present an additional example illustrating differences between nonscientific and scientific approaches to the study of learning. Suppose we are concerned with minimizing forgetting. Are some conditions under which learning occurs more effective than others in maintaining memory of what is learned? A student might introspectively arrive at the conclusion that cramming is ineffective for learning, since he recalls that he made better grades than those of a classmate who crammed, whereas the first student studied systematically during the semester. In other terms, he would argue that distributed practice is superior to massed practice. However, we have no way of knowing that the amount of study under the two methods was equal for both students! Nor can we assume that the two students were of equal ability. Perhaps the total time spent studying was greater for the distributed study than for cramming, or the first student was more intelligent than his classmate. Still other alternative explanations may exist.

Rather than rely on the impressions of one student, we might make systematic natural observations of a number of students. Comparing only students who study the same total time, we might compare those who employ long study sessions with those who employ shorter but more frequent study sessions. Again, even if we find differences in learning, there may be alternative explanations to the distribution-of-practice hypothesis. Perhaps, to start with, the students who follow the type of study method associated with better learning are more intelligent or better motivated than those whose learning is less.

In an experimental approach to the problem, we would examine the effects of distribution of practice on learning and retention under conditions which rule out alternative explanations. We might randomly assign subjects to two conditions such that we could assume that learning ability and motivation levels were equal. On a laboratory learning task one group could be given distributed practice, whereas the other group could receive massed practice. Any differences in performance between the two groups would be attributed to the method of practice. The reason for using a laboratory learning task rather than one of learning in an academic course is that control of conditions for the former is easier than for the latter. But while it is more feasible and economical in time and effort to employ laboratory tasks, there does exist the problem of generalizability. Suppose we determine that distributed practice leads to better learning of our laboratory task. Can we safely conclude that learning of algebra, or of experimental psychology, would also benefit from distributed practice? The dilemma is that natural situations are generally too complex to study for obtaining conclusive cause-effect relationships. On the other hand, while laboratory investigations permit the determination of the effects of various factors, the situations are so artificially simplified that the conclusions may not be generalizable to real life! The best we can do is work from the ground up: We determine relationships in the laboratory; then we test their limits of generalizability by applying them to increasingly more complicated situations.

A Definition
of Learning

Now that we have examined the significance of learning and some of the differences between natural and laboratory learning situations, a more explicit definition of learning is in order.

Learning is a process by which the behavior of an organism is modified by experience. It is possible for learning to occur in an organism without an overt performance of the learned habits; however, before we can measure learning there must be observable modifications of some behavior. In other words, learning is a process inferred from examination of differences in some overt performance by an organism at two or more points in time. We assume that the modification of behavior stems from the experiences which occur between the two sets of observations. Without these changes in performance, we are not able to detect what learning, if any, has taken place.

Not all observed changes, however, may be attributed to learning. Other processes—such as maturation, warm-up, and fatigue—leading to changes in observable behavior overtime are not considered to involve learning. One major difference between the nature of changes in behavior due to learning and those due to other factors is the relative permanence of the modifications. We generally view learning as involving relatively permanent changes, whereas we consider warm-up and fatigue as transitory changes. We usually regard practice as another factor influencing the learning process whereas it does not affect maturation. Thus, changes of a permanent nature which are aided by practice are attributed to learning, whereas maturational changes are considered to be independent of practice.

Learning occupies a strong interest among psychologists because so much of man's behavior is affected by this process. The capacity to apply to future situations the experience gained through learning is of great importance to an organism; an individual organism which fails to learn or benefit from experiences tends to repeat past mistakes, whereas one which learns from experience succeeds in its interactions with the environment.

Relationship with Other Processes

In order to understand the process of learning, we need to consider two related processes, forgetting and transfer of training. The three processes are closely interwoven and we might better consider them as concurrent processes rather than distinct phenomena. However, learning, forgetting, and transfer are generally treated separately so that different aspects of the whole learning situation can be emphasized.

When our concern is primarily with improvements in ongoing behavior that result from practice and experience, we refer to the process of *learning*. On the other hand, *forgetting* generally involves decrements in performance of some previously learned behavior over a period during which practice is discontinued. The direction of the changes in learning and forgetting are opposed. Furthermore, these two processes differ in the time that elapses between successive measurements. Experiments concerned with the study of learning typically employ successive measurements within a single test session, whereas those examining forgetting generally involve measurements made after a lapse between test sessions.

The third process, which may affect both learning and forgetting, is *transfer of training*. Obviously each learner already possesses some associative habits when he approaches the new task to be learned. Unless we assume that such habits are passive and inert during the process of the new learning, it is necessary to measure these habits and to examine how they might influence ongoing learning and subsequent forgetting. It is possible that transfer from old verbal habits may either aid or interfere with the new habits to be learned; similarly, once new habits are learned, they might be more readily retained or forgotten depending on the nature of the old habits already present in the learner. In short, analyses of learning and forgetting must take into consideration the interaction of old learning with the new learning. Since virtually all learning involves a transfer situation, it is clear that we cannot understand how new learning occurs without examining the relationship between what has already been learned and what is about to be learned.

In the absence of a detailed record of all the past learning experiences of the learner before he comes to the new task, we can only speculate on the role of the interactions of his past and present learning. What is needed is controlled study, in the laboratory, of transfer training between tasks that bear different relationships to each other. Suppose we want to know the differential effect of past learning on present learning as a function of the degree of similarity between two tasks. We could have one group learn Task A, followed by similar Task B. A second group could learn Task X, which is dissimilar to Task B, before receiving Task B. Comparisons of performance between the two groups on B might then be related to the past experiences (A and X), differing in similarity to B, which are known to have existed for the two groups. Differences in B performance might then be attributed to the relationship of the first and second tasks for the two groups.

We have stressed the interrelationship of learning, retention or forgetting, and transfer. It should be apparent that these three processes are interwoven and can be studied separately only on an arbitrary basis. If sometimes one process is emphasized and the others are ignored, this is done partly for the sake of convenience. While in later chapters we shall analyze the findings with respect to each process, separately, we should keep in mind the interrelatedness of these processes.

SUMMARY

In this book, we will be concerned with a presentation of selected aspects of the findings, methods, and phenomena of verbal learning. This area of research, initiated by Ebbinghaus, has traditionally emphasized associative determinants of learning. Lists of nonsense syllables and words are used in tasks which allow a determination of variables which affect acquisition, retention, and transfer.

An implicit assumption in much verbal learning research is that "raw" learning is being observed. However, recent evidence and formulations emphasize the interaction or transfer between preexperimental verbal habits and the acquisition and retention of laboratory associations. At the same time, greater interest in the role of cognitive processes is developing. The orientation of the present work is toward an analysis of this transfer arrangement and the operation of past learning for an understanding of verbal learning and memory.

CHAPTER 2   The Learner

We shall first examine some conceptions of the nature of the learner himself before proceeding to an analysis of specific learning situations and factors affecting the learning process. For the sake of convenience, no distinction will be made concerning individual differences in learning as a function of intelligence, age, sex, motivation, or the like. While it is obvious that individuals differ in their ability to learn, it is also reasonable to assume that there are certain similarities in the basic process of learning which are invariant across individuals. Following the latter assumption, we shall consider the nature of the learner in general.

Associationist View

Traditionally, the associationist has considered the organism to be a *tabula rasa* at birth. On this blank tablet will be etched traces of associations that result from the direct experiences of the organism; each sensory event will produce its record, creating a mosaic of associations. By the time the organism becomes a college sophomore (suitable for participation in psychology experiments), he has formed a considerable backlog of past associations.

However, until recently the experimenters who studied human learning tended to overlook, in their approach, the fact that the college sophomore who served in their experiments possessed an enormous storehouse of preexperimental verbal habits. To be more accurate, although investigators knew that the learners had previous associations, they did not realize to what extent such preexperimental habits might affect the acquisition and retention of laboratory associations. Therefore, in the learning experiment the adult learner was treated as if he were a *tabula rasa*.

Cognitivist View

On the other hand, the traditional cognitivist insists that the learner thinks, devises and employs strategies, and develops cognitive structures in the course of learning. Certainly, the reader is apt to find the cognitivist view more appealing!

Instead of regarding learning as a passive process wherein events occur in the presence of the learner and simply leave a record of their occurrence, the cognitivist considers that learning involves active participation by the learner. The learner does not simply form associations; instead he perceives patterns and relationships. Cognitive learning involves insight into and learning of principles, not the rote memorization of isolated elements of a total task.

Much heat and controversy over the nature of learning have been generated between theorists of these rival orientations. Yet no one position has been able to demonstrate convincingly that its theoretical orientation is *the* correct view, while the other is an incorrect one. Could it be that each view is correct, each within certain limited domains? Perhaps some learning situations are typified by rote learning of simple associations of elements, whereas other tasks involve insight, strategies, and the learning of principles. Or perhaps the type of learning observed in a given situation is a function of the past knowledge of the individual learner. Thus, in the same learning situation some individuals may exhibit rote-like learning while other learners display insightful, cognitive-like performance. In other words, it is possible that learning is both rote and cognitive, depending on both the nature of the task and the past experiences of the individual learner. Many contemporary investigators cannot be classified as associationists or cognitivists in the traditional sense but seem to represent a combination of aspects of the two opposed positions. Other investigators disregard such theoretical issues and emphasize the study of empirical aspects of learning.

Aspects of Learning Tasks

Many learning tasks classified as rote learning situations deliberately utilize nonsense syllables or relatively unrelated words with which the subject has had a minimum of familiarity. The material to be learned is presented to the learner on an apparatus called a memory drum at a very rapid rate, usually 2 seconds per item. One reason for such a short exposure is that it does not allow some learners to get practice, in effect, by rehearsing during the presentation of each item. Such individuals might then have an advantage over those who did not rehearse material. In effect, the learner is restricted in relating his past learning to the present learning. He is "forced" to form the new associations required in the task, with a minimum of aid from both his past techniques or strategies of learning and his previous knowledge and associations.

On the other hand, suppose the learning material involved lists of related words. For example, each of the words in a long list might belong to one of a limited number of categories. Thus, Bousfield (1953) employed lists of sixty words which contained fifteen words from each of four categories: animals, vegetables, professions, and male names. A list of these words was presented to subjects once in a random order at a rate of about one word per second. The task of the learner was to recall as many of the words presented as he could, in any order. In a task such as this one, the learner would be able to apply his past learning, that is, to think. By noting that all the words in the list belong to one of four classes or categories, he might restrict his recall within these categories. Recall of one item in a category might aid in searching for other items from the same category. His pattern of recall might reflect the fact that the subgroups of words in the list are related, as indicated by the finding that sequences or clusters of items from a given category tend to be recalled together. In short, this task permits the application of certain past learning to the present task; hence, it appears that the performance is cognitive.

We have just seen how some tasks involve rote learning while others permit cognitive learning. However, depending on the past learning of the individual learner himself, it is conceivable that one can observe either type of learning in either situation. When a learner uses mnemonic devices or memory aids in a situation considered rote in nature, he is actually displaying cognitive learning; because of particular past experience, he is able to see some relationship between the task to be learned and some past learning of his own.

Similarly, a learner in the situation with categorized lists who failed to notice that categorization would probably fail to display cognitive or insightful learning. No organization such as clustering would appear in his pattern of recall if the learner himself did not notice the structure of the lists or devise a suitable alternative organization of the items.

In summary, conclusions about the nature of the learner are tied to the nature of the task from which the inferences are being drawn and to the nature of the learner's past associations. Even in the laboratory situation, the learner possesses and may employ a vast repertoire of learning techniques and acquired associations or knowledge. The extent to which he does use them so that we may infer them from his performance depends on the nature of the task. If we fail to recognize that fact, we could easily be misled into generalizing the conclusions obtained from one type of learning situation to all learning tasks.

Underwood (1964b) has noted that a particular learning task represents a mold which limits the learner to specific processes whereas other tasks may require different processes. As a result, the conclusions made about the nature of learning may be limited to the particular task involved. Use of a few standard tasks has the advantage of permitting an accumulation of facts regarding learning in those specific situations. Because such facts may not apply to other tasks, it is important that we devise and study other tasks to test the generalizability of findings with standard or traditional tasks.

Cognitive Factors
in Associative Situations

There is increasing evidence that no laboratory learning task involves pure rote associationistic learning. Nonassociationistic or cognitive factors play a role in any task.

In the typical rote learning task, the subject is provided with a list of nonsense syllables or unrelated words which he is to memorize according to certain procedures selected by the experimenter. However, the process by which this formation of new associations is made in the laboratory is not a passive one in which material is simply repeated over and over again until it is drilled in. Instead, the learner plays an active part by relating his past associative learning to the new learning material being presented to him.

Stimulus Selection In some tasks, the learner must associate pairs of items. When one item of each pair is presented by the experimenter, the subject's task is to respond with the other member. This member is termed the *response*, whereas the one presented by the experimenter is called the *stimulus*. In forming these associations, cognitive operations may occur, especially with respect to the stimulus members. For example, if the stimuli are highly similar, that is, look alike, sound alike, or have similar meanings, it may be difficult for the learner to differentiate among them. In order to improve the discriminability among the stimuli so that he may associate the appropriate response with its stimulus, some mode of transforming the stimuli may be used by the subject.

One strategy the learner may employ involves selecting a portion of each stimulus to attend to, rather than attempting to learn the entire stimulus, since he does not need to respond overtly with the stimuli. Any strategy which enhances the discriminability of the stimuli, such as stimulus selection, may be successfully adopted by the subject. Stimulus selection emphasizes a distinction between *nominal* and *functional* stimuli.

Weiss and Margolius (1954) performed an experiment which illustrates this distinction in rote learning. The *nominal* stimulus refers to the objective, experimenter-defined stimulus whereas the *functional* stimulus refers to the one utilized by the learner, which may or may not be the same as the nominal stimulus. Compound or hyphenated nonsense syllable stimuli were paired with word reponses. Each of nine such pairs was presented on a different color card; thus, each stimulus consisted of a compound nonsense syllable and a color cue. Retention was measured after 24 hours under several different conditions. One group received stimuli identical to those from the original list; one group received as stimuli the original nonsense syllables placed on gray cards; and one group was presented, as stimuli, only the different colored cards without the nonsense syllables. Retention was highest with the original compound stimuli. When only one of the two components was presented, the color cue alone was more effective than the nonsense syllable cue alone. We should point out that the relative effectiveness of the color and syllable cues may depend on the difficulty of the syllables. With stimuli containing words rather than nonsense syllables in combination with color components, it may be that the color cues would be less efficient.

Underwood, Ham, and Ekstrand (1962) repeated the Weiss and Margolius study, employing trigrams of high difficulty in combination with a color background to serve as compound stimuli for single-digit responses. After learning the list, three groups were given different second lists. One group continued to learn with the original compound items, one received only the trigram components as stimuli, and one group received only the color cues. Performance was equal for the group with the original stimuli and the one with only the color cues; the trigram cue group performed most poorly. Underwood *et al.* concluded that during learning, the subjects utilized the color cues as stimuli primarily and ignored the more difficult trigram component, since the group which was tested with only the color cues was able to do as well as the group which had both color and verbal cues.

Response Encoding Unlike the stimulus terms, the response terms not only must be differentiated but also must be accessible or available for overt responding. *Availability* refers to a condition such that an item can be reproduced rather than merely recognized. One factor affecting response availability is the material itself, words, for example, being more available than nonsense syllables. Presumably, this reflects differences in preexperimental associative characteristics of different materials. In addition, availability of the response terms may be enhanced by associative factors within the experiment, such as the number of times each item is presented or the similarity among the total set of items.

Words are readily available in recall on the basis of preexperimental frequency of experience. The learner may increase the availability of nonsense syllable response terms, such as DAP or HOS, by transforming them into other forms, such as DAPper and HOSpital. This process of associating nonsense syllables to familiar words might aid the learner in storing the responses, although when the responses must be elicited overtly, he would have to decode the transformations correctly. In this example he must give only the first three letters of the transformations as his responses. If a more difficult syllable, such as STM, were presented, the learner might transform it into "Short Term Memory," but again he would have to remember how to decode his transformation when called upon to respond overtly with the exact original trigram response.

Any transformation of an item which makes it more meaningful to the learner should enhance its availability as a response. Underwood and Keppel (1962a) and Underwood and Erlebacher (1965) examined the role of encoding on free recall of certain trigrams, each of which formed two meaningful words if the letters in the original trigram were properly rearranged. For example, BSU is a trigram which may be transformed to either of two more meaningful and better integrated units, SUB or BUS. The investigators used a list of such transformable trigrams for a series of alternate study and test trials. In some conditions recall of each trigram with its letters in exactly the same order as it was presented, for example, BSU, was required. Underwood and Keppel hypothesized that subjects who noticed or who were informed of encoding possibilities might transform the trigrams into their more meaningful arrangements to aid their memory. However, on the test trials, they would have to decode each stored unit back into its less meaningful trigram version. Performance was poorer for this condition than for another which allowed learners to recall each trigram with its letters in any arrangement. In addition, conditions in which subjects were required to recall trigrams in their original arrangement were altered, after differing numbers of trials, so that subjects were allowed to recall items with their letters in any arrangement. Performance improved markedly after this switch in requirements. Prior to the switch, any encoded items would have to be decoded on the test trials; following the switch, decoding was no longer required and thus performance improved, as shown in Figure 2.1. Underwood and Keppel concluded that encoding aided subjects as long as recall could be given with the letters of each trigram in any order. If coding were used, interference might occur when recall of trigrams was required with letters in the same order as originally presented. Of course, most learning situations do require responses to be recalled verbatim. Does this contradict the notion that encoding helps? The experiment

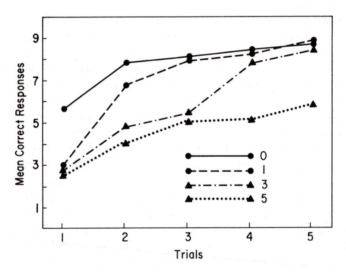

Figure 2.1. Acquisition curves for all groups. Group 0 could write the letters in any order on all trials, Group 1 only after the first trial, Group 3 only after the third trial, and Group 5 was always required to write the letters in the order presented. Responses were counted correct only if they conformed to the instructions prevailing on a given trial. [From B. J. Underwood and G. Keppel: Coding processes in verbal learning. *Journal of Verbal Learning and Verbal Behavior,* 1962, **1,** 250–257. Reprinted by permission of Academic Press, Inc., and the authors.]

done by Underwood and Keppel involved encoded forms which necessarily are incompatible with decoded or original items, since the same letters are involved in both forms. In other cases, encoding may be more universally beneficial. For example, BSU might be encoded as "Boston Seminary Union," which can more easily be decoded, thereby aiding recall.

Thus it appears that differentiation of stimuli and the attainment of response availability may be facilitated by various techniques which relate prior learning to the new learning. In addition, the learning of the association between each stimulus and its response may also be affected by past experience. From his previous learning, the learner possesses innumerable other associations to both the stimulus and the response members of each pair to be associated. While some of these past associations may aid, others may hinder the formation of the new association.

Mediation Suppose the learner has some strong past associations to the stimulus which are identical to some he has for the response term. For example, one pair in the list might be *black–light*. Most learners have a strong association, *dark*, to both *black* and *light*. The existence of such strong common associations as *dark* may aid the learner in forming a new association between *black* and *light* as follows: *black–dark–light*. This process of utilizing other associations to facilitate the acquisition of new associations is *mediation*. Mediation may be viewed as a process based on past common associations or as an active strategy or learning technique employed by the learner to improve his performance.

James Mill, the British philosopher of the early nineteenth century, long ago employed the mechanism of associative aids in answering the question of how we remember. He concluded,

> All men invariably employ the same expedient. They endeavor to form an association between the idea of the thing to be remembered, and some sensation, or some idea, which they know beforehand will occur at or near the time when they wish the remembrance to be in their minds.

The role of mediators in learning can be examined by providing assumed mediators to subjects in an experiment. Dallett (1964a) compared learning in groups provided with relevant mediators, irrelevant mediators, or no mediators. Consider the pair, BAC–EGGS, from Dallett's list of materials. Figure 2.2 suggests that a number of associations may be assumed to exist from past experience for most individuals. Among the many associations to the stimulus BAC are the words, *back* and *bacon*. For one group, the word BACON was presented following BAC and

Stimulus – (associative hierarchy) – – – – Response

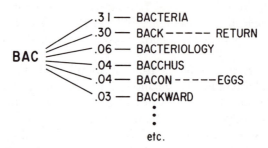

BAC

.31 — BACTERIA
.30 — BACK – – – – – RETURN
.06 — BACTERIOLOGY
.04 — BACCHUS
.04 — BACON – – – – –EGGS
.03 — BACKWARD

etc.

Figure 2.2. Conceptual model of a paired-associate item, including the stimulus, its associative hierarchy, and two possible response words. [From K. M. Dallett: Implicit mediators in paired-associate learning. *Journal of Verbal Learning and Verbal Behavior,* 1964, 3, 209–214. Reprinted by permission of Academic Press, Inc., and the author.]

preceding EGGS. It was assumed that BACON might act as a relevant mediator and aid learning. A second group received BACK between BAC and EGGS as an irrelevant mediator which might hinder learning. A third group received no mediator from the experimenter. The three conditions were repeated in such a way—by pairing BAC with the word RETURN instead of EGGS—that BACK was relevant and BACON was irrelevant. Thus, each mediator word was relevant for half the subjects and irrelevant for the other half.

Using a list of twelve pairs, Dallett found that learning was equal in the relevant-mediator and no-mediator control conditions, but both were superior to the irrelevant-mediator condition. He concluded that the no-mediator group was able to perform as well as the relevant-mediator group because subjects probably devised their own mediators, which, of course, would be highly relevant.

Montague, Adams, and Kiess (1966) have also examined the role of mediators. However, unlike Dallett who inferred the nature of the mediators from association norms, Montague *et al.* had their subjects devise their own mediators, which these investigators termed *natural language mediators.* During the first phase of the study, subjects were asked to respond with any natural language mediator, such as a word or a phrase they could devise, for each of several pairs of nonsense syllables. A day later, the stimulus terms of each pair were presented, and the subjects had to recall both the mediator they had devised and the response term for each stimulus.

Montague *et al.* found that response recall was high for pairs for which the subjects also recalled original or similar mediators, but low for pairs where either they had forgotten mediators or the reported mediators were dissimilar from the original ones. One interpretation of these findings is that the presence of self-generated mediators at recall favors performance. It is possible, of course, that items for which mediators can be readily generated and remembered by subjects are easier than those lacking this property. The correlation between recall and the amount of recalled mediators does not prove that mediators produce the higher recall; it may simply reflect the fact that easier items also possess stronger mediators.

The technique used by Montague *et al.*, however, can certainly be useful in determining more precisely what mediators are used by individual subjects than the procedure employed by Dallett based on norms. But whereas the former method is inconclusive as to the effect of mediators on learning and recall, one can answer this question with the latter method, where the experimenter rather than the material controls the degree of mediation present. In either situation, however, it would seem that the more associates elicited by the items of each pair, the more likely it is that mediational processes will occur to aid the learning of that pair. This prediction is based on the associative probability theory of Underwood and Schulz (1960). It is similar to William James' (1890) account of the role of associates in memory, which stated,

> In mental terms, the more other facts a fact is associated with in the mind, the better possession of it our memory retains. Each of its associates becomes a hook to which it hangs, a means to fish it up by when sunk beneath the surface.

We should add that Underwood and Schulz (p. 46) noted that the associative probability theory contained an interference paradox. Not only could associative learning be facilitated as the number of associates increased, but also there could develop greater interference from this greater number of associates. They hypothesized that the positive effects might be greater than the negative ones, thus permitting learning to improve as the number of associates increased.

Similarly, James was also concerned with situations where many associates existed. He wrote,

> We *recognize* but do not *remember* it—its associates form too confused a cloud. . . . There are cases where too many paths, leading to too diverse associates, block each other's way, and all that the mind gets along with its object is a fringe of felt familiarity or sense that there *are* associates.

The preceding evidence on mediation is concerned with the role of pre-experimental associations on the acquisition of a single list. In a later chapter we will describe studies of mediation in which associations are assumed to interact from several lists learned within the experimental setting.

To summarize, in forming a new association the learner has recourse to aid from past learning. By transforming stimuli as well as responses with the aid of past learning, and by mediating between stimuli and responses with past associations, the subject is able to acquire the new learning. The simple principles of associative learning—such as frequency, contiguity, and similarity—undoubtedly still operate, but they are accompanied by nonassociative factors as well. The typical rote learning situation has tended to minimize the operation of nonassociative factors in preference of a study of the former factors. Given a chance to operate, the cognitive factors may be more powerful than the associative ones in many situations.

Associative Learning
in Cognitive Situations

We have just seen the importance of such nonassociative, or cognitive, factors as stimulus selection, response encoding, and mediation in typical rote learning situations where associative formulations of learning are dominant.

The operation of cognitive learning involving insight, learning of principles, use of strategies and organization, and the like, is much more apparent in concept learning and concept identification tasks. Consider the list of pairs of names and numbers in the left column below. A careful inspection should disclose that the four names associated with each number have some feature in common which is not shared with the four names paired with the other number. All names paired with 1 are masculine names, whereas all names paired with 2 are feminine names. An alternative method of classification, shown in the right-hand column, is based on the number of syllables in each name, those with one syllable being paired with 1 and those with two syllables being paired with 2. In both cases there is a principle, or logical basis, for assigning one number to four of the names and another number to the other four names. An insightful learner will readily discover this relationship, and he will be able to remember the number associated with each name easily by applying the principle. Furthermore, given a new name he can assign it a number consistent with the classification rule governing the pairings given on the next page.

Bob	1		Bob	1
Richard	1		Richard	2
Billy	1		Billy	2
George	1		George	1
Jane	2		Jane	1
Mary	2		Mary	2
Sue	2		Sue	1
Betty	2		Betty	2

Suppose, on the other hand, that the following pairings of four names to each number were to be learned.

Bob	2
Richard	2
Billy	1
George	1
Jane	2
Mary	2
Sue	1
Betty	1

In this instance, where no principle is involved in forming the pairings, it would not be surprising if the learner failed to show principle or concept learning. Association of the names and numbers would be forced to occur in a more rote-like fashion, possibly modified by some nonassociative factors, as demonstrated earlier.

However, we should not suppose that learning is entirely cognitive, even in the two examples where the sets of pairings involved principles among the items. It is still necessary to learn or associate the specific pairings before the operation of cognitive processes, such as discovering a principle, can occur. If the learner forgets from one moment to the next which number is paired with which name, he will not be able to notice that all names paired with one number are of one class while those names paired with the other number are of another class. Such forgetting might occur readily if the pairs are presented successively, as in the typical experiment, rather than in a simultaneous display as done here.

It is of course conceivable that a learner may fail to notice the principle, when one is involved in the classification, and learn all the pairings by rote. However, it does not appear that cognitive learning can occur unless associative learning of the pairings themselves precedes it.

Motivation and Learning

Most persons would contend that motivation is essential for learning to occur. A student is often heard to explain his low grade in a course by citing his lack of motivation. Teachers attempt to "get their students motivated" so that learning will occur. This point of view argues that motivation is necessary for learning; it does not follow, of course, that learning will automatically occur, even if high motivation is present.

The level of motivation needed for learning is assumed to be maintained by the attainment of reinforcement for performance on the learning task. *Reinforcement* is loosely defined here as the stimulus conditions, such as praise, food, money, and sense of accomplishment, which are obtained by the learner as his performance improves. Some definitions of reinforcement involve speculation about the mechanisms by which reinforcement operates. For example, if a hungry rat turns left in a maze and receives food there, it may be said to have been reinforced for left-turning responses or for going to the left side. The food would be considered effective as a reinforcer because it reduced the hunger drive of the organism. Other definitions of reinforcement are merely descriptive; they simply state that conditions which increase the probability of given behaviors recurring are termed reinforcers, but they make no attempt to explain why or how.

Reinforcement is an important construct in learning theory, although some learning theories deny that it plays a role in the actual learning process; in this book reinforcement will rarely be mentioned. Although the role of motivation and reinforcement is of central importance in studies of learning in animals, it has been of surprisingly little direct interest among students of verbal learning. In studies employing animals, it is virtually essential to deprive subjects of primary needs, such as food, in order to obtain any overt behavior in the test situation. Such is obviously not the case with human subjects, for whom verbal instructions are generally sufficient to obtain cooperation on the experimental task. The person who consents or volunteers to serve in an experiment is generally highly motivated and eager to achieve a high performance to please either the experimenter or himself or both. Thus, the intrinsic level of motivation of subjects in verbal learning experiments is sufficient to guarantee some learning. Achievement in an experiment is a reward in itself. The level of motivation can be considered sufficiently high so that it is difficult to manipulate it by experimental treatments such as instructional variations.

Incidental Learning One exception to the foregoing statement is incidental learning. In this situation, no explicit instructions are provided to the subject to the effect that a subsequent test of learning will be administered. Instead, the instructions given to the subject mislead him into believing the task is unrelated to learning.

A comparison of the performance under these instructions with that under explicit instructions to learn generally discloses superior learning when learning is "intentional" (for example, Postman and Senders, 1946).

This paradigm, in which one group is instructed to learn and another group is not instructed to learn, is referred to as Type I incidental learning (Kausler and Trapp, 1960; McLaughlin, 1965; Postman, 1964a). It is typical to provide a cover task for incidental learning subjects so that they will not attempt to memorize the material. They may be instructed to rate the material for ease of pronunciability or esthetic appeal, or to produce associations to the items, so that they will not think a test of learning is involved.

A second situation, Type II incidental learning, compares the two types of learning within the same group of subjects. The learning of one task is explicitly called for by the instructions but, during the training period, the subject is also exposed to other cues or material which he is not instructed to learn. However, on the subsequent test, he is tested for his learning of these latter aspects of the material. For example, he might be told to learn a list of nonsense syllables but later be tested for incidental learning of the different colors in which the syllables are printed.

It is possible that incidental learning occurs in this latter paradigm as a consequence of a generalized tendency to learn that stems from the intentional learning component involved in this task. At the same time, however, there exists the possibility that the portion of the task in which intentional learning is involved may interfere with the acquisition of the learning which is assumed to occur incidentally. The brief time allotted for study may not be great enough to allow both intentional and incidental learning to occur. However, evidence is available to show that intentional learning is superior to the amount of incidental learning under Type II paradigms (for example, Kausler, Trapp, and Brewer, 1959).

The results showing superior intentional learning in both paradigms I and II could be interpreted as demonstrations of the effects of motivation on learning. We are here equating intentional learning instructions with levels of motivation higher than those which accompany incidental learning instructions with regard to the material to be tested. We should add that incidental learning subjects should be motivated to perform well on the irrelevant task. However, if we restrict our attention to the relevant task, we could attribute the better performance of the intentional condition to its higher motivation. Intentional instructions specify to the subject what he will be tested on and thus guide and direct his behavior toward the relevant goal. In similar fashion, motivational states, in general, lead to behavior appropriate to the attainment of specific goals.

Motivation to learn, like intent to learn, probably operates via attentional processes. When motivation is low or intent is absent, the cues relevant to the task are not well attended, so that when a test for learning is administered the performance obtained is low. As motivation or intent is increased, attention is directed toward the appropriate stimuli involved on the learning test, and performance improves.

However, there may be a limit to the benefits of increased motivation on learning. According to one theory (Spence, 1958), the effects of drive or motivation level on behavior vary as a function of the task difficulty. At extremely high levels of motivation, learning improves only if the material is simple. When the material is difficult and susceptible to interference, performance begins to deteriorate as higher levels of motivation are encountered. Some support of this theory has been given by studies of individual differences in which anxious subjects do better than non-anxious ones on easy tasks but not on difficult ones (Spence, Farber, and McFann, 1956; Standish and Champion, 1960). In these studies, anxiety level is considered to reflect motivational states.

Superior learning under intentional learning is not attributed to intent itself. Postman (1964a) suggests also that intentional instructions promote higher learning because they generally direct the subject's attention to the material relevant to the subsequent test better than do incidental learning instructions. In cases where the intentional and incidental instructions ensure equal attention to test relevant cues, it has been reported by Mechanic (1964) that there is no difference between learning under intentional and incidental instructions.

Mechanic manipulated the nature of the orienting task for intentional and incidental learning. He hypothesized that the factor responsible for differences between intentional and incidental learning is the orienting task involved. For intentional learners, a high degree of pronouncing responses to the material is assumed to occur, whereas less active attention is given to the material by incidental learners. Pronouncing is more likely to ensure that the subject is attending the materials than would mere inspection of the materials. By instructing incidental learners to pronounce the material at a fast rate for purposes ostensibly unrelated to learning, Mechanic found equal amounts of incidental and intentional learning.

Four groups were tested under all combinations of the two types of learning and two types of orienting tasks. In the high pronouncing task, both intentional and incidental groups were instructed to pronounce each item over and over for about 11 seconds before the next item appeared. They were told that the effects of fatigue and practice on pronunciation were being studied. In the low pronouncing task, intentional and incidental groups were told that the task involved extrasensory perception. They were to study each item and guess what number (between 0 and 99) had been previously assigned to it. A list of twenty-four trigrams was employed for a single trial.

Both intentional groups were told that the experimenter was also interested in how well they could learn the items and that they would be tested later. The incidental groups were not informed of such a future test. Immediately after the orienting task, a 5-minute test of free recall was administered. A comparison of performance under the different instructions regarding learning showed significant superiority of intentional learning when a low pronouncing orientation task was employed. However, incidental and intentional learning were equal under a high pronouncing orientation task. In addition, all groups in the high pronouncing task performed higher than those in the low pronouncing task.

These findings support the view that instructions, per se, or intent to learn do not produce the differences generally found in favor of intentional learning. Instead, the responses elicited by such instructions to learn, which can also be obtained by other means such as Mechanic's orienting task involving high pronouncing, appear to be responsible for the superior learning. Such responses probably maximize the subject's attention to the material and thus facilitate the learning of the material.

Arousal and Learning   Another exception to the observation that motivation is seldom manipulated in verbal learning studies is the work of Kleinsmith and Kaplan (1964), who examined the effects of arousal level on immediate and delayed recall of nonsense syllables. *Arousal level* is a motivational concept emphasizing that such physiological measures as galvanic skin resistance (GSR) underlie levels of psychological motivation.

Kleinsmith and Kaplan presented six nonsense syllables to subjects and recorded their GSRs to each syllable; differences in physiological responses were obtained from the syllables. Perhaps associations evoked by each syllable created different arousal levels in each subject. The examiners arbitrarily decided to term syllables producing the three highest GSRs "high arousal" and the syllables with the lowest three GSRs "low arousal" syllables for each subject. At the same time, each syllable was paired with a single digit and memorized by subjects who were tested after either 2 minutes, 20 minutes, or 1 week. On the test, the subject was shown each digit and asked to recall the nonsense syllable which had been paired with it.

Kleinsmith and Kaplan hypothesized that the low arousal syllables would be better recalled immediately than the high arousal syllables, since arousal is disruptive and prevents recall. However, they assumed that strong arousal at the time of learning would eventually lead to more permanent neural traces, so that recall after one week would be higher for items which produced higher arousal. Thus, an interaction was predicted between arousal level and recall interval. The results, shown in

Figure 2.3, confirmed their prediction. Similar results have been obtained by Walker and Tarte (1963).

Weiner and Walker (1966) examined motivational factors by varying the incentive for correct responses. Four incentive conditions were employed, and recall was tested after about 5 seconds or 15 seconds. If a response was correct, it resulted in 1¢ in one condition, 5¢ in a second condition, and nothing in a third condition. A fourth condition involved

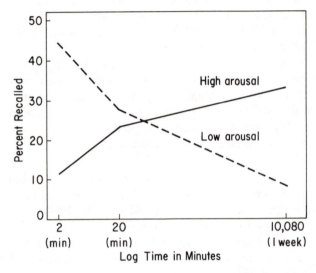

Figure 2.3. Differential recall of nonsense syllable paired associates as a function of arousal level. [From L. J. Kleinsmith and S. Kaplan: Interaction of arousal and recall interval in nonsense syllable paired-associate learning. *Journal of Experimental Psychology*, 1964, **67**, 124–126. Reprinted by permission of the American Psychological Association and the authors.]

shock for incorrect responses but nothing for correct responses. The results indicated that the different incentives had no effect for the short interval. However, with the long interval, the shock and the 5¢ reward conditions were both superior in recall to the 1¢ or no reward conditions. Thus, the amount of incentive was found to affect the amount of learning, but only at one of the two recall intervals.

These findings were explained in a manner similar to the account given by Kleinsmith and Kaplan (1964) for their data. The incentives differed in the arousal level involved, with the shock and 5¢ reward being high, and 1¢ or no reward being low, in arousal. Although the results of the two studies are not in accord for immediate retention, it does appear that high arousal at the time of learning is superior at longer retention intervals. Both studies support the hypothesis that high motivation or arousal may be inhibitory on immediate retention, since the traces interfere with each other, but facilitory on delayed retention, possibly due to the consolidation of neural traces over longer time periods.

The original observation that motivation is seldom varied in verbal learning still is valid. Since intentional instructions to learn are such strong motivators, it may not be possible to manipulate widely the level of motivation in verbal learning. However, there may be individual differences in motivational states among subjects which affect level of learning, but these are personality variables beyond the manipulations of the investigator. Our treatment of the tasks and variables involved in verbal learning will not give further consideration to motivational factors.

SUMMARY

The performance of the learner sometimes appears rote and associationistic, and at other times it appears cognitive and insightful. Rather than argue that all learning is of one variety, we maintain that both types occur under appropriate situations. Different conditions determine which type of learning can occur.

First we must consider the nature of the task, since it is a restricting factor on the types of behavior the learner may display. Associationistic learning dominates in rote tasks although it may be modified by stimulus selection, mediational processes, and response encoding. In concept learning, cognitive learning is prevalent although it also involves learning of a rote nature.

The stage of practice involved may affect the type of processes. Associationistic rote learning may be typical during early stages of practice. If the nature of the task involves a principle or logical classification system, cognitive-like behavior may occur at later stages of practice following the earlier rote stage.

We shall propose a schematic of a learner as he confronts a learning task. In most situations, the amount of material presented to the learner exceeds his limited intake capacity. This condition is deliberately imposed on the learner by the experimenter, who wants to be able to measure *changes* in performance. If the material falls within the limited intake capacity, the learner will be able to perform perfectly in "one trial" or presentation, thus preventing the experimenter from observing any changes which are necessary for inferring learning. "Overloading" the learner makes possible many trials or observations, and the course of learning may be measured and the variables affecting it can be determined.

Furthermore, not only may the intake be limited but there may be a priority of intake. It is as if a selective filter were present at the point of intake, screening the material that can enter. Aside from such factors as fluctuations in attention, the factors which govern the priority of intake are the past habits and associations already formed by the learner. Thus, the existing associations interact with the present materials to be learned, sometimes facilitating and sometimes interfering.

The materials to be learned require new associations, since the experimenter wants to see how new learning occurs. However, by stimulus selection, mediation, and response encoding the learner may relate his existing habits to the new ones to aid in their acquisition. If the new and old sets of associations are incompatible, learning will be difficult.

Since the preexperimental habits may differ widely from individual to individual, we may expect such interactions of old and new learning to lead to different results for different learners. A person trying to learn French may find it easy if he has studied Spanish, but someone who has learned to drive in England may have difficulty in driving in the United States. In any event, the need for the study of the interaction of past and present learning should be clear.

Finally, we should note that concepts which are central in animal learning situations, such as reinforcement and motivation, are rarely considered in verbal learning studies. Whereas usually animals must be deprived of primary needs before they will respond and must have such needs fulfilled as reinforcements when the correct responses are made, most human subjects find feedback concerning their level of performance to be more than adequate motivation for learning.

CHAPTER 3

Acquisition:
Major Variables
and Tasks

W e have already noted that the study of new learning must take into consideration the role of the past learning that has taken place throughout the subject's lifetime. Also, it is likely that the performance of a laboratory task may be facilitated or impeded by interactions with prior verbal habits acquired by the subjects outside the laboratory. While it is important that such habits be assessed, obviously it would be impossible to identify every past verbal association possessed by subjects. It would also be difficult to measure with much precision the strengths of such habits. Despite these difficulties, some approximate measures of the nature of the linguistic repertoire of the typical subject have been made.

By measuring some characteristics of an individual's present verbal behavior, we may infer the nature of that individual's past verbal learning. Some form of association test is commonly employed to induce subjects to display verbal behavior. A verbal unit such as a single letter, nonsense syllable, or word is presented to subjects, who are instructed to respond with the first association that comes to mind. Usually, responses are restricted to those of the same type as the stimulus word. In this manner we may obtain frequency distributions of the responses to a number of stimuli to show the type or strength of verbal associations already possessed by subjects at the time laboratory learning is initiated. Another approach is based on ratings of verbal materials as to the number of past associations, or as to the number of subjects who have associations, to each stimulus. Here the emphasis is on measuring characteristics of the stimuli as a function of past learning. No concern exists for measuring the specific association; the goal is to measure the quantity of past associations. Still another approach involves tabulating the frequencies of occurrence of verbal units in the natural language; stronger habits should occur more frequently in the natural language usage.

Characteristics of
Nonsense Syllables

When Ebbinghaus hit upon the idea of using combinations of three letters (with a vowel between two consonants) he assumed that such nonsense syllables were the basic elements of language. These materials, he thought, avoided the problems of past learning and meaning which were present with words and sentences.

Since the time of Ebbinghaus, psychologists have recognized the fact that while nonsense syllables have no specific meaning as words do, nonetheless they do possess associated meanings in varying degrees. Nonsense syllables may remind the learner of meaningful associations for one reason or another; such associations have been formed over the lifetime of the individual. Since past associations are assumed to affect learning, one goal of experimenters has been the assessment of the association values of nonsense syllables and other laboratory learning materials, such as trigrams and paralogs. Trigrams are nonsense syllables, that is, a trigram is any three-letter combination which does not form a word. Paralogs or dissyllables are verbal units containing two syllables and range from meaningless units to actual words.

An early scale of association value of nonsense syllables was devised by Glaze (1928). Although his use of a small sample of subjects has been criticized, his scale has been widely used. Fifteen subjects rated a set of over 2000 nonsense syllables according to whether or not they had an available association for each syllable within 2 or 3 seconds; it was not necessary for them to produce their associations. A determination of the *percentage* of subjects who reported having associations to each syllable was made, and this represented the association value for that syllable. No consideration was given to the *number* of associations elicited by each syllable. Later scalings (Hull, 1933; Krueger, 1934; Witmer, 1935) employed different methods, but the scale values for syllables common to different investigations have been found to correlate highly (Underwood and Schulz, 1960).

Some examples of more recent measurements of association value or meaningfulness of verbal units devised for learning tasks are the works of Archer (1960), Noble (1952a), and Underwood and Schulz (1960). *Meaningfulness*, the term favored by these investigators, should not be confused with the term *meaning*. The latter term refers to the referent of a word, that is, the thing to which a word refers. Meaningfulness, on the other hand, is used by these investigators to indicate the extent to which laboratory materials such as dissyllables and trigrams elicit previous associations. Thus, meaningfulness should contain the association of "association value."

Early attempts to scale the meaningfulness of nonsense syllables are limited because experimenters used few subjects or few syllables. Furthermore, ratings made many years ago may have become out-of-date. For these reasons, Archer (1960) made an ambitious reevaluation of the meaningfulness of 2480 trigrams. He chose the term *trigram* in preference to *nonsense syllable* because he thought the former a more appropriate term. The composition of Archer's materials involved only consonant–vowel–consonant (CVC) trigrams. When each of the 2480 possible CVC trigrams were presented, the 319 subjects considered whether it was a word, sounded like a word, reminded them of a word, or could be used in a sentence. Three sessions were employed to minimize the monotony of the task.

Archer determined the meaningfulness of each trigram by calculating the percentage of subjects who considered each trigram meaningful. Such ratings were tested for reliability and found to be stable. Furthermore, high correlations were obtained between the Archer and Glaze ratings, as well as between the Archer and Krueger values for the 1933 trigrams common to all studies. However, lower correlations were obtained among the studies when sampling was restricted to quartiles instead of using the total range, from 0 to 100, on the meaningfulness scale. As Archer indicated, most studies do deal with portions of the total scale more often than with the entire range. Since the older and more limited scales are not highly correlated with Archer's norms for restricted ranges, it appears preferable to employ the latter scale.

Noble (1952a) used 18 artificial two-syllable words and 96 actual two-syllable words, which he termed dissyllables. As each item was presented to the subjects, they were told to write down all associations that came

TABLE 3.1

LIST OF DISSYLLABLE WORDS (NOUNS) IN
RANK ORDER OF INCREASING MEANINGFULNESS (m) AS DEFINED BY MEAN
FREQUENCY OF CONTINUED ASSOCIATIONS IN 60 SECONDS ($N = 119$)

Rank	Word Number	m-Value	σ	Word	Rank	Word Number	m-Value	σ	Word
1	24	0.99	2.05	GOJEY	49	58	2.69	3.43	OVUM
2	53	1.04	1.60	NEGLAN	50	72	2.73	3.24	ROSTRUM
3	49	1.05	1.85	MEARDON	51	84	2.76	2.92	VERTEX
4	8	1.13	1.89	BYSSUS	52	5	2.80	3.27	BODICE
5	4	1.22	1.95	BALAP	53	76	2.89	3.20	TANKARD
6	86	1.22	2.17	VOLVAP	54	60	3.06	3.04	PALLOR
7	77	1.24	2.03	TAROP	55	74	3.21	2.85	SEQUENCE
8	90	1.24	2.20	XYLEM	56	1	3.34	3.34	ARGON
9	41	1.26	2.16	LATUK	57	68	3.36	3.22	RAMPART
10	66	1.26	2.01	QUIPSON	58	35	3.51	3.50	JITNEY
11	25	1.27	2.20	GOKEM	59	17	3.55	3.19	ENTRANT
12	52	1.28	1.96	NARES	60	59	3.62	3.26	PALLET
13	96	1.28	2.19	ZUMAP	61	51	3.64	3.48	NAPHTHA
14	63	1.30	1.98	POLEF	62	62	3.77	3.45	PIGMENT
15	73	1.33	2.06	SAGROLE	63	57	3.91	3.42	ORDEAL
16	55	1.34	2.37	NOSTAW	64	94	4.44	3.19	ZENITH
17	6	1.39	2.12	BODKIN	65	91	4.60	3.82	YEOMAN
18	81	1.50	2.78	ULNA	66	67	4.68	3.13	QUOTA
19	88	1.53	2.05	WELKIN	67	64	5.10	3.45	QUARRY
20	29	1.54	2.84	ICON	68	15	5.13	3.19	EFFORT
21	40	1.55	2.45	KUPOD	69	83	5.32	3.24	UNIT
22	13	1.60	2.46	DELPIN	70	18	5.33	3.46	FATIGUE
23	3	1.71	2.55	ATTAR	71	37	5.47	3.11	KEEPER
24	48	1.73	2.69	MATRIX	72	38	5.52	3.70	KENNEL
25	12	1.74	2.69	DAVIT	73	47	5.61	3.32	MALLET
26	89	1.78	2.77	WIDGEON	74	42	5.94	3.17	LEADER
27	7	1.79	2.65	BRUGEN	75	65	5.98	3.16	QUARTER
28	36	1.82	2.95	KAYSEN	76	69	5.98	3.70	REGION
29	46	1.84	2.85	MAELSTROM	77	28	6.02	3.33	HUNGER
30	79	1.84	2.95	TUMBRIL	78	95	6.15	3.05	ZERO
31	70	1.86	2.85	RENNET	79	30	6.24	3.50	INCOME
32	71	1.90	2.35	ROMPIN	80	82	6.57	3.79	UNCLE
33	22	1.95	2.55	GAMIN	81	92	6.75	4.12	YOUNGSTER
34	19	2.09	3.11	FEMUR	82	80	6.83	3.29	TYPHOON
35	45	2.09	3.42	LOZENGE	83	10	6.88	3.11	CAPTAIN
36	20	2.13	2.77	FERRULE	84	93	7.12	3.75	ZEBRA
37	75	2.14	2.75	STOMA	85	23	7.17	4.48	GARMENT
38	26	2.15	3.09	GRAPNEL	86	85	7.28	4.05	VILLAGE
39	21	2.19	3.25	FLOTSAM	87	31	7.39	3.09	INSECT
40	11	2.26	3.35	CAROM	88	34	7.58	3.69	JEWEL
41	54	2.26	2.65	NIMBUS	89	32	7.70	3.53	JELLY
42	43	2.28	3.06	LEMUR	90	27	7.91	3.86	HEAVEN
43	9	2.41	3.13	CAPSTAN	91	56	7.95	3.66	OFFICE
44	61	2.43	2.88	PERCEPT	92	87	8.12	3.67	WAGON
45	44	2.48	2.96	LICHENS	93	14	8.33	4.21	DINNER
46	33	2.54	3.53	JETSAM	94	50	8.98	4.27	MONEY
47	16	2.59	3.08	ENDIVE	95	2	9.43	4.30	ARMY
48	78	2.63	3.04	TARTAN	96	39	9.61	4.30	KITCHEN

Source: From C. E. Noble. An analysis of meaning. Psychological Review, 1952, 59, 421–430.
Reprinted by permission of the American Psychological Association and the author.

to mind in 60 seconds. Dissyllables were ranked on a scale of meaningfulness on the basis of the number of associations given to them. Table 3.1 indicates that the actual words received higher positions on his scale than did the artificial words, as one might expect.

The meaningfulness of trigrams was determined by Underwood and Schulz (1960). They had 273 subjects respond to each single letter of the alphabet with the first single-letter response that came to mind; then the subjects were presented with all possible two-letter combinations as stimuli and asked to provide the first single letter they thought of as a response. Underwood and Schulz tallied the frequencies of occurrence for each possible combination of three letters. Given any three-letter sequence, we can use their norms to determine the meaningfulness of that unit. The frequency with which the first letter of the sequence elicits the second letter in the norms is combined with the frequency with which the first two letters elicit the third letter in the norms. This value constitutes the generated frequency score, indicating its meaningfulness value.

The various scales described above clearly indicate that nonsense materials are not without associations as assumed by Ebbinghaus. Instead, materials can be devised ranging widely in association value. We can assume that such variations in scale value reflect the strength or amount of past associations to the materials.

Characteristics of Individual Words

Words are discrete units which actually occur in natural learning situations, whereas nonsense syllables are not intact or functional units. Some nonsense syllables, usually the pronunciable ones, are integrated and function as a unit, but nonpronunciable combinations are unintegrated as units and act like three items rather than one discrete item. This feature of nonsense syllables has even led to the suggestion that nonsense syllables are too complicated for learning tasks and should be discarded in favor of more integrated units (Deese, 1961).

In any event, we should now examine some features of meaningful words. Words, as shown in Noble's (1952a) study, possess more associations than do nonsensical dissyllables. However, among words there is little interest in scaling differences in degree or magnitude of meaningfulness as is the case with nonsense materials. Of greater concern with respect to words is the determination and specification of qualitative aspects, such as differences in meaning and association.

One method of measuring specific preexperimental verbal habits and their associative strengths is the word-association test (WAT). This procedure, dating back to the early days of experimental psychology with Galton in 1879, has had wide application in psychology. Although it has been used in clinical situations, the present interest centers on its usefulness in measuring the existing verbal habits of the learner. We shall examine the nature of the test itself and the factors which affect performance.

The WAT developed by Kent and Rosanoff (1910) has come to serve as the standard instrument. It includes 100 common words, mostly nouns and adjectives. The task of the subject is to "give the first word that comes into mind" in response to each stimulus word of the list. The test is in written form and there is no time pressure for responding. Norms showing the frequency with which various responses are given to each stimulus word on the test are available from the results of groups of individuals (Kent and Rosanoff, 1910; Palermo and Jenkins, 1964; Russell and Jenkins, 1954).

It is generally assumed that the most frequent response to a given stimulus word represents the one with the greatest associative connection. Thus, the WAT allows the underlying associations to be measured. Several problems exist for this interpretation. The norms are based on data from groups, and the most common response of a group may not reflect the strongest associate for each individual subject. Furthermore, data from groups in different studies may not always provide agreement on the most common responses for given stimulus words, since a variety of test administration procedures have been used for different norms. Several studies have demonstrated that procedural differences, including the type of instructions, may markedly affect the nature of responses given on WATs.

Horton, Marlowe, and Crowne (1963) reported that speeded instructions led to more common responses than relaxed instructions. Siipola, Walker, and Kolb (1955) found that even the grammatical class of responses differed for speeded and relaxed conditions. Adjective stimulus words tended to evoke responses of the same grammatical-form class under speeded conditions, but with relaxed conditions adjective stimuli produced more noun responses.

The order in which the stimulus list is presented may affect the response made, since the context of the stimulus words varies with different list orders. Wynne, Gerjuoy, and Schiffman (1965) employed a list in which some words possessed opposites and other words did not. For one condition these antonym stimuli occurred in the first part of the list; in another condition they were placed toward the end of the list; and in a third order the antonyms were evenly placed throughout the list. Thus, although the total list was exactly the same, the order of presentation varied. When antonyms were placed in a block at either end of the list, more opposites were given as responses than when the antonyms were evenly distributed in the list. These results imply that the specific response to a stimulus word depends on the context of the stimulus word. Since WAT norms typically have employed only one serial order of the list, it is possible that their generalizability is limited to WAT data employing the same serial order used in collecting the norms. Most studies, however, do not meet this requirement.

Such unreliability of responses to WAT has led the writer (Jung, 1966) to question the view that associative factors are the primary determinants of the responses obtained on WATs. Due to the ambiguity of the WAT paradigm, responses of subjects may be affected by their interpretation of the purpose of the task. For example, individuals who view the WAT as a personality test might respond differently in many ways from those who think it measures verbal intelligence.

Thus, both associative and nonassociative factors, such as administrative procedure and task perceptions, are probably operative on most WATs. Nonassociative factors cannot be eliminated completely. The WAT, at best, measures associative habits approximately.

Words also differ in their relative frequencies of occurrence in the language. Thorndike and Lorge (1944) tabulated the frequency of usage of different words in a wide range of printed material including newspapers and magazines. If we assume that differences in frequencies of occurrence of words determine the differences with which individuals experience words, high-frequency words should be stronger items, and hence more easily learned, than low-frequency words. However, one practical consideration in continued use of these norms, widely employed since 1944, is whether or not they can predict the linguistic usage of today more adequately than contemporary norms can.

Sets of Verbal Units

The measurement of characteristics of individual verbal units—such as association value, meaningfulness, and frequency of occurrence—ignores the fact that learning tasks involve units in the context of many other units. In the laboratory task, the subject is presented with more units than his immediate memory span can hold so that the learning process can be lengthened sufficiently for examination. Verbal units which may be similar as individual units may differ considerably in their characteristics as groups of units.

Intralist similarity refers to the degree to which the units comprising a learning list are alike. Highly similar items tend to be confused with one another and are difficult to distinguish, whereas items low in similarity are initially easily discriminable. Similarity is an index of the interrelationship among items and is not a feature of the individual items.

Formal or physical similarity is usually defined in terms of the number of different elements involved in generating the total set of items. Its use is limited to nonsense materials. If many different letters are involved over the set, there is low similarity since there is less overlap in the composition of individual items. With few different letters, the items are of high similarity and the items in the set share more common letters.

If words are considered, similarity can be defined in terms of meaningful relationships among the items. At one end of the similarity continuum are groups of words selected at random and considered to be relatively unrelated to each other meaningfully. At the other end, lists can be selected which have words with related meanings, such as synonyms, words with similar connotations, or words related to a common area. In addition, items with conceptual similarity may be grouped by using words from a common logical category, such as TREES or BIRDS. Obviously, sets of words defined in terms of meaningful or conceptual similarity may be highly similar without any physical or formal similarity.

The distinction between meaningful and conceptual similarity may be unnecessary if we consider the manner in which degree of similarity is measured. One method is to consider the extent to which different words in the list possess common direct or indirect associations. For example, Deese (1960) measured the similarity among sets of words with his index of inter-item associative strength (IIAS). This measure reflects the extent to which each word elicits other words in the list as responses on a free association test. This index can be viewed as measuring meaningful similarity if we assume that the more associations shared by a set of words, the more similar they are in meaning. Thus, *butterfly, summer, bird, fly, sky, sunshine,* and *flower* comprise a group of words which possesses many inter-item associations and can therefore be considered as being high in IIAS and meaningful similarity. Yet, it is obvious that these words do not come from any one logical category such as TREES or BIRDS. On the other hand, items which do come from the same logical category, such as *elm, pine, maple, spruce, cedar, walnut, birch,* and *willow,* contain many interassociations compared to most groups of words from unrelated categories. In other words, groups of items of high conceptual similarity may also be high in associative or meaningful similarity.

There are indices of associative relationships among words other than the one developed by Deese. Most of them are based on some form of free association test which provides information on the direct associations for various individual words. Marshall and Cofer (1963) list several of these methods and their applications.

Serial Learning

The majority of verbal learning studies have employed two standard tasks, the serial and the paired-associate paradigms. We shall examine the nature of these paradigms and the specific problems of interest associated with each task.

Many of our everyday learning situations involve sequential aspects. Serial tasks require not only the learning of particular components but also the order or arrangement among them. Thus, a housewife must not only remember what ingredients to put into a dish but also the order in which they should be added. A sports fan must know the order of the league's teams with respect to wins and losses as well as the names of the teams. Our language possesses a grammatical structure such that certain words follow others; a sentence is a particular serial order of words.

These daily learning situations have their laboratory counterpart in the serial anticipation learning task in which the subject must memorize the items of a list as well as their serial order. One interesting aspect of the task is the nature of the errors committed. The errors that occur in the learning of this task might be of three types; omissions, importations, and intrusions. Omissions are failures to respond correctly or incorrectly, whereas importations refer to erroneous responses which do not even come fom other parts of the list. The intrusion, or misplaced response, is a correct response insofar as it belongs in the list but is an error because it occurs in an incorrect serial position.

One reliable phenomenon of serial learning involves the relationship of errors to the serial position of items in the list. Although some aspects of the particular material and learning situation used may modify the findings, the errors generally occur most frequently in the middle portions of the list, followed by the end positions, with the least number occurring at the initial positions. The same relationship obtains between the ease of learning (number of correct responses) and the serial position of an item. Thus, learning occurs fastest for items at the beginning, then at the end, and slowest for those items in the middle of a serial task.

Several attempts have been made to account for this phenomenon, known as the bowed serial position curve. Similar views of Hull (1935) and Lepley (1934) suggested that correct and incorrect associations are formed to each item in learning the list. Traces of previous stimuli exist when items later in the list are presented, so that remote associations are formed between nonadjacent items. The formation of such associations interferes with the correct association to the adjacent item. This interference is assumed to be greater for items in the middle of the list than for those at the ends of the list. Consequently, more errors or poorer learning occurs for the items in the middle of the list.

One aspect of this explanation is the assumption that interference dissipates over time. Therefore, a reduction in the amount of bowing of the serial position curve should result with distributed practice during learning. Hovland (1938), in a much cited study, compared serial learning when the intertrial interval was either 6 seconds or 2 minutes and 6 seconds. His results suggested less bowing with the longer intertrial interval, as predicted from the Lepley–Hull hypothesis.

However, McCrary and Hunter (1953) challenged this interpretation and reanalyzed Hovland's data. In addition, they conducted a study of their own. Since distributed practice facilitates learning or reduces the absolute number of errors, these investigators concluded that the flatter serial position curve obtained by Hovland under distributed practice is an artifact. McCrary and Hunter determined the percentage of total errors occurring at each serial position rather than the absolute number of errors. Here they found essentially identical bowed curves, with maximal errors in the middle of the list for both massed and distributed practice. In their own experiment, McCrary and Hunter compared serial learning of names with that of nonsense syllables. Thus, they varied the meaningfulness of the material rather than the distribution of practice. Comparing the absolute number of errors, they found more bowing for the nonsense syllable list, but when an analysis was made of percentage errors, they found equivalent serial position curves for both types of material. These results are shown in Figures 3.1 and 3.2.

Similar results were reported by Braun and Heymann (1958). They examined the effects of meaningfulness as well as distribution of practice on serial position curves. Twelve paralogs of either high or low meaningfulness were given under serial learning. In one study, the intertrial interval was either 2 or 4 seconds, while in another study it was either 6 seconds or 2 minutes and 6 seconds.

As in an experiment by McCrary and Hunter (1953), more bowing occurred with low meaningfulness, but only if absolute curves were considered. The findings on distribution of practice agreed with the McCrary–Hunter reanalysis of Hovland's (1938) data. When absolute curves were viewed, greater bowing was obtained with massed practice, but on percentage curves there was little difference due to this variable.

The combined results of McCrary and Hunter (1953) and Braun and Heymann (1958) raise questions as to whether previous studies such as

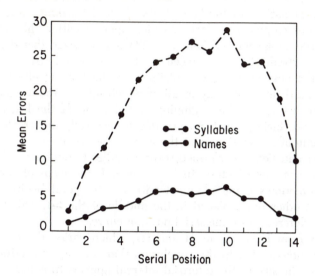

Figure 3.1. Mean errors as a function of serial position.

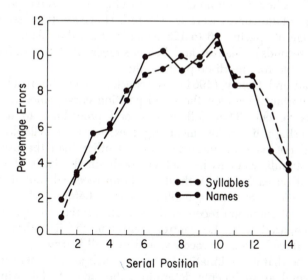

Figure 3.2. Percentage errors as a function of serial function. [Figures 3.1 and 3.2 are from J. W. McCrary, Jr., and W. S. Hunter: Serial position curves in verbal learning. *Science,* 6 February 1963, **117**, 131–134, Figs. 3 and 4. Copyright 1963 by the American Association for the Advancement of Science. Reprinted by permission of *Science* and the authors.]

Hovland's provide any critical evidence in evaluating the inter-item interference explanations of the bowedness of serial learning curves.

Instead of emphasizing factors which operate within the list of items to be learned, Glanzer and Peters (1962) hypothesized that the temporal gap, or intertrial interval, between the last item of one trial and the first item of the next trial might contribute to the bowing effect. This gap serves several functions, any or all of which might produce the bowing. It acts to distinguish the beginning and the end of the list, provides a short period during which no practice is received, and creates a break in the chain of association from the first to the last item.

Glanzer and Peters performed several studies to determine the relative importance of these factors. In Experiment I, the locus of the gap was varied, sometimes being identical with the temporal beginning of the list but at other times placed in the middle of the list. This factor produced no differences on the serial position curve.

Results from Experiments II and III, which varied the length of the intertrial interval, led to the conclusion that the gap is a critical factor. Increasing the size of the intertrial interval appears to enhance the magnitude of the bowing of the curve. Glanzer and Peters suggest that the increased spacing may favor the acquisition of the items at either end. Other studies (McCrary and Hunter, 1953; Braun and Heymann, 1958), it will be recalled, found no effect of spacing on the serial position curve when percentage curves were considered. However, these studies used a wider range of spacing (6 to 126 seconds) than did Glanzer and Peters (0 to 16 seconds). Glanzer and Peters suggest that this difference may be responsible for the discrepant results.

Lippman and Denny (1964) also considered the intertrial interval to be an important factor on the serial position curve, since it serves as a discriminative cue. They followed several procedures to test this hypothesis, using a list of low meaningfulness nonsense syllables. One condition did not have an intertrial interval other than the usual interval between stimuli, whereas in another condition the locus of the interval was varied on each trial. A third condition received four filler items of zero-association nonsense syllables, inserted before the relevant serial list. A control condition received the standard serial anticipation method. When compared with the control condition, the first three conditions showed reduced primacy, recency, and over-all learning.

It may be that a combination of factors such as inter-item interference and temporal arrangements determines the amount of bowing in serial learning. The intertrial interval probably aids the subject by providing a discriminative point, an "anchor" from which he can attempt to learn the remainder of the list. This factor is more perceptual than associative in nature. Items at the ends of the list may be better learned due to the greater saliency of their positions. Items in the middle of the list are not only less discriminable but also subject to more inter-item interference. In other words, it may be that one set of factors is responsible for the better learning of the items at either end, whereas other factors lead to the poorer learning of middle items.

The Stimulus in Serial Learning Although we have examined serial learning as a function of the position of items in the series, we have not asked how the learning process occurs. Does one item serve as a stimulus for the next item in the series? Researchers have attempted to analyze serial learning into stimuli and responses, although it seems that one characteristic of serial learning tasks is the lack of a clearly identifiable stimulus for each response. Young (1962) offered three possibilities as to the nature of the stimulus in serial learning: the item preceding a response, a cluster of two or more preceding items, or the serial position of the item in the list. Experimental tests of these hypotheses were performed. In Experiment I, subjects learned a serial list followed by a paired-associate list derived from the preceding serial list. In the derived paired-associate list, half of the pairs consisted of nonadjacent items from the serial list. Consider the items in the serial list as A, B, C, D, E, F, and so on. In the derived list, A–B would be an example of a pair of adjacent items whereas C–F would be a pair of nonadjacent items. If the chaining or specificity hypothesis which holds that the stimulus is the immediately preceding item is correct, then the learning of pairs of adjacent items should be higher than that of pairs of nonadjacent items. The results showed no differences, except for early trials on the transfer list.

The compound-stimulus hypothesis, which assumes that the stimulus involves several preceding items, was examined in Experiment II. A serial list of fifteen pairs was learned, followed by a derived paired-associate list of five pairs. A pair consisted of an item from the serial list as a response term, with the two items which preceded that item in the serial list serving as a compound stimulus in the paired-associate task. A control group received similar treatment except that the compound stimuli did not consist of adjacent preceding items. No support for the hypothesis was obtained, since performance was actually higher for the control group.

In the third experiment, the serial-position hypothesis was tested. Here it is assumed that the ordinal position of an item in the list serves as its stimulus. Subjects learned a serial list, followed by a second serial list derived from the first one such that half of the original items retained their original serial positions whereas the other half were relocated randomly. If the serial position served as a cue for each item in the serial list, learning would be similar to paired-associate learning, with serial positions acting as stimuli paired with verbal responses.

In effect, the subject would be forming the following associations: 1–A, 2–B, 3–C, 4–D, 5–E, 6–F, and so on. On the transfer list, items placed in their original locations would essentially be the same "pairs." Thus, 1–A would be the pair for the first item A if it were assigned the same position in both lists. On the other hand, if A were first in the first list but fourth in the second list, it would be necessary to learn two contradictory pairs, 1–A in the first list and 4–A in the second list. It was predicted and found that learning of items in the same position on both lists was faster on the second list than the learning of items occurring in different positions on the two lists. Thus, of the three hypotheses mentioned by Young, support was obtained for only the serial-position hypothesis.

Ebenholtz (1963) also obtained support for the serial-position hypothesis. In one study he compared the learning of a serial list of ten nonsense syllables for a condition in which the starting point varied nonsystematically on each trial with that of a condition in which the starting point was identical on all trials. He reasoned that learning should not differ in the two conditions if associations between successive items were critical for serial learning; however, if serial position acted as a cue for each item, learning would be poorer for the group which received items in different ordinal positions over the trials. Ebenholtz found differences in favor of the condition with a constant starting point, which agrees with the serial-position hypothesis.

A second study of Ebenholtz was similar to Experiment III of Young described above. After learning a serial list, subjects were presented with a second serial list, with half of the items coming from the first list and half of the items being new. In one condition, the old items occupied the same position in both lists, whereas they were in different positions in the two lists for another condition. Support for the serial-position hypothesis was obtained, with better learning when old items occupied the same positions in the two lists.

Thus far, the strongest support obtained has been for the serial-position hypothesis. Even then, alternative views have been suggested (Jensen, 1962). Rather than analyzing the serial learning task in terms of stimuli and responses, Jensen considers the task as one of response learning only. The entire series is a response chain, just as a consonant trigram such as TRW is a series of elements. Serial learning occurs by using the first item or the gap between trials as an anchor point for attaching each of the items in the list. Jensen avoids the search for the stimulus for each response, preferring to view the entire list as a complex response or unit in itself. Although such a conception avoids the problem of determining the stimulus in serial learning, we are still faced with the question of how each link in the complex response chain is joined together in the proper sequence.

Paired-Associate Learning

Some of the problems encountered in serial tasks are absent in the paired-associate task. In this paradigm the experimenter has substantially more precision in specifying the stimulus for each response. The task involves the formation of associations between a list of pairs of items, one member of each pair being designated by the experimenter to serve as the stimulus for the other member, which acts as the response. Since each item is involved in only one pair, it serves as either a stimulus or response but not as both as in serial learning.

An everyday situation analogous to paired-associate learning is the acquisition of a foreign language vocabulary. Here each foreign word is paired with its English equivalent and the subject's task is to form these associations. Learning of an association between the two members of one pair is somewhat independent of the associations to be formed for other pairs. However, when there is high similarity among the total set of items, some associations may adversely affect other associations. Nonetheless, theoretically each pair is independent of the other pairs, whereas in serial learning the interrelationship among all items is an inherent feature of the task.

A widely used procedure in the paired-associate paradigm involves an anticipation method of presentation in which the stimulus term of a given pair is presented alone briefly (usually 2 seconds), followed by the presentation of that stimulus on the left-hand side paired with its response term on the right-hand side, for an equal exposure time. Then the next stimulus is presented, followed by the presentation of that stimulus paired with its response, and so on, until each pair in the list has been exposed. This constitutes the first study trial, which serves to familiarize the subject with the entire list. Starting with the next trial, the experimenter can begin to measure any learning that occurred during the first study trial. When any stimulus term is presented alone, after the first study trial, the subject's task is to respond aloud, that is, anticipate, with the correct response to that stimulus. Two seconds are usually provided before the same stimulus is shown again, paired with the correct response either to confirm the subject's response or to provide additional study of that pairing. Then the stimulus term of the next pair is presented to test for anticipation, and then the next, until the entire list has been tested. Credit for correct responses is given only if the response is made in anticipation of the actual presentation of the correct stimulus-response pairing.

Trials are continued until the subject reaches some criterion of performance (*performance criterion*) specified by the experimenter, such as one perfect trial, or until a fixed number of trials (*trials criterion*) have occurred. The order of the pairs in the list is varied from trial to trial in some unsystematic manner in order to minimize the possibility that serial learning might occur instead of paired-associate learning. That is, if the pairs of the list occur in the identical serial order on each trial, it is possible for correct responses to be made even if the subject ignores the stimulus-response pairing and simply learns the serial order of the response terms as if they represented a serial task. Since one goal of the paired-associate paradigm is to study the acquisition of associations between members of the pairs, it is considered necessary that the list order of the pairs should be varied over successive trials to force the subject to attend to the specific stimulus-response pairings. In this respect, it should be acknowledged that the functional stimuli employed in learning the pairs may not correspond to the nominal or list stimuli. As noted in an earlier section, the subject may modify or encode the stimuli in forming the required associations. In this sense we still cannot identify the stimulus in paired-associate learning any more than we could determine it for serial learning. On the other hand, the stimulus is more closely defined than in serial learning, since the only consistent cue for each response must be some aspect of the nominal stimulus.

Early studies (for example, McGeoch and Underwood, 1943) indicated that learning of paired associates was better if the pairs on each trial occurred in a constant order rather than in a varied order. It was assumed that the serial-position cues either substituted for or augmented the verbal associations within pairs for the constant order condition.

More recently, Newman and Saltz (1962) repeated and extended the study of this variable. Five trials were given on a list of paired associates, with the pairs occurring in random order on each trial for one condition and in constant order for another condition. Performance was compared on a sixth trial, which showed superior scores for the constant order condition. However, one additional condition, which also received the five constant order trials, received the stimuli in random order on the sixth trial. Performance here was equal to the condition which received all six trials in constant order. Thus, although serial cues may have aided learning in the constant order condition, it appears that these cues become less important on later trials. The higher learning of both of the constant order conditions shows that serial cues are an aid, but the lack of difference between the two constant order conditions suggests that the serial order cues lose their importance as more trials are given.

However, we should note that in a further study (Martin and Saltz, 1963) the random order condition was slightly better than the constant order condition. In this study, more meaningful items and more trials were used so that a higher degree of learning was involved than that attained in the Newman and Saltz study. To complicate matters more, Battig, Brown, and Nelson (1963) found few differences between constant and random orders except on later trials in two of their five studies. But the late trial effect obtained by Battig *et al.* was in favor of the constant order, whereas Martin and Saltz found just the opposite. It appears that the exact effects of the input order are more ambiguous than one might initially assume.

Components of Paired-Associate Learning

The nature of the paired-associate task has lent itself to more precise analysis than the serial learning task. In the paired-associate task each item serves either as a stimulus or response, whereas in the serial task each item serves as both. The separation of stimuli and responses in the paired-associate task allows one to assess the effects of various factors on the stimulus terms and response terms.

When the anticipation method is employed, the subject must learn different aspects of the stimulus and response terms. Since the stimuli need not be overtly produced by the subject under anticipation learning, he is free to learn the stimuli as given on the list or to transform them in ways which may facilitate learning. As mentioned earlier, the stimuli need not be available to the subject in the sense that the response terms must. It is sufficient that the stimuli be recognizable or discriminably different from each other. However, for the responses, which must be overtly produced, recognition is inadequate. The response terms may not be given in a transformed manner on the test trials but must be learned and given exactly as specified by the experimental list in paired-associate anticipation learning.

Finally, there is the process of associative learning. Not only must the subject be capable of differentiating the stimuli and overtly producing the responses but he must know which stimulus goes with which response. *Associative learning* refers to the correct pairing of stimuli and responses. Although others have proposed such stage analyses, the work of Underwood (Underwood, Runquist, and Schulz, 1959; Underwood and Schulz, 1960) has contributed the most influence. This formulation concentrated on response and associative learning as the two stages, or components, of paired-associate learning. The factor of stimulus differentiation did not receive much attention in their analysis, although other researchers (for example, McGuire, 1961) consider it as a component in the paired-associate paradigm.

The usefulness of the distinction between two stages of paired-associate learning is evident in a study by Underwood, Runquist, and Schulz (1959). They investigated the effects of intralist response similarity on the two stages. They hypothesized that response learning would be favored with high intralist response similarity since the recall of one response would aid the recall of highly similar responses. Yet, because it was known from other studies that paired-associate learning itself is handicapped by high intralist response similarity, they argued that associative learning must also be handicapped by high intralist response similarity if this same factor aids response learning.

Ten pairs of nonsense syllable stimuli and adjective responses were used to form a paired-associate list. High similarity responses consisted of synonyms such as *happy, jolly, gleeful,* and the like, whereas low similarity responses included unrelated words such as *spicy, rounded,* and *hairy.* Response learning conditions were stopped after either 1, 2, 3, 5, 8, or 13 anticipation trials, and subjects were asked to recall as many responses as possible without any other aid. Control conditions simply learned under standard procedures for 15 anticipation trials without interruptions. As indicated by other studies, over-all paired-associate learning was poorer with high intralist response similarity. Furthermore, as predicted, more response learning occurred, as measured by the response recall test, for high intralist response similarity conditions. It was inferred that associative learning was poorer with higher intralist response similarity, since over-all learning is the combined result of the two stages.

The writer (Jung, 1965b) replicated and extended the Underwood *et al.* (1959) study. He directly measured the two stages of paired-associate learning. In addition to assessing the effects of intralist response similarity on the two stages, he examined the effects of response meaningfulness.

Lists of eight pairs of single-digit stimuli and nonsense syllable responses were learned under a procedure in which the study and test parts of each trial were separated temporally. Each pair was shown for 2 seconds during the study part; then, after each trial, a test of free recall was given to measure the amount of response learning, while an associative matching test was given to assess associative learning. Each test lasted 45 seconds. In free recall the subject was simply asked to recall as many responses as he could without any aids. Associative matching involved presenting the subject with each of the list stimuli and responses, printed on separate cards, in a shuffled arrangement. The task was to match the stimuli with their appropriate responses.

Four conditions were involved, one for each combination of the two levels of formal similarity and meaningfulness of responses. In Experiment I, each subject was tested first for response and then for associative learning. Because it is conceivable that the administration of each type of test might affect the performance on the other type of test on subsequent trials, Experiment II was performed with half of the subjects in each condition receiving only response learning tests while the other half received only the associative learning test. Meaningfulness was not a variable in this second experiment.

The results of both Experiments I and II were in close agreement. High intralist response similarity failed to affect response learning, whereas it hampered associative learning. It will be recalled that Underwood *et al.* found that high similarity aided response learning; one reason for this discrepancy may be that they used meaningful words, whereas the writer's study used trigrams as response terms.

The results of Experiment I confirmed the predictions and findings of Underwood and Schulz (1960) with respect to response meaningfulness. Higher values of this factor aided both response and associative learning.

In addition, this study provided evidence on the relative rates of the two types of learning. Response learning was higher than associative learning, especially on early trials, provided meaningfulness and similarity were both high. Perhaps response learning was aided by high meaningfulness while the associative learning was depressed by the high similarity, thus creating the wide difference in favor of response learning. However, when both factors were low, there were no differences between the levels of the two stages of learning. These relationships are illustrated in Figures 3.3 and 3.4, which show the results from Experiment I. It appears that the relationship of the two stages is not fixed, but instead varies with the type of materials employed.

Many conclusions about paired-associate learning have been based on studies using the anticipation method and may not be generalizable to variations of this task. For example, Underwood and Schulz (1960) concluded that variables which affect learning, such as meaningfulness, are more powerful on the response terms than on the stimulus terms. Similarly, Hunt (1959) found greater differences in learning as a function of variations in response meaningfulness than with stimulus meaningfulness. Both studies used the anticipation method. These results are easy to understand, since it is necessary for the response terms to be available in recall whereas the stimulus terms need only be recognized in paired-associate learning when anticipation is employed.

In situations where the stimuli as well as the responses must be recalled, or where neither stimuli nor responses must be recalled, the evidence disagrees with the conclusions obtained with anticipation learning. Epstein and Streib (1962) made use of a recognition test so that no response learning was necessary. When presented with a stimulus,

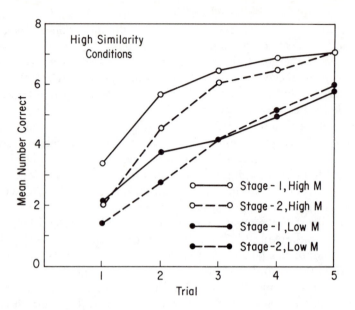

Figure 3.3. Mean number of correct responses recalled and matched on Trials 1 to 5 for high similarity conditions of Experiment 1 as a function of response meaningfulness (*M*). [From J. Jung: Two stages of paired-associate learning as a function of intralist response similarity (IRS) and response meaningfulness (*M*). *Journal of Experimental Psychology*, 1965, **70**, 371–378. Reprinted by permission of the American Psychological Association.]

the subject chose one of three response alternatives. Stimulus-response pairs were formed with paralogs to form low-high or high-low meaningfulness lists. It was predicted that the list with high meaningfulness responses would be better learned under the anticipation method, but that the use of a recognition test method would lead to equal learning of the two lists. The results supported the predictions except when the similarity of the recognition alternatives was high. In this case, learning was better with the high-low list.

Another method of avoiding the unequal recall requirements on the stimulus and response terms inherent in anticipation learning involves recall of both stimulus and response terms. Epstein and Platt (1964) studied free recall of paired associates with the following combinations of stimulus and response meaningfulness: high-high, high-low, low-high, low-low. Study trials were given on which all pairs in the list were shown; then test trials were interspersed on which the subject was to recall all the stimuli and responses in any order. In this situation, variations in stimulus rather than response meaningfulness had a greater effect on performance.

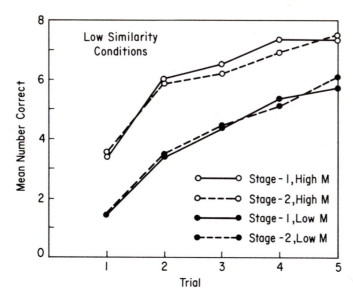

Figure 3.4. Mean number of correct responses recalled and matched on Trials 1 to 5 for low similarity conditions of Experiment 1 as a function of response meaningfulness (*M*). [From J. Jung: Two stages of paired-associate learning as a function of intralist response similarity (IRS) and response meaningfulness (*M*). *Journal of Experimental Psychology,* 1965, **70,** 371–378. Reprinted by permission of the American Psychological Association.]

SUMMARY

Verbal learning studies employ a variety of materials including trigrams, paralogs, and words. The ease with which such materials are learned is assumed to depend on the extent to which subjects have encountered them in their past learning. Numerous attempts have been made to measure such characteristics of learning materials as association value, meaningfulness, and frequency of occurrence, to name a few. Sets of materials also vary in such aspects as formal, meaningful, and conceptual similarity, which also affect learning.

Two tasks have been used primarily in experiments on verbal learning: the serial and the paired-associate paradigms. Although each task has some analogues in daily experience, the tasks are not used primarily because such parallels exist. In order to study learning and the factors which influence the process, some task must serve as a vehicle so that some learning can occur. Learning in general, rather than learning of a specific task or skill, is also important to understand. Of course, while there may be features common to all learning tasks, there are many unique aspects of different paradigms.

Items must be differentiated and made available in the subject's repertoire, and associations must be formed among items in both serial and paired-associate learning. On the other hand, the learning of the order among the items is a feature of serial learning which does not apply to paired-associate learning. While the subject need make only the response terms available in the paired-associates task, he must integrate all items in the serial task, where the same items serve both as stimuli and responses.

learning "trial." A trial of 10 seconds is not the same type of trial as one containing 100 seconds; it is reasonable to consider the latter trial as equivalent to ten of the former variety.

Part versus Whole Methods Another situation dealing with temporal characteristics of practice conditions has been that of part versus whole learning. Suppose we are confronted with a task requiring many trials to learn. Would our efficiency differ depending on how we distributed our total practice time over the various sections of the total material? This practical question is involved in studies of part versus whole learning. In *part learning*, a limited part of the total material is presented on each trial for a specified amount of practice, then another part is presented, and so on, until all the parts of the total are presented. Then the whole material is presented in its entirety. Usually the parts are of equal size and difficulty. In the case of *whole learning*, each trial involves the presentation of the entire material. Comparisons of learning under the two conditions have yielded ambiguous results.

Postman and Goggin (1964) compared part and whole learning procedures for serial learning. Subjects learned nonsense syllable lists that represented the four combinations of high and low meaningfulness and of high and low similarity. Although individual parts of the list required less time to learn than the total list, there was but a slight advantage to the part method when the time needed to combine the parts into the whole was considered.

These investigators concluded that learning is equivalent under the two methods. Learning involves a number of processes, such as response integration and differentiation among the items of the list; however, for a given set of material the amount of learning involved is constant. Variations in input procedure, such as part versus whole, produce no differences in learning since the total amount to be learned is identical.

A similar comparison of part and whole learning was made for paired-associate learning (Postman and Goggin, 1966). In addition to part and whole learning, the investigators included a third condition, in which each stage of the part condition involved the repetition of previous parts plus the addition of a new part. The results showed no differences between part and whole learning, as was the case with serial learning. However, performance was superior for the repetitive part condition. Unlike the pure part condition, it was unnecessary for the parts to be combined *after* each part was learned, since each part was progressively combined with larger parts until the whole was attained. This feature of the repetitive part condition may account for its superiority.

The writer (Jung, 1964) employed a procedure similar to the repetitive part method, which he labeled a *cumulative* method. During the first portion of the session, subjects were presented the list in cumulative fashion. First, a single item was presented, then it was repeated with a second (new) item, and so on, until the entire list had been exposed. Control conditions received "standard" trials on which all items of the list appeared on each trial. The total amount of practice was equated; however, for the standard method conditions, each item appeared equally often, whereas with the cumulative method, the earlier an item was introduced to the list, the more presentations it was given. Consider a five-item list presented for three trials. Under the standard method, each item would appear three times since each item occurred on each trial. For the cumulative method, the first item would receive five exposures, the second four, the third three, the fourth two, and the fifth only one. The total amount of practice would involve fifteen individual exposures for both conditions.

Following this phase of the experiment, subjects then received the entire list for additional full-length learning trials, on which performance was compared. No consistent differences were obtained between cumulative and standard method conditions for a wide range of materials under either serial or paired-associate methods.

Thus, the evidence on the efficiency of the repetitive part or cumulative method is conflicting at best.

Blocking versus Anticipation   In the anticipation method of paired associates, a stimulus cue is first presented alone; the subject is supposed to produce the correct response within a few seconds, before the response is provided for feedback or additional learning. An alternative procedure was used by Battig and Brackett (1961). First, the stimulus-response pairs were presented one at a time without any interspersed test trials, as with the anticipation method. Then a test trial, consisting entirely of test items, was given. Thus, this method separated the study and test portions of each trial.

Battig and Brackett presented twelve pairs of nonsense shapes and two-digit numbers at a 5-second rate. They found better learning for their method, which is somewhat surprising since this procedure involves greater delay of reinforcement or knowledge of results. They accounted for their finding in terms of the greater opportunity to develop stimulus differentiation under their method, which provides two separate runs through the stimulus set.

However, a later study (Lockhead, 1962) failed to support the Battig and Brackett study. Three methods were employed: the standard anticipation, a blocking method (same as the Battig–Brackett method), and a random method. In the last method, the presentation of the stimulus of each pair alone and the exposure of the stimulus of each pair with its response were in random order for all list pairs. The list contained nine pairs of nonsense syllables. Lockhead found no significant differences among the three methods. Learning again was found to be independent of procedural variations.

Confirmation versus Prompting   Cook and Spitzer (1960) refer to the anticipation method of paired associates as a confirmation method, since the correct answer is provided *after* the subject has an opportunity to make a response to the stimulus. On the other hand, they speak of prompting when the procedure involves the presentation of the correct pairing immediately before a test for that very same pair. Under prompting, the subject is prevented from making errors, which is not the case with the confirmation method. Cook and Spitzer found that prompting led to better learning. They attributed such superiority to the shorter delay between the stimulus and the response of each pair. They also found that prompting was better when no overt practice was allowed. This suggests another reason why prompting is better than confirmation, since overt rehearsal is more typical of the latter method. This study is one situation where a procedural variable produced differences in learning.

However, another study (Hawker, 1964) obtained results that weaken any firm conclusions about the effects of prompting and confirmation. Hawker examined prompting and confirmation procedures in paired-associate learning as a function of stimulus similarity, response similarity, and type of pairs. Pairs were either nonsense line-figure stimuli and adjective responses, or just the reverse order. A modification of the paired-associate paradigm was employed which involved a multiple-choice test trial. Under the confirmation method, a stimulus was followed by four alternative responses. The subject chose until he made the correct response; then a bulb above the correct response lighted to confirm his response. For prompting conditions, a stimulus appeared with four response alternatives and the correct one had a lighted bulb above it to indicate that it was the correct one. In order to measure learning, test trials which did not provide feedback were interspersed among study trials.

Although prompting led to better performance on early trials, there were no over-all advantages in either method. The task was administered at the subject's pace rather than in an automatic manner. Comparisons of performance speed revealed that subjects under the prompting conditions proceeded faster through the lists, although they did not produce any better learning in terms of number of correct responses. The two methods failed to produce differences over a variety of conditions which involved variations of both stimulus and response similarity as well as the type of pair.

Invariance Hypothesis It appears that a wide variety of procedural variations does not alter the amount of learning under either serial or paired-associate learning. Postman and Goggin (1966) offered an invariance hypothesis in which they proposed that variations of method are ineffective when the same amount of total time is provided for learning a given amount of material.

The findings of invariance refer to the effects of variations of stimulus input and do not necessarily include the effects of different strategies or techniques of learning. The method of stimulus input could itself be considered as a strategy, but we must recognize that other strategies exist, such as mnemonics and organizational devices. A related point to consider is the fact that the invariance findings have involved rote materials. If the learning content involves organized and logically related materials, the programming of stimulus input may then be an important factor in learning. In fact, this assumption underlies much of the research and application of teaching machine programs.

Measurement of Learning

Regardless of the particular learning paradigm we may employ, certain common considerations exist in the measurement of learning. We must decide on specifications with respect to the length of learning trials, the nature of a list, and the criteria for learning, for both serial and paired-associate paradigms.

Our inference that learning occurs depends on our observations that improvements in performance take place from one observation to the next. Multiple opportunities for performance on the learning task are referred to as *learning trials*. Usually, a trial involves one presentation of the total task. However, the exact definition of a trial is arbitrary and obviously depends on the particular task. Thus, in both serial and paired-associate anticipation tasks, a trial actually includes a combined study and test trial. However, both paradigms can be employed with distinctly separated study and test trials. On the other hand, in the free recall task—which will be discussed in Chapter 7—these two components are separated temporally. In some situations, such as studies of part versus whole learning, the amount of material presented varies on different trials.

The definition of a trial is still vague and imprecise. No mention has been made of the temporal duration of each trial. Is a trial of 1-minute duration the same as one encompassing 2 minutes on the same material, or is the latter trial actually two trials? Obviously the total time involved is unequal. It is not easy to determine the equivalence of trials defined in different units.

Suppose we have a list of ten nonsense syllables which we want the learner to memorize in serial order. (Here we will define a trial as involving the presentation and testing of each item in the list once.) In order to minimize rehearsal of items by some learners, which would in effect provide more repetition, we will keep the exposure time for each item as short as possible, while still allowing sufficient time for stimulus inspection. Since exposure times as short as 2 seconds per item are commonly used, a complete trial for this list should require 20 seconds.

The list is administered trial after trial until it is learned to a criterion of performance acceptable to the investigator, typically one perfect recitation or a given number of trials. If the list is extremely short or easy, it will require few trials, perhaps only one, to attain perfect performance.

In order to require more trials (observations) for the learner to attain the particular criterion desired, the investigator may deliberately lengthen the list or employ more difficult items, The reason for devising tasks which require more trials to learn is so that more detailed observations of the course of learning can be made.

If, for example, conditions allowed learning to occur in only one trial, we would have no opportunity to examine the effects of different factors on learning. By using very short lists or easy items so that learning occurs in fewer trials, we would not be able to determine how learning differs under different variables, since it would be perfect under all conditions. Nor could we detect individual differences among learners under easy conditions, because of their homogeneously high or perfect performance; however, the use of more difficult situations—such as longer lists or more difficult items—would permit the appearance of individual differences in performances. Similarly, differences in performance as a function of different factors might be measurable.

We have already pointed out that learning is an inference from improved performance on a trial following practice as compared with a trial preceding practice. However, the actual learning must occur only while the learner is practicing on the material. If the measurement of learning is to be accurate, some attention should be given to having the "before" and "after" practice tests for measuring learning as close as temporally possible to the period during which learning is actually taking place. If the before test is made too far in advance of the actual training period, it is possible that during the interim the learning of extraneous material may occur, which might affect performance on the subsequent learning task provided by the experimenter. On the other hand, if the after test is delayed too far beyond the end of training, it is possible that the learner may either forget some of the learned material or learn some additional material from other sources, which may affect performance of the relevant learning task given by the experimenter.

Criteria of Learning

How does one determine when the learning of a task can be considered completed? Is it the first trial by which all items in the list have been given correctly at least once previously? Is it the trial after which no errors are ever made?

We could choose these and other criteria, since any decision is arbitrary as to what level of performance represents "complete" learning. In everyday life, we decide learning is complete if it enables the individual to perform at a certain level on some task. One common criterion for completion used in experiments is the first trial on which all items in the list are correctly given. However, errors can still occur on trials beyond the criterial trial. If one insisted on using ten consecutive perfect, or errorless, trials as the criterion of complete learning, there should be fewer errors on subsequent trials, but there might still be some. In a relative sense, more stringent criteria constitute more complete learning, but what represents complete learning on an absolute basis is not specifiable.

In contrast to the above performance criteria, one could employ a constant number of trials as a criterion of learning. In this case, the investigator arbitrarily selects a constant number of trials to be given to all learners. Individuals will differ in the levels of performance they will attain in a given number of trials, but practice is discontinued after the same number of trials for all learners. Comparisons are then made of the number of correct responses; there is no implication that any given number of trials represents complete learning.

Definition of a List

The set of materials given to the learner is generally referred to as a *list*, regardless of its length. It is common procedure to use a list whose length exceeds that of the immediate memory span, so that the process of learning can be examined.

Since the length of the list governs the amount of material to be learned, it should affect the ease of learning. Another aspect of the list is the interrelationship among the items comprising the list, such as the level of intralist similarity or internal structure. One may devise lists in which all members are physically similar, conceptually similar, or logically related. Learning is affected not only by length of list but also by type of list composition.

Unless one is specifically interested in examining these quantitative and qualitative aspects of lists, he should follow some general precedents in the formation of his lists for learning experiments. Suppose he is interested in comparing the learning of normal subjects and schizophrenic subjects. Since neither the length nor the type of list is of interest as a variable, the investigator might use a list whose length exceeded the immediate memory span so that an opportunity for improvement would exist. The list composition would employ "unrelated" materials inasmuch as degree of interrelationship would not be of interest. These decisions, like many others in the design of a study, are arbitrary or based on experience gained from other experiments. Conventions develop as research accumulates in an area, and unless the investigator is interested in manipulating some specific variable, he adopts as values of the variables those similar to the values typically used, in order to facilitate comparisons among studies.

Mixed versus Unmixed Lists One factor influencing the composition of a list is the type of experimental design employed. Suppose that we are interested in assessing the effects of three levels of meaningfulness on learning. One procedure might be to use independent groups of subjects, one for each level of the variable being studied. This procedure is called a *between-groups design* and employs different lists, each of homogeneous or unmixed difficulty. An alternative design calls for the use of a single group of subjects for all conditions; when the same group is used for all levels of the variable, we have one type of the *within-groups design*. For this single group, a mixed list is devised which contains items from all levels of the variable used for the study. In our example, suppose twelve-item lists were being used for the independent groups procedure. Each list would contain twelve items from one of three meaningfulness levels, and would be regarded as "unmixed." For the mixed-list group, however, there would be four items from each of three meaningfulness levels in the twelve-item list presented in random order.

The mixed-list design is used when the experimenter wishes to minimize the variability in his results due to individual differences among subjects. Since the same subjects serve under each condition, individual differences are held constant over conditions. This benefit is especially welcome when there are few subjects available for testing.

The obvious question is whether or not the results obtained under the unmixed- and mixed-list procedures are comparable. The subject may notice the heterogeneous characteristics of the mixed list and produce differential performance to the several levels of the variable being examined, a result which might not occur in a comparable experiment using an unmixed design. It is also conceivable that the subject may become confused by a mixed list. The technique he uses for learning one part of the list may interfere with the learning of other parts. Relative to an unmixed design, poorer performance may occur.

Johnson and Penney (1966) have provided evidence that the type of design can affect the results. They formed strongly or weakly associated pairs of adjectives, and employed three conditions: an unmixed list of strong pairs, an unmixed list of weak pairs, and a mixed list of strong and weak pairs. The lists contained twelve pairs, all of the same level of intrapair association for the unmixed conditions, and half from each level for the mixed condition.

One comparison of the effect of associative strength was made between the two unmixed-list conditions, whereas the other comparison was made within the mixed-list condition on the two subsets of the lists. Regardless of which design was considered, learning was better with the strongly associated pairs.

Johnson and Penney made several other comparisons. The learning of the strong pairs of the mixed-list condition occurred at a slower rate than did the learning of the same pairs when presented in the unmixed-list condition. On the other hand, the weak pairs of the mixed-list condition were more rapidly acquired than the same pairs when presented in the unmixed-list condition.

It appears that the use of a mixed list led to slower learning of strongly associated pairs while it produced faster learning of the weakly associated pairs. The results of the Johnson and Penney study illustrate that unmixed- and mixed-list designs may produce different results.

Theoretical Problems

We suggested earlier that the conclusions made about the nature of learning are dependent upon the nature of the learning task. Nonetheless, some common processes are involved in most learning tasks. Thus, even though serial and paired-associate learning situations differ in many details, both involve stimulus differentiation, response learning or integration, and associative learning.

The distinction between stimuli and responses in serial learning is less clear than in paired-associate situations, and perhaps one can refer only to items. Thus, serial learning can be viewed as involving differentiation among items, the integration of items so that they become available, and the formation of associations among items. In addition, associations may occur between items and their serial positions. In any case, perhaps the variables affecting these processes within both paradigms do so in similar ways.

Differentiation of Stimuli

Learning requires that the items themselves be differentiated from each other. On early trials many of the stimuli tend to be confused with each other. Gibson (1940) suggested that incorrect as well as correct response tendencies to each stimulus are formed early in learning. Due to stimulus generalization, the responses to some stimuli may become associated with other stimuli. As learning proceeds, the stimuli become more differentiated and distinct from one another through differential reinforcement. Thus, the correct responses to stimuli are reinforced but the incorrect tendencies are nonreinforced.

An additional assumption made by Gibson is that the stimulus differentiation is transitory, being susceptible to dissipation over time. As time passes, stimulus generalization tendencies tend to recover spontaneously, disrupting subsequent performance.

The differentiation hypothesis of Gibson can account for the effects of stimulus similarity on learning. With materials of high intralist stimulus similarity, there is low differentiation at the outset of learning, whereas with low intralist stimulus similarity, initial differentiation is high. It would therefore be predicted that learning would be faster with material of low similarity.

Gibson (1942) tested the effects of variations in stimulus similarity. Lists of paired associates consisting of nonsense geometrical-form stimuli and nonsense syllable responses were used in which several degrees of stimulus similarity existed. As predicted, learning was inversely related to degree of stimulus similarity. An analysis of error tendencies showed that they increased initially, and finally decreased as learning proceeded. Gibson interpreted this relationship to mean that generalization tendencies were low initially, then increased, and finally decreased as learning proceeded.

Another test of Gibson's theory was performed with serial learning by

Underwood (1952). Lists of fourteen nonsense syllables were constructed so that the formal similarity within lists varied from low to medium to high. Learning was inversely related to the degree of intralist similarity, thus supporting Gibson's prediction.

Comparison of the learning of materials of different similarity is one method of obtaining evidence regarding the differentiation hypothesis. If one assumes that more differentiation is needed for high similarity material, then faster learning is predicted for material of low similarity. Such was Gibson's (1942) approach to this problem.

A more direct procedure for assessing the role of stimulus differentiation involves manipulation of the opportunity for differentiation to occur within the experiment. In this situation, the characteristics of the material are not varied but the type of practice is varied for different conditions.

Predifferentiation Procedures   In stimulus predifferentiation studies (Arnoult, 1957), the subject is provided with some form of pretraining with the items which are to serve as stimuli on a subsequent task. Typically the procedure calls for the attachment of verbal labels to each item in order to make each stimulus more discriminable from other stimuli. Thus, it is assumed that stimuli become differentiated when they are associated to more distinct responses, such as verbal labels. Such acquired distinctiveness of the stimuli should enable subsequent learning that involves these items as stimuli to proceed more rapidly.

One danger with the predifferentiation treatment is the possibility that the response associated with each stimulus during pretraining may interfere with the acquisition of a new response to each of these stimuli on the test list. An alternative method of predifferentiation which avoids this problem involves the use of different stimuli during pretraining from those to be used on the test list. Pretraining would then be assumed to aid the process of differentiation, per se, rather than the differentiation of the specific stimulus terms which would appear on the test list. Any associations formed between pretraining stimuli and responses should not affect the associations called for on the test list, which involve different stimuli and responses.

Predifferentiation procedures could conceivably aid test list learning simply due to the subject's becoming oriented to the task or receiving warm-up. Thus, differentiation itself could be irrelevant as a factor aiding performance on the test list. Consequently, it is necessary to include control conditions that receive pretraining which provides warm-up but which does not also produce differentiation.

In summary, a number of methodological problems exist in predifferentiation studies. If no facilitation is obtained from predifferentiation, it could be due to interference between pretraining and test list associations. A lack of difference between the experimental and control conditions may be due also to the possibility that the control condition, which is instructed to passively inspect the stimuli during pretraining, actually supplies its own verbal labels for each stimulus. In fact, the labels selected by the subjects in the control condition might be more successful in providing stimulus differentiation than the ones arbitrarily selected by the experimenter for the predifferentiation condition. On the other hand, positive findings that show higher test list performance in the predifferentiation condition are questionable unless a control condition for warm-up is included, since the latter factor itself could have produced the improved test list performance.

Availability of Responses

In any learning task, it is necessary that certain items called *responses* be learned so that they can be overtly produced to permit measurement of the learning process. Availability of responses refers to a condition such that items can be overtly recalled although not necessarily in response to specific stimuli. In serial tasks, the items which must be available as responses also serve as stimuli for other items; in paired-associate learning, different items serve as stimuli and as responses, but only the latter items must be available.

Frequency and Pronunciability The extent to which an item is available is related to the degree of integration of that item. Nonsense syllables are less available than words since the latter items are better integrated units. Words have more associations, usually occur more frequently in the natural language, and are more pronunciable than nonsense syllables. These are some of the differences which make words better integrated units and more available units.

Underwood and Schulz (1960) attribute the availability of items to the frequency with which the item has occurred in the language. They discount association value as a primary determinant of availability and consider this characteristic of materials to be affected also by frequency.

The experimental support for Underwood and Schulz's so-called spew, or frequency, hypothesis is mixed. Their comparisons of the learning of materials differing in frequency of occurrence in norms supported the spew hypothesis for lists of either single letters or bigrams, but for lists of trigrams the results obtained were negative. Other analyses indicated that rated pronunciability of items was a better predictor of learning than frequency. However, pronunciability and frequency of items were highly correlated. Underwood and Schulz concluded that pronunciability may be more important than frequency in accounting for availability of items. Nonetheless, they felt that future evidence for the frequency hypothesis might be more positive.

Meaningfulness It may be difficult to determine the particular variable correlated with association value and meaningfulness that is responsible for their effects on learning. However, much evidence is available that there is an effect.

Noble (1952*b*) evaluated the effects of variations in rated meaningfulness of material on serial learning. Lists of twelve dissyllable words of either low, medium, or high meaningfulness were learned under the serial anticipation procedure. Noble found learning to improve as the meaningfulness of the material increased.

An examination of the effects of meaningfulness on paired-associate learning was made by Noble and McNeely (1957). Lists of paired associates were devised which represented ten equally spaced points on Noble's (1952*a*) scale of meaningfulness. A comparison of the mean number of errors as a function of the median meaningfulness of the pairs in each list showed a strong relationship. The more meaningful the pairs in a list, the fewer errors were obtained. Noble and McNeely recognized that further studies were needed in which comparisons were made for variation in meaningfulness of stimulus and response terms, separately.

Three such investigations (Cieutat, Stockwell, and Noble, 1958; Hunt, 1959; L'Abate, 1959) were conducted using paired-associate lists. Four combinations of high and low stimulus and response meaningfulness were employed: high-high, high-low, low-high, and low-low. Learning was a direct function of response meaningfulness but there was no effect of variations of stimulus meaningfulness on learning as a rule. The results obtained by Cieutat *et al.* are presented in Figure 4.1.

It may appear circular to the student to learn that more meaningful material is better learned. However, it should be noted that independent measures were taken of this characteristic of the material and of the rate at which it was learned. It is not a matter of first noting what material is learned fastest and then labeling such material as more meaningful.

In the preceding studies relating meaningfulness and learning, the materials already possessed whatever level of this factor they contained before the experiment. In other words, we have shown that a correlation exists between one aspect of material and learning. The question "Why does meaningfulness lead to faster learning?" cannot be clearly answered by this obtained correlation. Many other variables may be correlated with meaningfulness, and which one (or combination) of

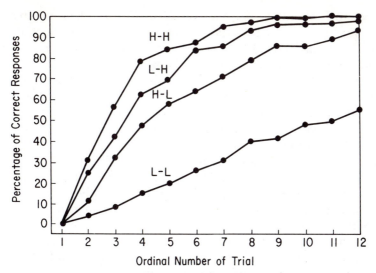

Figure 4.1. Acquisition curves for lists of ten paired associates as a function of practice. The four S–R combinations of low (L) and high (H) meaningfulness represent the parameter. [From V. J. Cieutat, F. E. Stockwell, and C. E. Noble: The interaction of ability and amount of practice with stimulus and response meaningfulness (m, m′) in paired-associate learning. *Journal of Experimental Psychology*, 1958, 56, 193–202. Reprinted by permission of the American Psychological Association and the authors.]

these variables "causes" the better learning associated with more meaningful material is difficult to determine.

Familiarization One correlate of more meaningful material is the frequency with which it occurs in the language. Attempts to assess the role of frequency experimentally fall under a class of studies of familiarization. The materials to be learned are typically given different amounts of familiarization before the actual learning task. For example, the subject may be instructed merely to pronounce each of the items in the list without being told that later he will be required to learn this material. The frequency can be varied by having different numbers of familiarization trials for different groups. Then all groups are required to learn the material, and comparisons of learning as a function of amount of familiarization can be made. The familiarization paradigm is aimed at measuring the effects of frequency of exposure as manipulated within the experiment. It is very similar to the predifferentiation paradigm described earlier, except that the subject is not instructed to attach any verbal responses to the items during the familiarization phase.

In familiarization studies, the subject is presented with a pretraining task before the learning task. Subjects in control conditions are given no pretraining or irrelevant pretraining on items which will not be encountered on the learning task, in order to equate all conditions on such nonspecific factors as warm-up from the pretraining task.

Sheffield (1946) examined the effects of amount and locus of prefamiliarization on paired-associate learning. He gave different amounts of prefamiliarization on either the stimulus or response terms. The results indicated significant benefits from prefamiliarization for the response terms but not for the stimulus terms.

A similar study (Underwood and Schulz, 1960, Experiment I) also indicated that the more familiarization trials, the greater the benefit on learning when the response terms were involved. However, with stimulus terms, performance actually decreased slightly as a function of amount of familiarization.

The amount of familiarization and the locus of familiarization in paired-associate learning were varied by Gannon and Noble (1961). The results of some previous studies indicated that familiarization was more effective on the response than on the stimulus terms, whereas other studies suggested that familiarization had no effect at all.

Four familiarization conditions were involved: 20 trials on both the stimulus and response terms ($S_{20}R_{20}$); 20 trials on the stimulus and zero trials on the response terms ($S_{20}R_0$); zero trials on the stimulus terms and 20 trials on the response terms (S_0R_{20}); and zero trials on both the stimulus and response terms (S_0R_0). To equate warm-up, the total amount of pretraining was equated in all four conditions by providing added familiarization on materials which were irrelevant to the test list. A fifth condition, which served as a control group for warm-up, received no familiarization training.

No instructions to learn were given during pretraining; subjects were instructed instead to pronounce each of fifteen items aloud as they were presented. Then a list of five paired associates was learned, containing ten of the fifteen pretrained items. The remaining five items were included to provide the same total number of exposures for all conditions.

The procedure for paired-associate learning differed in one respect from the typical procedure. The subjects were required to pronounce the stimulus terms in addition to anticipating the response terms. Gannon and Noble felt that this procedure would ensure maximal stimulus reception.

The results indicated significant benefits on performance for conditions receiving stimulus familiarization but not for those given response familiarization. Gannon and Noble interpreted this finding, which departed from those in previous studies, to mean that stimulus terms were more important in the learning process than the response terms. Their

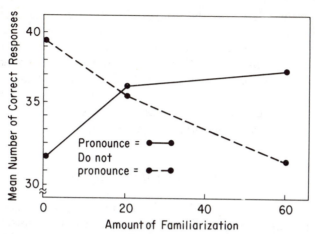

Figure 4.2. Mean total number of correct responses during seventeen anticipation trials as a function of instructions and number of stimulus familiarization trials. [From R. W. Schulz and I. F. Tucker: Supplementary report: Stimulus familiarization in paired-associate learning. *Journal of Experimental Psychology*, 1962, **64**, 549–550. Reprinted by permission of the American Psychological Association and the authors.]

results with variations of frequency of occurrence of items disagree with those obtained in other studies for variations of rated meaningfulness. Gannon and Noble take this discrepancy as evidence against a frequency hypothesis, such as that of Underwood and Schulz, to explain the effects of meaningfulness on learning.

One factor which may account for the discrepancy between results of the later study and earlier findings has already been mentioned. Schulz and Tucker (1962) hypothesized that the procedure employed by Gannon and Noble, which called for articulation of stimulus terms during paired-associate anticipation learning, may have produced the higher performance in the stimulus familiarization condition. Due to acquaintance with the stimulus terms during pretraining for this condition, subjects could pronounce them faster than the nonfamiliarized subjects during the actual learning task. The importance of this difference lies in the fact that familiarization conditions would gain more time in which to anticipate on the test list.

As a test of their explanation, Schulz and Tucker compared paired-associate learning with articulation and nonarticulation of stimulus terms after either zero, 20, or 60 trials of stimulus familiarization. When articulation was employed as in Gannon and Noble's study, significant benefits of stimulus familiarization were obtained. However, when articulation of stimulus terms was not required, performance was found to be inversely related to the amount of stimulus familiarization as shown in Figure 4.2.

A seemingly small procedural difference has been found to markedly affect the results. This example illustrates one of the dangers of employing highly standardized procedures. It is difficult to arrive at any firm conclusion regarding the effects of familiarization. The effects of this variable on stimulus terms must be weak if opposite results are obtained, depending on whether or not articulation was required during pretraining.

Associative Learning

In addition to forming stimulus differentiation and response integration, it is necessary that the subject acquire associations between specific stimuli and responses before learning is completed. In theoretical discussions, an association refers to the *connection* or *bond* between two items. In the study of current learning, it is the investigator who determines which associations will be learned on the task. He selects certain items which he instructs the subject to associate. On the other hand, he can make inferences about previously learned associations, which are beyond the control of an investigator, from observations of verbal behavior.

Associations between items appear to be formed in both the forward and the reverse (or backward) direction. Suppose the subject learns an association between the stimulus *A* and the response *B*. When he is presented with *A*, he can respond with *B* if learning has occurred. Not only can the subject give the forward association, *A–B*, but it appears that the backward association, *B–A*, also exists. Thus, if he is tested with the response, *B*, he can respond with the proper stimulus term, *A*. Usually however, forward associations have been found to be stronger than backward associations (Ekstrand, 1966).

Backward associations can be considered a form of incidental learning, since no instructions are provided to the subjects at the outset that they will be tested for backward associations. In many respects, backward associations follow the same laws as forward associations. For example, Jantz and Underwood (1958) demonstrated that both types of associative learning improve as a direct function of the number of practice trials provided for forward associative learning, although forward learning reaches a higher level than backward learning.

An alternative view (Asch and Ebenholtz, 1962a) holds that forward and backward associative tendencies of equal strength are formed during associative learning. The view that associations are of equal strength in either direction is referred to as the *symmetry* position, whereas the *asymmetry* position holds that forward associations are stronger. Asch and Ebenholtz maintained that findings of superior forward associative learning are an artifact stemming from the use of transformed stimuli on the part of subjects in learning the list. Suppose you were required to learn an association between CQW and DPX. Under the anticipation method of learning, you would need to learn the response term exactly but could modify the nominal stimulus into a form which aided your learning. When the test for backward association occurred, you might very well remember your transformed modification of the stimulus. However, since the backward association test requires the recall of the nominal stimulus and not the functional stimulus, B–A performance may be lowered.

Ekstrand (1966) suggested that the extent to which the Asch–Ebenholtz hypothesis is tenable depends on the type of nominal stimuli used. If they are complex and stimulus selection is probable, then the situation should favor asymmetry. However, with highly available stimulus and response terms, a better chance for symmetry is possible. Such a demonstration was made by Houston (1964*b*), who compared forward and backward recall of paired associates consisting of compound stimuli (colors and CVCs) and single-digit responses. Asymmetry was obtained when a comparison was made of forward recall of the digits and backward recall of either the compound stimulus or the trigram component. However, backward recall of the color component of the stimuli was equal to the forward recall condition. The color component was considered easier than the trigram component. Thus, asymmetry occurs if the stimuli are difficult since it leads to more stimulus selection, whereas with easy stimuli, backward recall is equal to forward recall.

Another problem of associative learning is the nature of the role of previously learned associations in the formation of new associations. When an association common to both the stimulus and response exists, it may facilitate the formation of the new association. This process is generally referred to as *mediation.*

The fact that mediation, or the use of intermediary past associations, occurs in the learning of new associations is commonplace. However, such evidence does not mean that all associations are formed with the aid of mediation. It is conceivable that some "raw" or direct learning could occur in which an association occurs between a stimulus and response in one or more trials simply on the basis of contiguity.

In fact, Spear, Ekstrand, and Underwood (1964) suggest that associations can be formed by contiguity alone. In two of their three experiments, they used a verbal discrimination task. In this task, the subject was presented with a list of pairs of items, and his task was to learn which member of each pair was the "correct" one. Before the experiment, the experimenter arbitrarily designated which member of each pair was "correct."

After this task, Spear *et al.* had subjects learn a paired-associate list containing the same items involved on the verbal discrimination task. In Experiment II, one group received the original pairings while another group received altered pairings of items from the verbal discrimination task. Better learning occurred in the group receiving a paired-associate list containing the original pairings. Similar findings were obtained in their other studies using different procedures. Since subjects were learning discriminations rather than intrapair associations on the verbal discrimination task, Spear *et al.* concluded that their results showed that associations can be formed by mere contiguity of items.

On the other hand, Spear *et al.* do suggest that subjects generally use mediators and past associations. They view contiguity as a more primary mechanism and one which may have aided the formation of prior associations, which then affect new learning. In short, with adult subjects, it is difficult to observe direct learning by contiguity because so much indirect learning occurs spontaneously via mediation.

Our evidence for mediation in the learning of a single list is mostly introspective and based on the verbal reports of subjects after the experiment (for example, Bugelski, 1962). The experimental manipulation of the mediational process involves the learning of two or more successive related lists and will be discussed in Chapter 8.

One-Trial versus Incremental Learning

A theoretical issue dividing associationists and cognitivists is the role of repetition on associative learning. For some theorists, associations are considered to involve the gradual or incremental build-up of habit strength with repeated trials. The alternative view maintains that an association is formed in one trial in an all-or-none manner. Suppose a learner misses an item on the first N trials of an experiment and gets it correct for the first time on Trial $N + 1$. The incremental position argues that associative strength was being gradually formed on trials preceding the first correct response; the one-trial view holds that no learning occurred prior to the trial on which the correct response first appeared. Learning of that item then occurred completely on that one trial. An illustration of the different conceptions for an item correctly given for the first time on Trial 4 is shown in Figure 4.3.

An experiment by Rock (1957) obtained results in favor of the one-trial

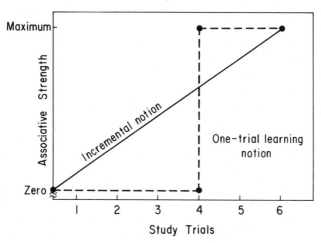

Figure 4.3. Schematic representation of the learning of a single paired associate as interpreted by a one-trial theory and by an incremental theory. The single item was first given correctly following the fourth study trial. [From B. J. Underwood and G. Keppel: One trial learning? *Journal of Verbal Learning and Verbal Behavior,* 1962, 1, 1–13. Reprinted by permission of Academic Press, Inc., and the authors.]

learning view. He utilized a "drop-out" procedure of administering a list of eight paired associates of single- or double-letter stimuli and number responses. On each trial, Rock replaced all unlearned items with new items from a pool of similar items. He continued with this procedure until the subject was able to learn all eight pairs presented on a given trial. The number of trials required to learn the list to one perfect trial in this manner was compared to that required by a control group which did not receive drop-out procedures. In other words, the control group received the same eight pairs on all trials as in the usual paired-associate task.

A comparison of these two groups provided Rock with a test of the role of repetition in learning. If repetition is important, then the experimental group which received the drop-out procedure should be poorer since every item that they eventually learned must have been learned in one trial. That is, since an item was dropped out of the list if it was not learned on a trial, there was no opportunity for incremental learning to occur. Since Rock found no difference in trials-to-criterion for the two conditions, he concluded that repetition was unnecessary for learning.

Proponents of the incremental view of associative learning (Postman, 1962*b;* Underwood, Rehula, and Keppel, 1962) attempted to demonstrate the role of artifacts in Rock's evidence. Both studies were based on the premise that the drop-out procedure developed by Rock allowed item selection such that the ultimate list learned by each subject in the experimental condition tended to consist of the easier items.

Postman (1962b) replicated Rock's study twice with the addition of a second control group who received the lists which the individual subjects of the drop-out condition ultimately learned. Since different individuals in the drop-out method eventually ended with different lists, the list for the added control condition varied for different subjects.

Eight pairs of nonsense syllables were selected for each subject from a pool of 202 items. In Experiment I, corrective feedback was presented, whereas it was omitted in Experiment II. Since the missed items would be dropped out in the experimental condition, it was assumed that feedback might not affect performance. However, with the control conditions, informative feedback might be useful for subsequent trials. In both experiments, the two control groups were significantly better than the drop-out condition, whereas Rock reported no difference between his one-control condition and drop-out condition. Postman attributed this discrepancy to the fact that selective rehearsal was more likely to have occurred in Rock's study, since subjects did not have to pronounce the items as in Postman's study. Evidence indicated that item selection was apparent only in Experiment I, where the control condition receiving lists assumed to be easier than those given to the drop-out condition eventually learned faster than the standard control condition.

Similar evidence that item selection occurred in the drop-out procedure was also reported by Underwood et al. (1962). The same set of basic materials used by Rock was employed in several replications. As in Rock's study, pairs of single- and double-letter stimuli and digit responses were learned under either a drop-out or a control condition. In addition, Underwood et al. tested the item-selection hypothesis by adding the second control condition, which learned the lists eventually learned by subjects in the drop-out condition. The evidence indicated that the drop-out procedure did lead to easier lists, thus supporting the item-selection explanation of Rock's results.

Another approach to the question of how repetition affects learning is the RTT (Reinforcement–Test–Test) paradigm (Estes, 1960; Estes, Hopkins, and Crothers, 1960). One study trial on a list of eight pairs of word stimuli and single digit responses (1 to 8) was followed by two successive test trials. On test trials, the subject was required to give the response to each stimulus as it was presented. Since no opportunity for additional reinforcement or feedback was provided between the two test trials, Estes et al. reasoned that no learning could occur between the two test trials.

Several aspects of the data are worth considering here, such as the percentage of items which were correct on both tests (C_1C_2), incorrect on both tests (NC_1NC_2), correct on the first but incorrect on the second test (C_1NC_2), and incorrect on the first but correct on the second (NC_1C_2). The last measure is of most relevance to the theoretical controversy.

On the basis of the one-trial position, the value of NC_1C_2 should be zero, since no opportunities for learning occur between tests. However, the response terms used by Estes *et al.* were the digits 1 to 8, and hence likely to be correctly guessed on some occasions. Thus, it is possible for items missed on the first test to become correct on the second test due to guessing one out of eight times, or 0.125. In fact, the results showed that 0.09 of the items incorrect on the first test were correct on the second test, which is close to chance expectation.

The incremental view, on the other hand, would predict that the value of NC_1C_2 would exceed chance. Although items may be incorrect on the first test, this position assumes that some increment of association is formed for those items so that their probability of being correct is actually greater than zero. The incrementalists assume that those items which were missed and those which were correctly given on the first trial have equal chances of being correct on the second test without any intervening reinforcement. The basis for this prediction involves the view that there is a threshold or minimal value of associative strength required before an item will be correctly given. This threshold varies from moment to moment just as does one's attention. On one trial, certain items of a given strength might be given correctly while others of the same strength might be missed. On the next trial, the same process occurs so that the items correctly given then will be independent of whether they were correct or incorrect on the first test. This prediction assumes that the items are all approximately equal in difficulty.

However, Estes (1960) views the data as strong evidence for the one-trial position, since the value of C_1C_2 was 0.71 and that of NC_1C_2 was 0.09. Contrary to the incremental view, the probability of an item's being correct on the second test is much higher for items that were correct than for those incorrect on the first test.

One possible alternative for explaining these results was suggested by Underwood and Keppel (1962*b*). If one assumes that the items correct on the first test are easier than those missed on the first test, then the Estes *et al.* results do not necessarily require the one-trial view of associative learning. Items correct on the first trial would be more likely also to be correct on the second trial than items which were incorrect on the first test, simply because they are easier items.

Estes *et al.* were aware of this interpretation and included control comparisons designed to show that items which were correct on the first test were equal in difficulty to those missed on the first test. However, Underwood and Keppel (1962*b*) point out that the controls used were equivocal for several reasons too complicated to describe here. It is still possible that items correctly given on the first test were easier than those missed on the first test. If this is the case, then the Estes *et al.* results are not convincing support for the one-trial learning view.

Postman (1963*b*) questioned the RTT evidence for the one-trial view and reported studies which supported the incremental theory. He varied the number of successive reinforcements preceding the tests. It was found that the value of NC_1C_2 increased as a function of the number of reinforcements preceding the first test, thus supporting the incremental view.

To summarize, the evidence on the one-trial learning issue is conflicting. Incrementalists have openly criticized the methodological soundness of studies proposed by the one-trial learning theorists. Unless studies of sound procedure are available, there is no way of beginning to evaluate the findings or arrive at any conclusions.

A considerable part of the confusion and emotion caused by this controversy stems from the ambiguous definition of a "trial." Trials vary in length and conditions of practice. A single trial on a list of one item is not the same as one on a list containing fifty items; yet, the present controversy seems to ignore such a simple observation. There may be no way of answering the question of the role of repetition on associative learning until a definition of a trial is reached.

Associative Hierarchy

A learning situation is typified by the fact that the correct response is initially absent or improbable. By the process of learning, the correct response is made increasingly probable until it becomes the dominant or exclusive response in that situation. It may be assumed that for any stimulus situation a hierarchy of responses exists. Initially, the correct response is low in the hierarchy, and incorrect responses higher in the hierarchy are more likely to occur. As learning occurs, the correct response tendency is elevated until it eventually attains the highest rank in the hierarchy of associative responses.

Some direct evidence on the nature of associative hierarchies may be obtained for verbal habits with the 100 words of the Kent–Rosanoff WAT. The frequency with which a response occurs to a stimulus word in the WAT norms may be considered to define its position in the associative hierarchy of that word. It is assumed that the associative hierarchy for each word was formed according to the laws of association during the lifetime of individuals. Whenever the learner is confronted with a new

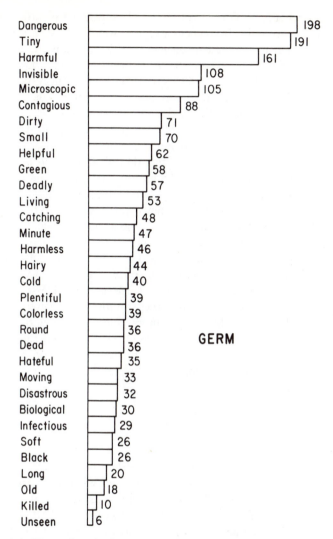

Figure 4.4. Hierarchy of adjective associations to germ. [From E. B. Coleman: The association hierarchy as a measure of extra-experimental transfer. *The Journal of Psychology,* 1964, **57,** 403–417. Reprinted by permission of The Journal Press and the author.]

learning task, these preexisting habit hierarchies interact with the habits to be formed and affect their acquisition.

In the laboratory situation, the investigator presents the learner with a task calling for the formation of new associations. If the task involves responses which are already dominant in strength to a given stimulus, no *new* learning is actually required; merely the performance or execution of existing associations. On the other hand, suppose the task requires responses which are unlikely to occur to given stimuli. That is, a response is called for which is assumed to be low in the associative hierarchy of the stimulus to which the response is to be attached. Here, new associative connections must be formed. The preexisting dominant response must be lowered, and the weaker response designated for the learning task must be elevated in the hierarchy of the stimulus involved.

An investigation by Coleman (1964) illustrates the application of the associative hierarchy concept. He assumed that the strength of a response to a given stimulus varied as a direct function of its location in the associative hierarchy of the stimulus. Coleman determined the nature of the hierarchies for a number of stimuli by instructing forty subjects to give continuous word associations. A continuous word-association test requires the subject to product a series of successive associative responses to each stimulus word. It is assumed that each successive response represents a lower position of the hierarchy. Figure 4.4 provides an example from Coleman's study of the associative hierarchy for the word *germ.* From these types of data, he constructed lists of paired associates. All lists contained the same stimuli but the stimuli were paired with responses from different levels of their hierarchies. A strong relationship was obtained between the number of correct responses and the assumed position of the response in the hierarchy. The earlier a response occurred in the continuous word-association test, the better it was learned as a response on the paired-associate task.

SUMMARY

There is considerable variation among experimenters in the procedures actually employed when they are all supposedly using the same task. There is no one standard serial or paired-associate learning paradigm; instead, there are varieties of both paradigms in present use. The demands of the task on the subject vary with the particular procedures employed by the experimenter. For example, what the subject must learn on a paired-associate task can be slightly different, depending upon whether the anticipation or study-test procedure is used.

Each variation of a given paradigm has just as much "validity" as any other; however, such a philosophy does lead to difficulty in allowing comparisons across experiments. Unless the investigator is primarily interested in the effects of procedural variations, it might be more useful in the long run for investigators to use some set of procedures which allow the formation of a body of knowledge obtained under comparable conditions.

One difficulty, of course, is in getting agreement as to which particular procedures should be defined as the standard ones.

The analysis of the acquisition process may be conveniently divided into three parts: stimulus differentiation, associative learning, and response learning or availability. Differentiation involves the ability of the subject to discriminate among items and should be inversely related to the similarity of the material. The formation of associations between stimuli and responses raises the question of whether learning is incremental or all-or-none. Tests of the one-trial learning position seem to have been equivocal, partly because the definition of what a trial *is* varies with the theoretical biases of the investigators. Finally, response learning or integration has been found to be highly affected by the meaningfulness of the material. However, a number of factors are correlated with this characteristic of material, such as pronunciability, frequency, or familiarity. Any or all of these factors may be responsible for the better learning obtained with higher meaningfulness.

CHAPTER 5

Transfer of Training

W henever new learning occurs, it takes place in the context of previously acquired learning; preexperimental habits play a role in the ease or difficulty with which the new learning proceeds. Nonetheless, in some situations the previous learning is ignored or assumed equivalent in all experimental conditions, since the precise nature of the past learning is often unknown. If the main concern of a study is to determine the effects of concurrent conditions on learning, then past learning is not taken into consideration. Similarly, retention studies which examine how the conditions of acquisition affect subsequent retention do not assess preexperimental habits. Such "selective" procedures are convenient when our major interest is the study of certain aspects of learning and retention. This is not to say that pre-experimental learning is unimportant or that it does not affect the processes of learning and retention: on the contrary. But it is a truism to assert that the learner possesses other verbal associations at the time he begins the laboratory task. Without more exact knowledge of the nature of his past learning, we are uncertain as to how it might interact with the new learning, if at all. Clearly, in order to describe the ways in which past learning affects new learning, we need information specifying the nature of the past learning and its relationship to the present learning.

How We Study Transfer of Training

The formal study of relationships between two tasks and the nature of transfer between the tasks investigates what is known as *transfer of training*. Rather than make inferences or assumptions about the nature of past learning, transfer studies require the subject to learn two successive tasks, both in the laboratory. In this situation the experimenter knows and controls the nature of the past learning. By systematically varying some of the aspects of relationships between the two tasks, he makes some determination of the principles underlying transfer between tasks. Of course, transfer is involved also when more than two tasks are concerned, but such situations are too complicated for analysis here. As will soon become evident, the aspects of transfer are many, even when there are only two tasks under consideration.

Generally speaking, in the study of transfer we are interested in how the learning of some first task affects the learning of a second task. An answer to this question necessitates a comparison between the learning of a given task when it is preceded, and when it is not preceded, by some other task whose transfer effects we wish to assess. Briefly, one procedure used in early studies was as follows: In the experimental condition, one task was followed by a second one, whereas only the second task was assigned in the control condition. If no other factors were operative, then any differences between the experimental and control performances on the second task were attributed to the effects of the first task, which only the experimental condition received. The control condition was needed to tell us what level of performance might have occurred had the first task not been administered to the experimental condition.

However, due to other processes which invariably operate in actual practice, it is not possible to attribute all, or perhaps any, of the differences between an experimental and a control condition to *specific* transfer from the first task to the second task in the experimental condition.

The transfer between tasks that occurs when some particular aspect of one task affects the learning of another may be referred to as *specific* transfer. If a first task leads to better performance on a second task relative to a control condition, we refer to *positive* transfer, but if it leads to poorer performance then we speak of *negative* transfer. In addition to the possible occurrence of specific transfer, invariably *nonspecific* transfer occurs between any two tasks. Due to the extended practice involved in learning the two tasks in the experimental condition, the subject may acquire warm-up which will enhance his performance. Furthermore, he may actually learn how to learn, that is, acquire techniques which are facilitative for learning a general class of tasks. These nonspecific factors, to be discussed at length later, operate even when there is no specific transfer between two tasks.

For this reason it is not proper to measure specific transfer effects by simply including a control group which receives only the second task, as

TABLE 5.1

AN EXPERIMENTAL DESIGN FOR TRANSFER

Condition	Task 1	Task 2	Type of Transfer
Experimental group	Learn A	Learn B	Specific transfer from A Nonspecific transfer over tasks
Control group (one-task)	(rest)	Learn B	Neither specific transfer from A nor nonspecific transfer over tasks
Control group (two-task)	Learn X	Learn B	Nonspecific transfer over tasks

was typical in early studies of transfer. Differences between the experimental and control groups may still stem partly or entirely from nonspecific effects which are present only in the experimental group, as indicated in Table 5.1. The first task may contribute no specific transfer to the performance of the experimental group on its second task. However, there could still be improved second-task performance in the experimental condition due to nonspecific sources of transfer. It is also possible that a combination of unknown percentages of specific and nonspecific factors could account for any differences in the experimental–control comparison.

The one-task control condition is inadequate because it leads to an overestimation of true positive transfer from specific sources by failing to control for such nonspecific effects as warm-up and learning-to-learn. At the same time, lack of control for such nonspecific factors permits an underestimation of true specific negative transfer between tasks in the experimental condition.

To provide adequate control for nonspecific transfer effects, it is necessary to employ a base-line condition in which subjects learn two tasks between which no specific transfer is involved, such as two unrelated tasks. The two-task control condition provides a base line against which other conditions that learn two related tasks can be compared to determine the amount of specific transfer.

Specific Transfer

One does not obtain in the same amount or direction of specific transfer between different pairs of tasks. The transfer between learning French and Italian is different from that between learning how to hit a baseball and how to solve calculus problems. An early suggestion (Thorndike and Woodworth, 1901) was that transfer occurred via the exchange of identical elements. Thus, if two tasks shared common elements, then learning of one would facilitate the acquisition of the other. If two tasks are similar, one would expect positive transfer.

Some tasks may be similar in some aspects but dissimilar in other aspects. Running is involved in both football and track, but the nature of the running and the conditions under which it can be performed differ markedly. Are the two tasks to be considered similar?

A closer analysis of laboratory tasks involves the distinction between interlist similarity of stimuli and of responses. (Interlist similarity refers to the similarity *between* lists and should not be confused with intralist similarity, mentioned earlier, which refers to the similarity *within* a single list.)

Suppose we examine the learning of two paired-associate lists. The relationship between the two lists might vary along the entire continuum of similarity on either the stimulus side or the response side, or both. Two tasks may be of high similarity in one locus but of low similarity in the other locus. Thus, it is not unequivocal whether such tasks are similar or dissimilar. How variations in interlist stimulus and response similarity affect the amount and direction of transfer has been a major concern in transfer studies.

A major difficulty in determining the effects of interlist stimulus and response similarity is agreeing on a definition of "similarity." In one sense, similar items are those that look alike and tend to be confused with each other, whereas dissimilar items are those that are readily discriminable from each other. In the case of nonsense syllables and geometrical forms, this definition seems appropriate. But when we deal with meaningful words, physical similarity is not as important as the meaningful similarity, or synonymity, among items. More serious is the problem that words of high similarity tend to be more closely associated than words of low similarity. Thus, *happy, joyful,* and *gleeful* are synonyms and are also strong associates of each other, whereas *placid, robust,* and *agile* are low in similarity of meaning and also lack strong interassociations. In addition, there may be strong associative strength between two words quite dissimilar in meaning, such as opposites like *black* and *white.* Sets of words which are similar seem also to be strongly associated, but not all sets of highly associated words need be similar.

Consider the subject who is presented with two lists of pairs on nonsense syllables to learn in which both the interlist stimulus and the response similarity are high. A representative pair from each list might be KEX–WOG and KIX–WUG. The high formal similarity between pairs of the two lists may hinder learning by confusing the learner. However, in the case of meaningful similarity, a representative pair from each list might be LAWYER–DOCTOR and ATTORNEY–PHYSICIAN. In this example of high interlist similarity of words, learning of the pairs in the first list may facilitate learning of those in the second list. Thus, formal and meaningful similarity may produce opposite effects.

One could speculate that the two situations just described represent the difference between a person's learning pairs of foreign words and pairs of his native words. The latter words would have meanings which enable him to see semantic relationships between pairs of two lists and eliminate interference due to any physical similarity.

Similarity is often discussed as if it were a single dimension along which items are easy to locate, but apparently such is not the case. The dimension of similarity for words may be closely tied to the dimension of associative strength, which is not based on physical similarity. Perhaps the dimension of associative strength is the more appropriate one to consider for prediction of transfer relationships. It can account for the positive transfer obtained sometimes from such opposites as *black* and *white,* which are high in associative strength. On the basis of similarity of meaning, these words are opposed, or low, in similarity and should be expected to produce little, if any, transfer if similarity is considered the basis for transfer.

Basic Transfer Paradigms

Variations in the degree of similarity between the stimuli as well as between the responses of the two lists serve to define the basic paradigms for the study of transfer. Since an analysis of the relationship of the stimuli and responses of the two tasks involved is desirable, the paired-associate task is most appropriate because it allows explicit separation of stimuli and responses. The basic transfer paradigms and the conventionally used notation for each are presented in Table 5.2.

Transfer paradigm labels are often confusing to the student. It is convenient for psychologists to refer to each paradigm in a type of shorthand, or code. The *A–B, C–B* paradigm, for example, refers to the situation in which the subject learns two lists which contain different sets of stimulus items but involve the same set of response terms. If QTW–*friendly* is one pair in the first list, the corresponding pair in the second list might be GKY–*friendly*.

On the other hand, if QTW–*friendly* is a pair from the first list and its corresponding pair in the second list is QTW–*sleepy*, we have a paradigm in which the stimuli are the same on both lists but the responses are

TABLE 5.2

BASIC TRANSFER PARADIGMS

Interlist Similarity		Paradigm	
STIMULUS TERMS	RESPONSE TERMS	LIST 1	LIST 2
Identical	Unrelated	A–B,	A–D
Unrelated	Identical	A–B,	C–B
Unrelated	Unrelated	A–B,	C–D
Identical [a]	Identical [a]	A–B,	A–Br

[a] Stimuli and Responses of the first list were re-paired to form the second list.

different. We would designate it as *A–B, A–D*. It should be emphasized that this paradigm has often been labeled *A–B, A–C*, but in order to have a more internally consistent code or system for all paradigms we will use the new label. However, you should equate these two labels (*A–B, A–D* and *A–B, A–C*) as referring to exactly the same situation.

This example serves to illustrate the arbitrariness of the code. The letters designating each transfer paradigm do not mean that there are actually *A*s, *B*s, *C*s, or *D*s in the lists. The letters are simply ways of labeling the stimulus and response loci of each list of a transfer paradigm. By examining the label, we can quickly decide what the relationship is between the two lists of a paradigm with respect to each locus.

In addition to the stimulus-response arrangements between two lists as shown in Table 5.2, there are paradigms with intermediate degrees of interlist stimulus and response similarity possible. For example, the stimuli or responses between the lists may not be identical but can vary along a continuum from identical to dissimilar such as $A, A', A'' \cdots C$ for stimuli, and $B, B', B'' \cdots D$ for responses. Table 5.3 provides some idea of the large number of paradigms possible. However, the paradigms described in Table 5.2 are the major interlist similarity relationships to be considered here.

TABLE 5.3

SOME COMBINATIONS OF DIFFERENT DE-
GREES OF INTERLIST STIMULUS AND RESPONSE SIMILARITY

	Interlist Stimulus Similarity						
	HIGH						LOW
HIGH	A–B,	A–B	A–B,	A′–B	A–B,	A″–B . . . A–B,	C–B
	A–B,	A–B′	A–B,	A′–B′	A–B,	A″–B′ . . . A–B,	C–B′
Interlist	A–B,	A–B″	A–B,	A′–B″	A–B,	A″–B″ . . . A–B,	C–B″
Response							
Similarity							
LOW	A–B, ↓ A–D		A–B, ↓ A′–D		A–B, ↓ A″–D . . . A–B, ↓ C–D		

Measurement of Transfer

Before we examine the evidence on the effects of interlist similarity, let us consider some problems in measuring the magnitude and direction of transfer effects in general.

The simplest measure of transfer is a difference score (E–C) between the mean performance of the experimental and the control conditions on the second, or transfer, task. One shortcoming of this absolute transfer measure, however, is that comparisons with results from other studies are meaningless, since the number of trials, length of lists, and other procedures vary from study to study. A conversion of absolute transfer scores into relative, or percentage, scores allows comparisons across studies. The difference between the experimental and control condition is viewed in proportion to the performance level attained by the control condition:

$$\frac{E - C}{C} \times 100 = \text{percentage transfer}$$

Both measures are used in transfer studies since there is no common agreement as to which is the better index. Consider the results of some hypothetical experiments in Table 5.4. Experiment A has a score of 100 for the experimental group and of 50 for the control group. There are 50 units of positive transfer by the difference score, and there is 100 percent transfer by the percentage score. In Experiment B, the experimental group obtains a score of 200 while the control group gets 100. Now we have

100 units of absolute transfer and 100 percent transfer on a percentage basis. If we use absolute scores, we argue that Experiment B shows twice as much transfer as Experiment A, but if we use percentage scores we conclude that there are no differences.

On the other hand, suppose we consider two additional studies. In Experiment C, the experimental group score is 200, and the control group score is 150. There are 50 units of absolute transfer, and there is a percentage transfer of 33 percent. In Experiment D, the absolute transfer is 50 units, whereas there is a percentage gain of 67 percent. Again, depending on our index, we may conclude either that there is no difference in transfer, or that there is twice as much transfer, in one study as in the other.

TABLE 5.4

RESULTS AND TRANSFER SCORES IN FOUR HYPOTHETICAL EXPERIMENTS

Experiment	Experimental Group	Control Group	Difference Score (E − C)	Percentage Score $\frac{(E - C)}{C} \times 100$
A	100	50	50	100
B	200	100	100	100
C	200	150	50	33
D	125	75	50	67

Other indices have been developed for measuring transfer (Gagné, Foster, and Crowley, 1948; Murdock, 1957) which are variations of the percentage score. Gagné *et al.* take into consideration the maximal level of performance possible in the situation under study. However, many transfer situations do not have a known maximal score. Murdock's formula

$$\frac{E - C}{E + C} \times 100$$

has a maximum value of 100 percent positive or negative transfer. However, there are no logical reasons for this formula other than ones of convenience. The addition of the E and C scores to provide the denominator of the formula has no psychological meaning and is arbitrary.

There is still no universally employed measure of transfer. Obviously, it is difficult to make precise quantitative comparisons across studies which use different indices of transfer; comparisons of the general effects in different studies are more sound. Now that some of the problems of measuring transfer have been pointed out, we can return to the examination of interlist similarity.

Stimulus Similarity Varied, Response Similarity Maximal In order to assess the effects of interlist similarity on transfer, let us vary similarity in one locus while holding it constant on the other side. Otherwise, if we vary interlist similarity simultaneously on both stimulus and response terms, we cannot possibly determine how much of the over-all effect is due to variation of stimulus or response similarity separately.

Yum (1931) had subjects learn paired associates consisting of nonsense syllable stimuli and word responses. The next day they were required to learn a list with the *identical* set of responses but with stimuli ranging from identical to dissimilar (to the extent of four different degrees) to those of the first day. The greater the dissimilarity between the stimuli of the two lists, the poorer was transfer performance.

Similar findings were obtained by Hamilton (1943), who used *identical* sets of nonsense syllables as responses in both lists but varied the similarity of the geometrical-form stimuli across lists from identical to three other points of less similarity. Decreases in positive transfer occurred as the stimuli decreased in similarity.

Stimulus Similarity Varied, Response Similarity Minimal Unlike either Yum or Hamilton, Gibson (1941) assessed the effects of interlist stimulus similarity under conditions in which the responses of the two lists were *different*. However, interlist response similarity was not systematically varied. Under these conditions, stimulus similarity led to results opposed to those found by Yum or Hamilton. In Gibson's study, there was decreasing positive transfer as the stimuli between lists became more similar. Apparently the effects of degree of interlist stimulus similarity depend on the degree of interlist response similarity.

This pattern of findings can be related to Gibson's (1940) theory based on stimulus generalization, which accounted for some basic facts of learning and transfer. Similarity was considered as a single dimension along which stimuli were ordered. Although her theory was aimed at verbal learning situations, we should keep in mind that her use of geometrical nonsense forms as stimuli may not have yielded the same results as verbal stimuli might have.

In applying her theory to transfer situations, Gibson varied interlist stimulus similarity while holding the interlist response similarity constant, making it either identical or dissimilar in the two lists. The effects of similarity of stimuli between lists differed depending on the interlist similarity of the responses. If the sets of responses were *identical,* positive transfer was obtained with increasing stimulus similarity (Yum, 1931; Hamilton, 1943); if the sets of responses were *dissimilar,* negative transfer was obtained with increasing stimulus similarity (Gibson, 1941).

Underwood (1961), in evaluating the Gibson theory, observed that no account of the effects of variations of interlist response similarity was included. The situations Gibson used involved either identical or dissimilar responses between lists, but no systematic variation of the interlist response similarity was made. In this respect, Gibson's report falls short of being a complete account of interlist similarity effects on transfer.

Response Similarity Varied, Stimulus Similarity Maximal The effects of interlist response similarity have been examined with the interlist stimulus similarity held constant, that is, either identical or dissimilar.

When the sets of stimuli were *identical* in the two lists and the response similarity was varied, it was found (Bruce, 1933; Underwood, 1951) that performance was better, the greater the interlist response similarity. Neither study allows conclusions about the absolute level of performance; although the performance of the second task was higher than that of the first in direct proportion to the degree of interlist response similarity, in the absence of a control for the beneficial effects of nonspecific transfer, it is not possible to conclude that improved performance on the second task was entirely due to positive transfer. However, one may say that there is relatively higher performance (less negative or more positive) transfer with higher interlist response similarity when the sets of stimuli are *identical* across lists.

Response Similarity Varied, Stimulus Similarity Minimal The effects of degree of interlist response similarity may also be assessed when the sets of stimuli on the two lists are *dissimilar.* Young and Underwood (1954) suggested that positive transfer could occur in this situation if the interlist response similarity was maximal. The differentiation that subjects formed among the response terms while learning the first list would aid in learning the second list if the same sets of responses were used on both lists. Thus, the investigators predicted that the higher the interlist response similarity, the greater the positive transfer of differentiation of responses.

Young and Underwood tested their notion by actually providing predifferentiation of the response terms before the experiment to some groups, while giving practice on irrelevant items during this phase to control groups. Predifferentiation of responses was assumed to eliminate response differentiation as a source of positive transfer between lists for the experimental conditions. Different groups received lists of low, medium, or high interlist response similarity. Variations in interlist response similarity did not affect the amount of transfer when responses were predifferentiated. But when predifferentiation involved irrelevant items, there was a slight increasing trend toward positive transfer as the level of interlist response similarity increased.

Thus, a trend toward increasing positive transfer from response differentiation occurs as a direct function of the amount of interlist response similarity, provided the sets of stimuli are *unrelated* in the two lists (Young and Underwood, 1954). Similar increases in positive transfer occur with higher interlist response similarity when the *identical* set of stimuli is used on both lists (Bruce, 1933; Underwood, 1951).

A Transfer Model

By this point, it should be obvious that the effects of interlist stimulus and response similarity are complicated and undoubtedly difficult to integrate. Some system for organizing the myriad findings would be useful in providing an overview.

In attempting just such a summary of the current evidence on transfer at the time, Osgood (1949) proposed a model of the effects of interlist stimulus and response similarity. Three laws of interlist similarity were proposed: (1) when the stimuli are identical, increasing negative transfer is obtained with increased response dissimilarity; (2) when stimuli vary and responses are identical, positive transfer increases with increased stimulus similarity; (3) when both stimuli and responses vary, negative transfer increases as stimulus similarity increases.

Figure 5.1 illustrates the principles of transfer proposed by Osgood. The dimensions of interlist stimulus and response similarity are indicated, with several levels for each. Since it was based on existing studies, the model allows for wider variations of response similarity (identical, similar, neutral, opposed, antagonistic) than for stimulus similarity (identical, similar, neutral). However, it would seem logical to provide equal ranges of similarity for both stimuli and responses. Any possible combination of interlist stimulus and response similarity can be located on this model by finding the location of the similarity level of the stimulus and response terms and determining their intersection on the top surface of the model. For convenience, we have located and labeled four major transfer paradigms on the model: A–B, A–B; A–B, A–D; A–B, C–B; A–B, C–D.

The vertical dimension of the model provides an estimate of the amount and direction of transfer for each possible combination of interlist

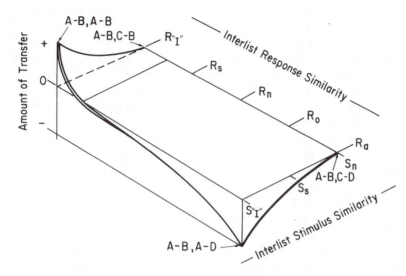

Figure 5.1. The transfer and retroaction surface: Medial plane represents effects of zero magnitude; response relations distributed along length of solid and stimulus relations along its width. [Based on C. E. Osgood: The similarity paradox in human learning: A resolution. *Psychological Review*, 1949, **56**, 132–143. Reprinted by permission of the American Psychological Association and the author.]

stimulus and response similarity. The flat rectangular surface on the horizontal plane is considered to represent zero transfer.

Consider a few aspects of Osgood's surface. In the left background, we see that positive transfer increases as stimulus similarity increases, provided the sets of responses are identical across lists (Hamilton, 1943; Yum, 1931). At the other end of the model, in the right foreground, we see the effects of varying stimulus similarity when the sets of responses are different on the two lists. As in Gibson's study (1941), negative transfer increases as interlist stimulus similarity becomes higher in this situation.

Next, examine the front side of the model, which portrays the effects of variation of interlist response similarity when interlist stimulus similarity is high. Transfer changes from positive to negative as response similarity moves from identical to different, agreeing with the results by Bruce (1933) and Underwood (1951).

Finally, the far side of the model illustrates the effects of interlist response similarity when the sets of stimuli on the two lists are different. There is almost no effect, and transfer is neither positive nor negative. Young and Underwood's study (1954) indicated a slight tendency for higher positive transfer with increased interlist response similarity in this situation. However, since the effect was small, it could be taken as confirmation of this side of the model.

The Osgood model is a summary, based on previous studies, which aids us in visualizing the effects of many possible combinations of interlist stimulus and response similarity. The model describes the relationships between these variables but does not represent an explanation. Its validity depends on the correspondence of the results of subsequent studies with its predictions.

Bugelski and Cadwallader (1956) made a test of Osgood's model, using a sample of the possible combinations of interlist stimulus and response similarity. Actually, these investigators were measuring the retention of the first list after both the first and second lists had been learned. Since retention and the learning of the transfer list were correlated, it is possible also to make conclusions about transfer from their data on retention.

They used geometrical forms as stimuli and adjectives as responses in paired-associate lists. Interlist stimulus similarity varied from identical to neutral at four different points, while interlist response similarity varied from identical to opposed, also at four points along the continuum. Bugelski and Cadwallader provided a more extensive study than those available before Osgood's model.

While predictions based on Osgood's model were upheld for variations in stimulus similarity, no support was obtained for these involving response variations. When the sets of stimuli varied, with the sets of responses being identical across lists, increasing positive transfer was obtained with higher stimulus similarity. If both stimulus and response similarity varied, negative transfer increased as stimulus similarity increased. However, when sets of stimuli across lists were identical, performance was poorer with higher response similarity, contrary to prediction.

One possible factor accounting for Bugelski and Cadwallader's failure to confirm the prediction may have been that their first and second lists were unequal in difficulty. Since the lists were not counterbalanced, it is possible that some conditions had more difficult transfer tasks (Underwood, 1961). The second tasks must be equal in difficulty for all conditions if one wishes to compare the effects of different first tasks on the transfer task.

Dallett (1962) also tested a number of combinations of interlist stimulus and response similarity represented on Osgood's model. He employed the same list as the second, or transfer, list for all conditions, allowing their first lists to differ. In this way, comparisons across conditions on transfer would be based on a list which was of equal difficulty for all conditions. Dallett's results led him to conclude that Osgood's model was valid for the most part.

Wimer (1964) conducted a thorough test of points on the transfer surface. He employed five levels of both stimulus and response interlist similarity, requiring twenty-five different experimental conditions. He used lists of paired associates comprised of common adjectives.

Wimer found that when the sets of stimuli were identical, negative transfer was obtained only if the sets of responses were unrelated or dissimilar. For situations with some degree of response similarity, positive transfer was obtained. Thus, Osgood's prediction for such paradigms was confirmed. When the sets of responses were identical across lists, positive transfer was found to increase as the stimulus similarity between lists increased. This finding also agreed with Osgood's prediction.

Finally, when both stimulus and response similarity varied, the results did not confirm Osgood's predictions that increased stimulus similarity would lead to increased negative transfer. Wimer obtained positive transfer for all combinations of stimulus and response interlist similarity.

Summary of
Interlist Similarity

The results of studies varying similarity between tasks are complex. One obvious conclusion is that transfer is maximal when both stimuli and reponses are identical between lists. In this limiting case of interlist similarity, the transfer situation actually consists of the two successive trials of a learning experiment on the same list.

But as both the stimulus and response terms between the two lists become less similar, less positive transfer occurs, although it is not necessarily the case that negative transfer is obtained. Some positive transfer may be obtained due to the generalization between tasks as a function of similarity. Stimulus generalization refers to the fact that a response associated with one stimulus may also occur when stimuli similar to the original one are presented. The analogous tendency for a stimulus to evoke responses similar to the one originally associated to that stimulus is called *response generalization*.

Simple conclusions are not possible in situations where the interlist similarity is high in one locus but varied in the other locus.

If the sets of stimulus terms on both lists are identical, there should be a component of positive transfer due to stimulus differentiation, regardless of the level of interlist response similarity. Since the stimuli have become differentiated on the first list, second-list learning involving the same stimuli should be aided. However, if the responses on the lists are different, we have the A–B, A–D paradigm in which there may be interference due to the competing associations required on the two lists. This negative component exceeds the positive factor so that negative transfer has been the rule in this paradigm.

On the other hand, as the sets of responses on the two lists become more similar, positive transfer has been obtained. The similar responses no longer form competing associations; in fact, a mediation chain of A–(B)–B′ may be formed to aid second-list learning, especially if the responses are words. If nonsense syllable responses are used so that the similarity is formal, response generalization may produce the positive transfer. In addition, stimulus differentiation would be an added source of positive transfer regardless of the type of responses.

If the sets of responses are identical across lists, there should be positive transfer of response learning, regardless of the level of interlist stimulus similarity. The magnitude of this factor varies as a function of the difficulty of the responses. However, when the stimuli are different on the two lists (A–B, C–B), the backward associations (B–A, B–C) of the two lists form a negative transfer paradigm themselves of identical stimuli paired with different responses (Twedt and Underwood, 1959). Transfer in the A–B, C–B paradigm should be a function of the relative magnitude of these two opposed factors; usually, transfer has been small in this paradigm.

On the other hand, identical sets of responses paired with highly similar sets of stimuli across lists (A–B, A′–B) favor positive transfer. There would still be positive transfer of response learning. Furthermore, the backward associations of the two lists (B–A, B–A′) would form a paradigm of identical stimuli paired with similar responses. This situation has been found to produce positive transfer. Both factors are conducive for positive transfer, which has been obtained in this paradigm. Since the stimuli are highly similar, positive transfer may also be explained in terms of stimulus generalization.

Finally, when the interlist similarity is minimal for both stimuli and responses (A–B, C–D), any changes in performance from the first to the second list cannot be attributed to similarity. Nonetheless, improvement does occur between lists for this paradigm, and it can be assigned to the nonspecific factors of warm-up and learning-to-learn. The A–B, C–D paradigm thus represents a base-line, or control, comparison for non-specific effects so that the specific effects of interlist similarity in the other paradigms can be isolated.

Considerable attention has been given to the effects of interlist similarity, since the various transfer paradigms are defined in terms of this variable. Now we shall consider other factors which are involved in transfer.

Intralist Similarity

Gibson (1940) suggested that the stimulus differentiation developed from learning the first list could be a source of positive transfer on the learning of a second list containing the same set of stimuli. The amount of such positive transfer should be a direct function of the degree of intralist stimulus similarity. However, there has been little direct evidence to confirm this prediction.

By analogy, intralist response similarity might affect transfer in situations where the sets of responses across the two lists are identical. More positive transfer of response differentiation from the first to the second list should occur if there is high intralist response similarity in the set of responses common to both lists. The Young and Underwood (1954) study described earlier provided some slight indirect support for this prediction. In general, however, the effects of intralist stimulus and response similarity have not been closely tested in transfer situations.

Degree of
First-List Learning

Transfer should vary as a function of the degree of the first-list learning since the first task is considered the source of transfer. Atwater (1953) and Underwood (1951) varied the degree of first-list learning in the A–B, A–D paradigm and found substantial decrements in negative transfer as more first-list training was given. However, they did not include control groups in these studies, and the drop in negative transfer might simply reflect the benefits of warm-up. Several later studies (Jung, 1962; Postman, 1962c; Spence and Schulz, 1965) included an A–B, C–D control condition for nonspecific transfer. These more recent studies found only slight, if any, decreases in negative transfer with higher first-list learning in the A–B, A–D paradigm. Jung and Postman both found some slight decreases, but the net effect of first-list overlearning was still negative transfer. Figure 5.2 shows Postman's results for several paradigms as compared to the A–B, C–D control. For the A–B, A–D paradigm, there appears to be an increase, and then decrease, in negative transfer as the degree of first-list learning increases. However, this relationship was not statistically significant.

Mandler (1962, 1965) has maintained that overlearning of the first list in the A–B, A–D paradigm leads not only to substantial decreases in negative transfer but possibly even to positive transfer. His position is based on the earlier uncontrolled studies and experiments using animal

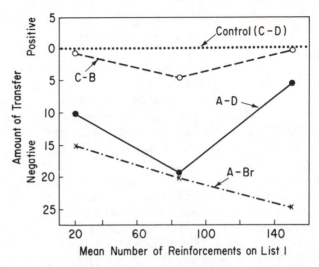

Figure 5.2. Amounts of negative transfer as measured by the differences between the control condition (C–D) and each of the experimental conditions in the mean number of correct responses over Trials 1 to 10 on the second list. [From L. Postman: Transfer of training as a function of experimental paradigm and degree of first-list learning. *Journal of Verbal Learning and Verbal Behavior,* 1962, 1, 109–118. Reprinted by permission of Academic Press, Inc., and the author.]

subjects. He suggested that overlearning produces cognitive structures of the first-list associations so that they no longer interfere with the associations to be formed on the second list. Jung (1965a) and Mandler (1965) have debated the facts and explanations of overlearning. There is no evidence for marked improvements in transfer as a result of over-learning when control groups for nonspecific transfer are utilized (Jung, 1962; Postman, 1962c; Spence and Schulz, 1965). Mandler maintained that studies of overlearning simply have not extended the degree of first-list learning far enough, and that when sufficiently high overlearning is employed, substantial reduction in negative transfer will result in this paradigm.

Degree of first-list learning in the Jung and Postman studies did not affect the amount of transfer in the A–B, C–B or A–B, C–D paradigms. However, as shown in Figure 5.2 for Postman's study, increased first-list learning led to marked increases in negative transfer in the A–B, A–Br paradigm, in which the stimuli and responses of the first list are re-paired to form a second list. Although stimulus differentiation and response learning on the first list are useful on the second list, substantial inter-ference exists from the competing associations involved between the two lists of this paradigm.

Response Meaningfulness

The effects of level of response meaningfulness in the A–B, C–B and A–B, A–D paradigms were examined by the writer (Jung, 1963). The A–B, C–D condition was also included for an estimate of nonspecific transfer.

In the A–B, C–B situation, the factor leading to positive transfer, response learning, was assumed to be greater with low meaningfulness responses. At the same time the formation of backward associations, B–A, B–C, which lead to negative transfer in this paradigm, was hypothesized to be minimized with low meaningfulness, since most of the effort would be concerned with response learning. It was predicted that low meaningfulness responses would lead to positive transfer, whereas high meaningfulness responses would lead to less positive or even negative transfer. The results supported the predictions.

Variations of response meaningfulness in the A–B, A–D paradigm cannot affect transfer between tasks via response learning since different sets of responses are involved on the two lists. However, if response meaningfulness affects the strength of associative learning, then it may affect transfer in this paradigm. Stronger competing associations should occur with responses of higher meaningfulness since response learning will be completed quickly and associative learning will occur, thus leading to greater negative transfer. The results showed slightly more negative transfer with responses of high meaningfulness.

Merikle and Battig (1963) also examined transfer as a function of response meaningfulness in different paradigms, the A–B, A–D and the A–B, A–Br. Their results also showed a slight tendency of greater negative transfer with higher meaningfulness responses in the A–B, A–D paradigm.

However, in the A–B, A–Br paradigm which generally leads to pronounced negative transfer (Besch and Reynolds, 1958; Porter and Duncan: 1953; Postman, 1962c; Twedt and Underwood, 1959), it was found that low meaningfulness responses led to positive transfer. Older findings of substantial negative transfer were replicated only with high meaningfulness responses.

Merikle and Battig applied the two-stage analysis (Underwood, Runquist, and Schulz, 1959) to their findings regarding the effects of response meaningfulness in the A–B, A–Br paradigm. In this situation, there is positive transfer of response learning but negative transfer of associative learning. When high meaningfulness responses are used, little response learning is required; as a result the associative learning which contributes interference is the major factor. However, with low meaningfulness responses, the negative transfer from associative learning is offset by greater positive transfer of response learning.

Components of Transfer

A theoretical formulation was proposed by Martin (1965) to incorporate transfer findings that have accumulated since Osgood's theory (1949). Martin considered that variations in degree of first-list learning and level of response meaningfulness accounted for findings which seem inconsistent with Osgood's predictions for different combinations of interlist stimulus and response similarity. We must consider the effects of these variables, as well as those of interlist similarity, in predicting the nature of transfer.

According to Martin, transfer between two paired-associate tasks involves the transfer of response learning, forward associations, and backward associations. The particular components involved differ for different paradigms. Thus, the A–B, A–D paradigm involves the transfer of forward associations between lists which produces negative transfer. In the A–B, C–B paradigm, backward associations of the two lists create interference which leads to negative transfer, whereas response learning is transferred from the first to the second list and leads to positive transfer. Figure 5.3 presents Martin's transfer surfaces for the different components.

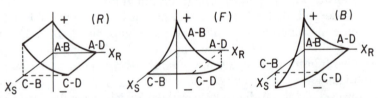

Figure 5.3. Component transfer surfaces. (The surfaces R, F, and B represent the transfer of response availability, forward associations, and backward associations, respectively.) [From E. Martin: Transfer of verbal paired associates. *Psychological Review,* 1965, **72,** 327–343. Reprinted by permission of the American Psychological Association and the author.]

Each of the surfaces shows the amount and direction of transfer of one of the components as a function of different combinations of interlist stimulus and response similarity. Consider the R surface, which shows how transfer of response learning differs for various paradigms. The square base of the model represents the level of zero transfer and also shows the combinations of different levels of interlist stimulus and response similarity. The corners are labeled, since they represent four basic transfer paradigms: A–B, A–B; A–B, A–D; A–B, C–B; A–B, C–D. The R surface suggests that positive transfer due to response learning increases as the interlist response similarity increases from different to identical. However, it is not affected by the interlist stimulus similarity.

The F surface shows the role of forward associations in different paradigms. There is zero or positive transfer in varying amounts from this component, except for the case where the interlist stimulus similarity is high and interlist response similarity is low. This case is the A–B, A–D paradigm, which generally produces negative transfer.

Finally, the B surface represents backward associations. As with forward associations, this component generally produces zero or positive transfer, which decreases as either interlist stimulus or response similarity decreases. However, in the case where interlist stimulus is low but interlist response similarity is high (A–B, C–B), the surface indicates strong negative transfer.

Such factors as degree of first-list learning (short of extreme degrees) and level of response meaningfulness affect the amount of these three components of transfer. Thus, a lower degree of first-list learning as well as lower response meaningfulness are beneficial to positive transfer in the A–B, C–B paradigm, since they maximize transfer of the positive component, response learning, while minimizing the negative component, backward associations. On the other hand, in the A–B, A–D paradigm, lower degrees of first-list learning and response meaningfulness produce less negative transfer, since such factors would presumably minimize the forward associative learning which is assumed to produce the negative transfer usually obtained there.

By considering the effects of such factors as degree of first-list learning and response meaningfulness on the postulated components of transfer in each paradigm, Martin has accounted for findings which do not conform closely to expectations based on Osgood's model.

Nonspecific Transfer

After this long discussion of specific transfer, we can now take a closer look at the evidence for nonspecific transfer. Regardless of the nature of two successive tasks, some form of nonspecific transfer may occur. Thus, in going from one task to another, a subject's performance may be enhanced due to transfer of warm-up. If, however, much effort is involved or the tasks are lengthy, performance on the second task may be impaired due to transfer of accumulated fatigue. Finally, if the two tasks are of the same form or involve similar skills, for example, paired associates, then the operation of learning-to-learn will facilitate second-list performance. The actual materials comprising one list may not even affect the learning of the second list, but since the two lists are both paired-associate lists, the learner may improve his performance on the second task as a consequence of becoming familiarized with the nature of such tasks and how best to proceed in mastering them.

Thune (1951) separated the warm-up and learning-to-learn components of nonspecific transfer. He had subjects learn three paired-associate lists on each of five days. The lists were considered to be equal in difficulty. The lists were counterbalanced or presented in different orders to different subjects. This procedure ensures that performance changes over successive lists can be attributed to the stage of practice rather than to the particular order of the lists.

As shown in Figure 5.4, the performance improved with each successive list within any given day. Furthermore, a comparison of the level of performance on the first list of each day for the several days revealed

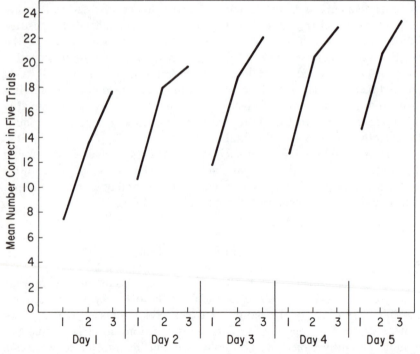

Figure 5.4. Mean total number of correct anticipations on the first five trials for each of the three lists learned on each of the five days ($N = 60$). [From L. E. Thune: Warm-up effect as a function of level of practice in verbal learning. *Journal of Experimental Psychology*, 1951, **42**, 250–256. Reprinted by permission of the American Psychological Association and the author.]

that it was also higher from day to day. There was, however, a drop in performance level from the last list of each day to the first list of the next day. In terms of nonspecific transfer factors, Thune concluded that the within-day changes reflected warm-up whereas the changes between days reflected learning-to-learn. The changes ascribed to warm-up were of greater magnitude than those due to learning-to-learn. Decrements in performance from the last list of one day to the first list of the next represented the dissipation of warm-up, which is temporary whereas learning-to-learn is more permanent.

Postman and Schwartz (1964) studied learning-to-learn and warm-up as a function of type of method and type of material. Each subject received one serial or paired-associate task of either trigrams or adjectives as his first list. Then, half of the subjects in each of these four conditions received a second list of serial adjectives, while the other half received a second list of paired-associate adjectives.

Postman and Schwartz were interested in assessing improvement in learning from one list to the second as a function of whether the materials were of the same class on the two lists, and whether the tasks involved on the two lists were of the same class. A control group learned only one list.

All experimental conditions showed improvement in proceeding from their first to their second list. The improvement was more substantial when the two lists involved the same type of task than when the type of task differed. A similar higher improvement was obtained if the materials in the two lists were of the same class. However, the effect of similarity of task was greater than that obtained for similarity of material. Postman and Schwartz concluded that certain techniques of learning involved in a specific task were being transferred between lists when the two lists involved the same type of task.

Postman (1964b) examined learning-to-learn as a function of the transfer paradigm involved. In the typical study of nonspecific effects, such as learning-to-learn, two unrelated tasks involving no specific transfer are used, such as an A–B, C–D paradigm for paired-associate lists.

Postman employed that paradigm plus three other widely used transfer paradigms: A–B, A–D; A–B, A–B′; and A–B, A–Br. Different groups learned three consecutive sets of two paired-associate lists of adjectives that conformed to one of the four transfer paradigms mentioned.

The results showed learning-to-learn in all paradigms, although the increase in the paradigm showing positive transfer (A–B, A–B′) was greater than the reductions in negative transfer occurring in the A–B, A–D and A–B, A–Br paradigms when the A–B, C–D paradigm was used as the control comparison.

It appears that improvement occurs over consecutive pairs of lists that constitute a given transfer paradigm. The differential improvement among paradigms could be due either to the acquisition of learning skills unique to each paradigm but differing in effectiveness, or to the development of general learning skills which also vary in applicability as a function of the paradigms.

Keppel and Postman (1966) attempted to answer the latter supposition by examining transfer from one paradigm to another. If general skills are involved in the improvement over pairs of lists, no impairment should occur when the paradigms involved are altered. On the other hand, this procedure will lower performance if specific skills are being acquired. Subjects learned two sets of lists corresponding to one of these paradigms: A–B, A–B'; A–B, A–D; A–B, A–Br; A–B, C–D. Then half of the

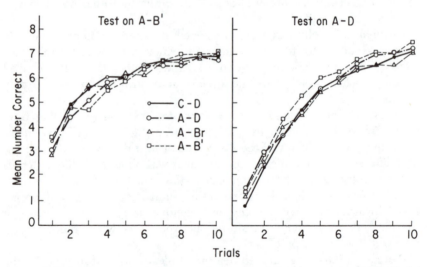

Figure 5.5. Performance on the transfer trials of Set 3 as a function of the paradigms used in training (Sets 1 and 2) and in the final common test (Set 3). [From G. Keppel and L. Postman: Studies of learning to learn: III. Conditions of improvement in successive transfer tasks. *Journal of Verbal Learning and Verbal Behavior*, 1966, **5**, 260–267. Reprinted by permission of Academic Press, Inc., and the authors.]

subjects learned a third set of lists forming the A–B, A–B' paradigm, while the remaining subjects learned lists representing the A–B, A–D paradigm. Keppel and Postman found that the type of training paradigm did not affect performance on the test paradigm, as shown in Figure 5.5. Performance was higher for the A–B, A–B' than for the A–B, A–D paradigm on the test list; but within each test paradigm, the type of training paradigm involved on the first two sets of lists did not affect performance.

They concluded that general rather than specific modes of learning were acquired over successive lists to account for the improved performance.

SUMMARY

Transfer of training studies involve the learning of two tasks in the laboratory environment. In this way, we may assess the effects of the first task on the learning of the second task. It is unnecessary to make assumptions or inferences about the nature of the past learning since we ourselves may specify its characteristics in transfer studies.

Performance on the second, or transfer, task is a function not only of factors derived from the specific first task learned but from such factors as warm-up and learning-to-learn, which are not specific to any particular task. It is necessary to include proper control conditions to separate the two sets of transfer factors.

The arrangements between two tasks may be examined in terms of the interlist similarity of stimuli and responses. Although many combinations of interlist stimulus and response similarity are possible, only a few major ones are investigated systematically: A–B, A–D; A–B, C–B; A–B, C–D; A–B, A–Br.

A summary of the transfer effects under different paradigms was made by Osgood. Studies conducted since this model was proposed have generally confirmed the predictions from it. Many of the findings which depart slightly from expectations based on the model have been incorporated by Martin's formulations based on three component models: response learning, forward associations, and backward associations. He suggested that these components play different roles under different paradigms. Furthermore, within a given paradigm, the principal components affecting transfer are modified by such variables as degree of first-list learning and level of response meaningfulness. From this framework it was shown that findings of small departures from those expected from Osgood's model are due to variations in these factors.

CHAPTER 6

Retention: Long- and Short-Term Memory

T he changes in performance attributed to learning are considered to be relatively permanent. Yet, an obvious fact of experience is that learned material is not perfectly retained. When retention is measured some time after the original learning has ended, we typically find that some forgetting has occurred. The longer the interval after learning, the greater the loss in retention. What are some of the factors responsible for this decrement in retention?

We shall examine some of the findings from experimental studies of forgetting. Most of the studies will deal with rote learning of unrelated materials. There are other aspects of memory which, while interesting, are not reported here because they are beyond the scope of this analysis. The selective forgetting or repression of emotionally unpleasant material is not included; nor is coverage of qualitative changes, that is, distorted memory, presented. Evidence for such aspects of memory comes primarily from naturalistic settings and is difficult to obtain in the laboratory because emotional and motivational factors are involved that are not easy to control experimentally.

The major aspects of memory that we shall examine here are quantitative changes in retention as a function of time. We shall also examine the variables found to produce such quantitative variations. Finally, we shall present a consideration of the theoretical analyses of forgetting.

Methods of Measurement

Three different indices of retention are the method of *recall,* method of *savings or relearning,* and method of *recognition.* The method of recall requires the subject to reproduce as much of the original material as he can without the aid of any external cues. Under the savings method, the initial time the subject needs to learn the task is compared with the time he requires to relearn the task. If forgetting is complete, there should be no savings in relearning as compared to original learning. On the other hand, if retention is complete, perfect performance should occur on the very first relearning trial. Finally, the recognition method actually provides the subject, on the retention test, with the original material in the context of other filler material which was not originally presented. Rentention is inferred if the subject can recognize the original material.

It has generally been found (Luh, 1922; Postman and Rau, 1957) that under a given set of conditions, estimates of retention are lowest under recall, intermediate with relearning, and highest with recognition measures. Recall is most difficult because the experimenter provides none of the original materials and the subject must recall them with a minimum of external cues. The method of relearning provides all the original materials and no additional material; however, if the subject has retained any of his learning it will be easier for him to relearn to his original level of performance. Recognition usually yields the highest index of retention since the subject does not have to make the responses available but only has to recognize them. However, there are a number of problems associated with such comparisons among methods, and we shall now take a more detailed look at the recognition method.

Recognition Memory On a recognition test, the correct item is presented with one or more alternatives which serve as distractors, on the assumption that if the item is remembered it can be identified from among several alternatives. If it has been forgotten, then it cannot be identified correctly except by chance. For this latter reason, recognition scores are usually adjusted for guessing by a factor of $1/N$, where N is the number of alternatives for each item. With only two alternatives, a person who has forgotten the correct answer (or someone who has never learned the task before) has a chance of 1 out of 2 of guessing the correct answer. The number correct on a recognition test must be adjusted for lucky guesses by subtracting $1/N$ of the total correct answers.

The guessing correction is often an underestimate, since it assumes that all alternatives are equally likely to be selected by someone who has forgotten the material. However, as anyone knows who has taken a multiple-choice examination—which is essentially a recognition test—it is usually possible to rule out some of the alternatives as being wrong and restrict one's guesses to the remaining alternatives. This process increases the chances of being correct by guessing.

This methodological problem makes it difficult to compare amount of retention under different methods. Earlier studies (Luh, 1922; Postman and Rau, 1957) led to the conclusion that estimates of retention are higher under recognition than under recall. Exactly how much more retention occurs under recognition depends on the assumptions one makes about the guessing factor.

A study by Postman, Jenkins, and Postman (1948) illustrates the possibility that all alternatives are not equally likely guesses. The study was essentially a comparison of recall and recognition and found retention to be higher under the latter method. Our interest in this study is primarily in the analysis of the wrong choices made on the recognition test. Each item had four alternatives, some of which differed from the original nonsense syllable by only one letter whereas others shared no common letters with the original item. Significantly more errors involved the choice of the more similar alternatives. Thus, the alternatives are not equally probable as guesses. It is possible to rule out dissimilar alternatives as being completely wrong and restrict one's choice to the remaining alternatives, which are similar to the original items. This process leads to more errors among the similar than among the dissimilar alternatives; it also increases the probability of getting an item correct by guessing. Since the guessing correction usually treats all alternatives as equally likely to occur under guessing, it may underestimate the number of items correctly guessed and overestimate the amount of retention.

What other factors distinguish recognition and recall? Response learning or integration is necessary under the recall method for an item to be retained, whereas it is not necessary on a recognition test since the correct item is always provided. On the other hand, because recognition tests place correct items among incorrect alternatives or so-called distractors, discrimination among alternatives is required.

Before an item can be recalled, the whole item must be available as an integrated response for the subject, but it may be recognizable at a lower degree of learning or retention. This difference in requirements favors the recognition method, but the exact amount of recognition depends on the similarity among the alternatives. Discrimination will be more difficult as similarity increases and will lead to reduced scores on a recognition task.

Furthermore, the range of possible answers from which the subject has to choose is quite restricted on a recognition test and substantially larger for a recall test. In attempting recall, the subject may think of a large number of possible responses and encounter interference between some of the correct and incorrect items he monitors. On a recognition test, he has only to cope with a few alternatives for each item.

In view of the foregoing considerations, it should be apparent that recall and recognition are methods involving different processes. Quantitative comparisons between them are somewhat like those between apples and oranges. Although retention can legitimately be measured by a number of different methods, quantitative comparisons of retention should be limited to situations where the same method is employed throughout.

Bahrick (1964) has noted that the superior retention claimed for recognition may simply stem from the fact that a higher degree of original learning occurs for recognition rather than recall tasks when the original training is provided under identical conditions. Suppose we give ten learning trials to two groups, one of which will later be tested for retention by recall and one by recognition. It requires fewer trials for recognition learning to reach a given criterion than for recall learning. If it takes ten trials before all items can be recalled correctly, it might take only five for all items to be correctly recognized.

However, if ten trials are provided for both groups, in effect, the recognition group actually receives a higher degree of original learning. One can obviously expect better retention if more practice is provided. Consequently, Bahrick concludes, higher recognition memory may represent just a carry-over of higher original learning. Here is another example of the difficulty in making legitimate quantitative comparisons of retention when different measurement techniques are employed.

A study by McNulty (1965) is a good example of evidence that shows the complex relationship between retention as measured by recall and by recognition. McNulty maintained that partial learning is often sufficient to enable correct recognition, whereas whole learning is required to make correct recall possible. Thus, one might not be able to recall that Sacramento is the state capital of California but he might recognize it among a set of alternatives. He might have remembered only that it started with "S" and contained several syllables; this partial learning would allow him to identify the correct answer if the other alternatives started with letters other than "S" or contained few syllables. On the other hand, if the alternatives all began with "S," such as San Francisco, Santa Barbara, Salinas, and Sausalito, the example of partial learning just described would not aid the subject, and the difference between recognition and recall scores should be smaller. When the alternatives are more similar, recognition becomes more difficult and a higher level of learning is needed for the correct answer to be selected from the alternatives provided.

In McNulty's study, the correct answer was paired with only one alternative for each original item on a recognition test. The alternative differed from the correct item either by one letter or by several letters. It was predicted that recognition would be higher when there was low similarity between the correct items and their alternatives. However, recall was still assumed to be poorer than under both forms of recognition test since it required whole learning of each item.

McNulty devised materials differing in the extent to which partial learning would exist after original training. He used lists of different statistical approximations to the structure found in the English language. Some items like *ewmemdnt* are unlike real words and are only first-order approximations; other items such as *legulati* are somewhat more like words and are designated as third-order approximations; and, finally, real words are the highest-order approximations.

Learning is lower with items that are of low-order approximation to English (Miller and Selfridge, 1950). However, more items are partially learned at this level, if at all, whereas actual words are likely to be completely learned. If partial learning aids recognition, McNulty reasoned that the superiority of recognition over recall would be greatest for the most difficult material. Partially learned items could not be recalled but could be identified on a recognition test, especially if the alternatives were dissimilar. However, with easy materials—such as lists of words—there would be little if any superiority of recognition since recall scores would not be limited by failure to learn each item completely as a unit. Similarly, the advantage of recognition should be smaller with similar alternatives because partial learning is not sufficient to identify the correct alternative.

McNulty's findings are presented in Figure 6.1, which shows that his predictions were supported. Recognition is generally better than recall, but the degree of superiority is a function of the similarity of the alternatives to the correct items as well as the difficulty of the items as indexed by degree of approximation to English. When alternatives are low in similarity (Recognition I) to the correct items, recognition is higher than

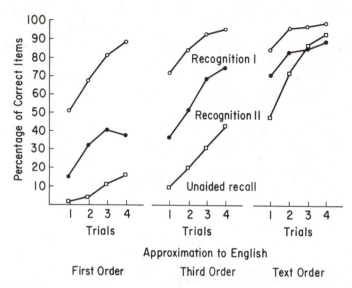

Figure 6.1. Percentage of items correctly remembered under the three methods of measurement. Data are plotted as a function of trials and approximation to English. [From J. A. McNulty: An analysis of recall and recognition process in verbal learning. *Journal of Verbal Learning and Verbal Behavior,* 1965, **4**, 430–436. Reprinted by permission of Academic Press, Inc., and the author.]

when this similarity is high (Recognition II). Finally, the biggest differences among the measures occur with the materials that have the lowest degree of approximation to English.

        Measurement Problems In order to determine the mechanisms responsible for forgetting, it is necessary to identify the variables which lead to decrements in retention. One may separate the possible factors into two classes: those variables which operate during original learning to affect later retention, and those variables which function during the retention interval after original learning has been completed. In the latter category there are other tasks which are acquired during the retention interval. In addition, learning which occurred before the task to-be-retained may exert its influence, during the retention interval, to cause forgetting.

It is with respect to factors which affect original learning of a task that there are special problems of measurement. As we shall see, it is difficult to determine whether factors which definitely affect the original learning of a task also have an influence on its retention. It is not surprising to learn that the degree of original learning is directly related to the amount of retention. As we might expect, higher degrees of learning lead to higher amounts of retention. But when we examine the effects of other variables, manipulated during learning, on the subsequent retention, we find, not infrequently, that clear-cut conclusions are difficult to reach. The reason for this indeterminacy is the very fact that retention is highly affected by the degree of original learning (Underwood, 1954; 1964a).

Any variable which produces differences in the original degree of learning makes it difficult to determine how that same variable affects retention. Suppose we compare the learning of high and low similarity material and find that low similarity material is more readily learned. If

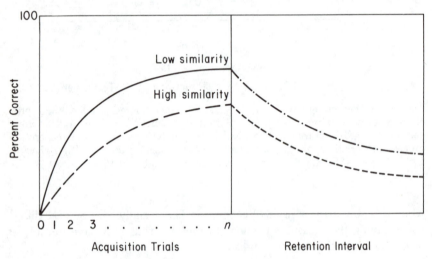

Figure 6.2. Hypothetical curves showing that differences in acquisition level may carry over to produce retention differences.

low similarity material is also higher in retention, this fact is partly or entirely due to a simple carry-over of its higher degree of original learning. It is the higher degree of original learning, not the low similarity of the material, per se, which leads to the higher retention. If, however, the low similarity material was less well-learned but was actually higher in retention, we could safely conclude that this finding is not due to any carry-over of higher original learning but occurs despite it! Figure 6.2 diagrams the problem under discussion.

How can one assess the effects of a variable on retention if that very variable leads to differences in degree of original learning? Any differences in retention might be due to either or both of the differences, that of the variable under study and that of degree of original learning.

One solution (Underwood, 1954; 1964a) might be to estimate how much more learning one condition is attaining compared to the other, and then to give the latter condition additional trials in order to bring it up to the same level as that of the first condition. If high meaningfulness words are learned to a higher degree in a given number of trials than are low meaningfulness words, then, if measures of retention also show higher retention for high meaningfulness words, this effect may not be due to meaningfulness, per se, but to the higher degree of original learning. By estimating from the learning curves, we can determine how many extra trials would be necessary for the low meaningfulness words to bring the degree of learning to the same level as that of the high meaningful-ness words. If we make this adjustment of original learning, any differ-ences in retention may then be attributed to the differences in meaning-fulness.

It would not be correct, according to Underwood (1964a), to assume that the problem of unequal original learning is solved by carrying learn-ing to a performance criterion. That is, rather than give a constant number of trials which would allow different groups to attain different levels of performance, the investigator might set a performance criterion that involved having all conditions learn to an arbitrary criterion, such as two consecutive errorless trials. The number of trials necessary to reach this performance criterion might differ for various experimental con-ditions, but the final level of acquisition performance would be the same. Nonetheless, according to Underwood, such a procedure does not ensure that learning is equal. Conditions in which learning reaches the criterion at a slower rate will receive overtraining compared to conditions which are faster in attaining the criterion. Thus, differences in original learning would still occur and "contaminate" conclusions drawn from measures of retention.

Underwood's conclusion is that the safest approach is to employ a con-stant number of trials for all conditions, and then provide additional learning trials for conditions lower in performance so that all conditions are equal in degree of original learning. Then it will be possible to draw conclusions regarding the effects of other variables on retention. It is important not to allow the level of learning in the highest condition to be too high because this would make it difficult to estimate how much additional training to give to conditions with lower levels of learning to equate all conditions.

When the adjustments for degree of original learning have been made, acquisition variables which produce differences in retention have been found only infrequently. According to Underwood, the single most ef-fective variable during learning on retention appears to be the degree of original learning. Variables which have powerful effects on acquisition, such as intralist similarity and meaningfulness, do not appear to produce differences in retention when the degree of original learning is equated. If these variables are reported to affect retention, it is usually because the degree of first-list learning has been unequal, thus creating the retention differences.

One conclusion that we can draw, regardless of the material, is that the more practice you have, the better you will remember it! This is exactly the point that William James expressed so eloquently in the following passage written in 1890.

> Briefly, then, of two men with the same outward experiences and the same amount of native tenacity, the *one who* THINKS *over his experiences most, and weaves them into systematic relations with each other, will be the one with the best memory.* We see examples of this on every hand . . . The college athlete who remains a dunce at his books will astonish you by his knowledge of men's "records" in various feats and games, and will be a walking dictionary of sporting statistics. The reason is that he is constantly going over these things in his mind . . . Let a man early in life set himself the task of verifying such a theory as that of evolution, and facts will soon cluster and cling to him like grapes to their stem . . . Meanwhile the theorist may have little, if any, desultory memory . . . An ignorance almost as encyclopaedic as his erudition may coexist with the latter, and hide, as it were, in the interstices of its web. Those who have had much to do with scholars and *savants* will readily think of examples of the class of mind I mean.

The next problem is to determine why a learned task is forgotten after a prolonged period without practice. Is the forgetting due to the time period, per se, or to certain events, particularly learned ones, which occur during the retention interval? We now turn to a consideration of the variables affecting retention after original learning has terminated.

Long-Term Memory (LTM)

The distinction between short- and long-term memory, from a strictly operational viewpoint, is based on the relative length of the retention interval. When the time between original learning and retention is more than a few minutes, long-term retention is involved. In most studies of long-term memory the retention intervals are anywhere from a few minutes to a day or a week.

Theoretically, there is disagreement about the mechanisms underlying both short- and long-term memory. The two major theories of forgetting are *decay or disuse* and *interference*. It is possible to find views attributing both short- and long-term forgetting to either decay or interference. In addition, some researchers view decay as the mechanism underlying short-term memory while they consider interference responsible for long-term memory.

Further discussion of these theoretical issues must follow an examination of the empirical facts of short- and long-term memory. Historically, work was first done on long-term memory, and only recently has research developed on short-term memory. We will follow this pattern by considering long-term memory first.

Proactive and Retroactive Inhibition   The laboratory paradigms of proactive (PI) and retroactive inhibition (RI) test the role of interference in forgetting. These paradigms involve the learning of two successive tasks, A and B, followed by a retention test of either the first task (RI) or the second task (PI). A rest interval is included between learning and retention for PI. The control group learns Task A and is tested for retention of that same task, without any practice on it during the retention interval, in both paradigms. The sequence of events in the RI and PI paradigms is diagramed in Table 6.1.

If a comparison of the experimental and the control groups shows poorer retention in the experimental group for Task A, we speak of *retroactive* or *proactive inhibition,* depending on the paradigm involved. (It should be noted that it is possible for the retention to be higher in

TABLE 6.1
RETROACTIVE AND PROACTIVE INHIBITION PARADIGMS

		Prior Learning	Original Learning	Interpolated Learning	Retention Test
Retroactive Inhibition	Experimental Group		Learn A	Learn B	Test for A
	Control Group		Learn A	rests or learns task unrelated to A	Test for A
Proactive Inhibition	Experimental Group	Learn B	Learn A	rests	Test for A
	Control Group	rests or learns task unrelated to A	Learn A	rests	Test for A

the experimental group than in the control group, in which case we would refer to retroactive and proactive *facilitation* rather than inhibition.)

The phenomena of RI and PI have been considered support for an interference theory of forgetting. It is assumed that the experimental groups will be poorer in retention because of interference from the task other than the task to be recalled in each paradigm. On the other hand, the performance of the control groups involves the retention of a task which was the only one that had to be learned. The control groups encounter no interference from other tasks and consequently should have higher retention than the experimental groups.

It should be obvious that the RI and PI paradigms involve a transfer paradigm since the experimental groups learn two tasks. The additional fact that retention measures are made of either the first or second task defines RI and PI paradigms, respectively. Since RI and PI paradigms involve a transfer situation, it would seem that principles of transfer of training might apply to RI and PI.

We have seen in the preceding chapter on transfer that the similarity between tasks determines whether positive or negative transfer is obtained. Similarity between two tasks should also affect the amount of forgetting of one due to interference from the other. As a matter of fact, Osgood's model for transfer (described earlier) was also proposed by him as a way to handle the effects of interlist similarity on retroaction paradigms. In other words, Osgood predicted that interlist similarity would affect RI in the same manner in which it affected transfer.

Bugelski and Cadwallader (1956) measured RI as a function of different combinations of interlist stimulus and response similarity. As with their findings for transfer, Bugelski and Cadwallader confirmed Osgood's predictions for variations of interlist stimulus similarity but not for interlist response similarity.

However, Dallett (1962), using materials similar to those of Bugelski and Cadwallader, confirmed all of Osgood's predictions for RI. He used the same second, or transfer, list for all conditions. He varied the interlist similarity by using different first lists for different conditions. In addition, Dallett examined PI by testing recall of the second list 20 minutes after it was learned. No differences were obtained as a function of interlist similarity; however, he did not consider that this negative finding ruled out the possibility that interlist similarity might affect PI. The lack of evidence for PI he attributed to the retention interval's being too short.

The effects of variations in degree of both first- and second-list learning on RI were examined by Briggs (1957). Original learning on the first list consisted of 2, 5, 10, or 20 trials, whereas the second list, referred to as *interpolated learning*, involved 0, 2, 5, 10, or 20 trials. Lists of ten paired adjectives were used. Following the interpolated task, Briggs took relearning measures on the first task to assess the amount of RI. The results he obtained are presented in Figure 6.3. He found that RI increased as the degree of interpolated learning increased. More interference is assumed for higher levels of interpolated learning. On the other hand, RI decreased with higher degrees of original learning. Briggs' results suggest that if a task is to be resistant to interference, it should be given overlearning.

Additional factors may affect the amount of RI besides the degree of similarity between tasks and the degree of original and interpolated learning. Bilodeau and Schlosberg (1951) hypothesized that interference in an RI paradigm would be diminished if the learning of the two lists

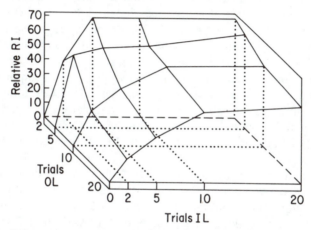

Figure 6.3. Relative retroactive inhibition as a function of the degree of original and interpolated learning. [From G. E. Briggs: Retroactive inhibition as a function of the degree of original and interpolated learning. *Journal of Experimental Psychology*, 1957, **53**, 60–67. Reprinted by permission of the American Psychological Association and the author.]

occurred under contrasting conditions. One group learned both lists under the same conditions, while a second group learned one list while standing in one room and the second list while seated in a different room. The method of study was also varied. A control group learned only one list. More RI was obtained in the condition where both lists were acquired under similar environmental conditions.

Schwartz (1963) manipulated the expectancy regarding the effect of interpolated learning. Some subjects were instructed that learning of the second list would aid, while other subjects were informed that it would hinder, subsequent retention of the first list. A control group was given neutral instructions regarding the effects of the second list. Although

such variations in task set toward the second list did not affect the learning of this list itself, those subjects led to believe that it would make recall of the first list more difficult actually showed less RI. It is possible
that such subjects rehearsed the first list or in some way incorporated it
in the learning of the second list, whereas subjects with the other task set
did not. In any case, here is another procedural factor which alters the
amount of RI.

Interference Theory A major develop-
ment in interference theory was the two-factor theory of RI proposed by
Melton and Irwin (1940). A study of the relationship between amount
of interpolated learning and RI was performed with serial lists of nonsense syllables. Melton and Irwin carried learning on the first list to a
criterion of one perfect trial. All experimental groups then learned a
second interpolated list for either 5, 10, 20, or 40 trials. No second list
was given to the control group. One day later, RI was assessed after all
groups relearned the first list. Savings scores based on the difference between trials for original learning and relearning were computed for the
experimental and the control groups. In general, it was found that RI
increased directly with the amount of interpolated learning. That is,
the more practice on the second list, the poorer the performance on the
relearning of the original task as compared with the performance of the
control group.

Melton and Irwin suggested that RI involved competition of associations from the two lists to the same stimuli. One observable index of
response competition should be the overt intrusions where responses were
being given incorrectly to the wrong stimuli. As Figure 6.4 indicates,
Melton and Irwin found that the number of intrusions increased as a
function of second-list learning up to a point, but then decreased with
higher interpolated learning. This reversal they ascribed to the build-up
of differentiation of list membership of the items by subjects as the relative amount of second-list learning increased.

However, a problem existed in the fact that, while response competition appeared to increase and then decrease with amount of interpolated
learning, the amount of RI continued to increase. Perhaps a second
factor was involved in addition to response competition; otherwise, RI
should also drop after second-list learning has progressed beyond a certain point, just as the frequency of intrusions drops. This second factor
they labeled Factor X, which they viewed as being similar to the process
of extinction in classical conditioning situations. *Extinction* refers to the
reduced tendency of a learned response to occur during a period without
reinforcement. Perhaps associations of the first list were "unlearned" dur-

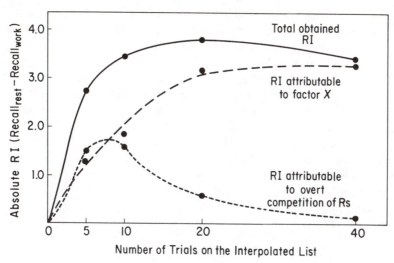

Figure 6.4. Relationship between the amount of RI and the degree of learning of the interpolated material. The total obtained RI is the number of syllables forgotten as a consequence of the interpolated learning. The RI attributable to the overt competition of original and interpolated responses has been taken as 2 times the average frequency of intrusions of entire interpolated syllables during the recall trial in order to take into account the unidentified overt intrusions of parts of syllables. The curve for Factor X represents the absolute decrement in recall attributable to the factor or factors other than the overt competition of original and interpolated responses. [From A. W. Melton and J. M. Irwin: The influence of degree of interpolated learning on retroactive inhibition and the overt transfer of specific responses. *American Journal of Psychology*, 1940, **53**, 173–203. Reprinted by permission of the *Journal* and the authors.]

ing the learning of the second list, since they did not receive reinforcement during the second-list learning.

In order to examine unlearning, Briggs (1954) interrupted subjects at different points during the second-list learning in an A–B, A–D paradigm. He presented subjects with each of the stimuli—which were the same for both lists—one at a time, and asked them to give the first of the two responses that came to mind for each stimulus. On this modified free recall task, Briggs found that more responses were recalled from the second than from the first list as more second-list learning was given. One possible implication of this result is that the first-list associations were being unlearned as second-list associations were strengthened, thus confirming Melton and Irwin's theory. It is possible, however, that these first-list responses were still available to subjects, but that they may have simply reported the second-list responses because they were stronger and more recent. Thus first-list responses occurred less frequently on recall due to a response bias, not because they were unavailable. Since Briggs' procedure allowed subjects to give only one response for each stimulus, there is no way to decide between the two explanations.

The limitations of the Briggs free recall test were avoided in an important study by Barnes and Underwood (1959). They had subjects learn two lists of paired associates in which the stimuli were identical but paired with different and unrelated responses. The first list was learned to one perfect trial. Different groups received 1, 5, 10, or 20 trials on the second list. After the second-list training was completed, Barnes and Underwood administered a modified free recall test (MMFR) similar to that of Briggs except that, if possible, the subject was to give *both* responses that had been associated with a given stimulus. Thus, the stimuli—which were the same for the two lists—were provided for the

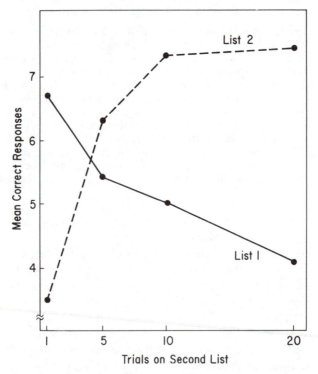

Figure 6.5. Mean number of responses correctly recalled and identified with stimulus and list in the A–B, A–D paradigm. [From J. M. Barnes and B. J. Underwood: "Fate" of first-list associations in transfer theory. *Journal of Experimental Psychology*, 1959, **58**, 97–105. Reprinted by permission of the American Psychological Association and the authors.]

subject, who had to recall both responses that had been paired with each stimulus on the two lists.

Figure 6.5 shows that recall in favor of second-list responses increased as a direct function of the number of trials on the second list. Barnes and Underwood's findings agreed with those of Briggs but permitted a more unequivocal conclusion. Since the subject was instructed to give *both* responses for each stimulus, his tendency to give fewer first-list responses is not as likely to be due to response bias or recency, as may have been the case in the Briggs test where the subject was requested to give only the *first* response to come into mind for each stimulus. A more direct measure of response availability is provided by the Barnes–Underwood procedure.

These findings lent solid support to the view that first-list associations undergo extinction during second-list learning in this paradigm. Consequently, the first-list responses are less available on the retention test. As the amount of second-list learning increases, more RI occurs due to the greater unlearning of first-list responses.

The fact that the magnitude of RI in laboratory situations has generally exceeded that of PI is consistent with the two-factor theory of Melton and Irwin. Response competition occurs in both paradigms, but unlearning of first-list associations during second-list learning represents a problem only for RI where first-list retention is being assessed. The magnitude of PI is lower for any comparable set of conditions because the list to be recalled is the most recent one learned and it does not undergo extinction.

However, the greater degree of RI compared to PI is transitory. Underwood (1948) compared RI and PI with either 5 or 48 hours between the second-list learning and the retention test of the list to be recalled. Whereas RI exceeded PI after 5 hours, this difference disappeared after 48 hours. Such a finding is in accord with the conception of unlearning, which is considered to be the major factor responsible for RI being greater than PI. Since PI involves retention of the second list, no unlearning occurs and PI is not as great as RI. But unlearning is viewed as analogous to extinction, a process which is capable of spontaneous recovery over time. Thus, the unlearned first-list associations are not permanently eliminated but may regain strength, that is, spontaneously recover, with the passage of time. Consequently, RI is reduced to the level of PI in magnitude when there is a long interval, such as 48 hours, between second-list learning and retention. However, since the assumed spontaneous recovery of the unlearned associations takes time, RI is still greater than PI when this interval is short, such as the 5 hours in Underwood's study.

One problem is that any evidence for this process of unlearning may be an artifact, since retention tests given immediately after the second list may give a bias in recall in favor of the second or more recent list due to the subject's set. With a delay between the second-list learning and retention test of the first list, this assumed set would dissipate, and it would then appear as if first-list responses gained in strength whereas the "gain" might be due simply to a drop in the bias for giving second-list responses. This bias has been termed *generalized response competition* (Postman, 1961*b*) to distinguish it from competition between specific associations.

Spontaneous Recovery   Evidence regarding spontaneous recovery has been weak. One study by Koppenaal (1963) measured associations with the MMFR at seven intervals from 1 minute to 1 week after the learning of an A–B, A–D paradigm. A control condition learned only one list.

The results obtained by Koppenaal, which appear in Figure 6.6, failed to show any spontaneous recovery of first-list associations. When an immediate MMFR was given, second-list responses were substantially higher than first-list responses, as found by Barnes and Underwood (1959). However, as the retention interval increased, the superiority of second-list responses on recall was reduced. Beyond 24 hours, there was no difference in recall of first- and second-list associations. However, there was no absolute increase in the number of extinguished first-list responses, except possibly between 90 minutes and 6 hours, but the increase was not statistically significant.

Similar results were obtained when retention was measured at intervals as long as 6 to 14 days (Birnbaum, 1965; Houston, 1966; Slamecka, 1966*b*). However, a study by Saltz (1965) provides some support for spontaneous recovery. First, subjects were required to give single-letter associations to a list of two-letter, or bigram, stimuli. From this data, Saltz determined the five most frequent responses to each stimulus for each individual subject. On all subsequent association trials, Saltz "extinguished" these responses by telling the subject he was "wrong" any time one of the five strongest responses was given. A retest was administered after 10 minutes, 1, 2, 3, or 24 hours. Spontaneous recovery of the extinguished "wrong" responses was obtained at intervals of 1 hour or more.

It should be noted that the substantial negative evidence regarding spontaneous recovery of first-list associations is not necessarily in conflict with the positive evidence reported by Saltz (1965). His task is quite different from the typical unlearning paradigm. Perhaps unlearning is not even involved. At short intervals, subjects rejected strong associates

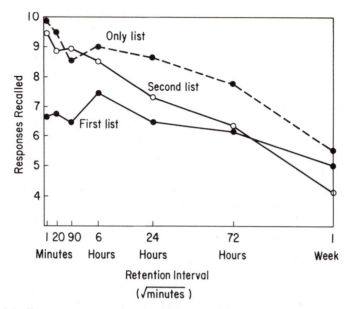

Figure 6.6. Retention curves for the first, second, and only lists. (From R. J. Koppenaal: Time changes in the strengths of A–B, A–C lists: Spontaneous recovery? *Journal of Verbal Learning and Verbal Behavior,* 1963, *2*, 310–319. Reprinted by permission of Academic Press, Inc., and the author.]

because they were "wrong." But at longer intervals, these responses "recovered" because subjects may have forgotten which responses were "wrong." In any event, Saltz used much stronger first-list associations involving preexperimental habits, whereas the negative studies employed laboratory produced first-list associations. The extent to which spontaneous recovery of associations is likely to occur is probably a direct function of the strength of those associations prior to extinction.

Additional support for this conjecture comes from some positive evidence for spontaneous recovery from a study made by Silverstein (1967). Although he used laboratory formed associations, he used higher levels of first-list learning than the studies that failed to find spontaneous recovery. He also employed a high degree of second-list learning. By so doing, he increased the chances that the first-list associations would be well-learned initially and well-unlearned during the acquisition of the second list. The results indicated significant spontaneous recovery after 1 or 2 days.

However, the over-all pattern of studies indicates equivocal support for spontaneous recovery. Yet, the failure to demonstrate reliable evidence of this process does not rule out unlearning as a process in A–B, A–D situations. It may simply be that the analogy drawn between unlearning and extinction by interference theorists is a misleading one. One may have unlearning without requiring spontaneous recovery.

In animal studies of extinction, a previously reinforced response is no longer reinforced but there is no alternative response for which reinforcement is provided. On the other hand, unlearning involves simultaneous nonreinforcement of a former response and reinforcement of a new response, so that it parallels the paradigm called counterconditioning. Furthermore, the responses extinguished in animal learning usually involve physical effort, such as running or bar pressing, whereas little physical strain is required for verbal learning responses. We should note that one explanation of spontaneous recovery is that some inhibitory factor develops during extinction and dissipates over the retention interval. If such is the case, then spontaneous recovery may be limited to situations which involve physical effort; since verbal learning does not, this difference may explain why it may be difficult to show spontaneous recovery of verbal associations.

Unlearning in Other Paradigms McGovern (1964) extended the Barnes and Underwood (1959) analysis of extinction in forgetting to several transfer paradigms. She analyzed the factors involved in four different transfer paradigms: A–B, A–D; A–B, C–B; A–B, C–D; and A–B, A–Br. Her basic goal was to identify any A–B, A–D-like relationships within any of the above mentioned paradigms. We should recall that in the A–B, A–D situations, it is assumed that unlearning of the first-list associations occurs during the acquisition of the second-list associations. That is, forward associations of the two lists interfere with each other.

However, it is possible that such unlearning paradigms exist for other transfer components besides forward associations. Table 6.2 presents a summary of McGovern's analysis. Thus, in the A–B, A–D paradigm, an extinction situation exists not only for forward but also for contextual associations. Contextual associations refer to connections between the responses and the environmental stimuli, such as the experimental setting, in general. That is, the responses are not only paired with the stimuli presented in the list but are also associated with stimuli in the experimental setting. One might consider the background as a constant additional portion of each stimulus term. Since two sets of responses are not only learned to a common set of stimuli in each list but also to a common set of environmental stimuli, it may be concluded that an A–B, A–D extinctive relationship also holds between contextual stimuli and the responses. The contextual associations formed on the first list are assumed to be unlearned when those required on the second list are formed. However, due to spontaneous recovery, the first-list associations eventually interfere with the second-list associations.

The Bilodeau and Schlosberg (1951) study reported earlier is related to this issue. McGovern's views are similar to those of these investigators in predicting more forgetting when the environmental stimuli are identi-

TABLE 6.2
LOCUS OF UNLEARNING

Paradigm	Forward Association	Backward Association	Contextual Association
A–B, C–D	0	0	+
A–B, C–B	0	+	0
A–B, A–D	+	0	+
A–B, A–Br	+	+	0

A + indicates the presence of an unlearning factor for the paradigm and a 0 indicates the absence of it.

cal for both lists of an A–B, A–D paradigm. However, McGovern's contextual stimuli are more hypothetical than those of Bilodeau and Schlosberg.

In the A–B, C–B paradigm, there is no extinction paradigm for either forward or contextual associations. However, the backward associations on the two lists, B–A and B–C, constitute an arrangement in which identical stimuli are paired with different responses. Thus, an extinction paradigm exists between the backward associations of the two lists in this paradigm. It, too, eventually leads to forgetting via interference.

For the A–B, C–D paradigm in which the stimuli and responses on the two lists are unrelated, there are neither forward nor backward interfering associations between lists. Still, since the contextual stimuli are the same for the two lists which contain different sets of responses, an extinction paradigm holds between the contextual stimuli and responses on the lists. Forgetting of the second list is due to the spontaneous recovery and interference of the first-list associations to the common contextual stimuli.

Finally, in the A–B, A–Br paradigm, McGovern noted that there are sources of interference from both forward and backward associations. For either factor each stimulus is associated with different responses on the two lists. However, no interference exists from the contextual associations, which involve the same stimuli and responses on both lists in this paradigm. Thus, extinction paradigms exist for both the forward and backward associations of the two lists in this paradigm.

In order to test these analyses of the different paradigms, McGovern administered either a free recall test or an associative matching test immediately after the subject had learned the two lists required in his particular paradigm. The free recall test simply required recall of as many first-list responses as possible in any order. This test was assumed to measure the response availability component of paired-associate learning. Other subjects were given an associative matching test in which all stimulus terms and first-list responses were provided and the task was to match these items correctly. The amount of associative learning was assumed to be measured by this test.

The results shown in Table 6.3 indicate that McGovern found that

TABLE 6.3

MEAN NUMBER OF RESPONSES RECALLED
FROM LIST 1 FOR EACH TRANSFER PARADIGM AS SCORED BY TWO METHODS [a]

Method	Paradigm				
	A–D	A–Br	C–B	C–D	Control
	Free-recall subgroup				
1	4.79	4.75	6.42	6.54	7.71
2	5.00	6.96	7.71	6.62	7.71
	Associative-Matching				
1	6.54	5.58	6.87	7.83	—

[a] In Method 1 a response is scored as correct only if matched with the correct stimulus. In Method 2 a response is counted as correct if merely recalled.

Source: From J. B. McGovern. Extinction of associations in four transfer paradigms. *Psychological Monographs*, 1964, 78 (16, Whole No. 593). Reprinted by permission of the American Psychological Association and the author.

free recall was lower in the A–B, A–D and A–B, A–Br paradigms compared with the A–B, C–B and A–B, C–D paradigms. She attributed this finding to the fact that two sources of extinction exist in each of the two former paradigms whereas only one factor is involved in each of the latter two.

It was predicted that associative matching would exceed free recall in paradigms where contextual associations underwent extinction but not in paradigms where such extinction did not occur. Thus, in the A–B, A–D and A–B, C–D paradigms, free recall would be lowered due to extinction of contextual associations, but associative matching scores would be higher in these paradigms since the stimuli and responses are provided to the subject on the test. Since no loss of contextual associations is assumed for A–B, C–B and A–B, A–Br, no differences were predicted between free recall and associative matching for these paradigms. The results supported these predictions.

Both the A–B, A–D and A–B, C–D conditions involved extinction of contextual associations. In addition, extinction of forward associations also occurs in the A–B, A–D paradigm but not in the A–B, C–D paradigm. Thus, it was predicted and found that A–B, A–D performance would be lower than A–B, C–D performance on associative matching where contextual associations were not a factor.

In the A–B, C–B paradigm, associative matching was assumed to be adversely affected by losses due to extinction of backward associations. Associative matching for this paradigm was found to be lower than that for the A–B, C–D condition, which does not involve backward associations.

Finally, a measure of the total losses due to the extinction of both forward and backward associations can be made by comparing the A–B, A–Br with the A–B, C–D paradigm on associative matching. Results in Table 6.3 show greater decrements in the A–B, A–Br paradigm.

McGovern included a control condition which learned only one list. No extinction of any type was assumed to occur for this condition, which provides a base line for measuring the amount of loss due to the extinction of contextual associations in the A–B, C–D paradigm.

McGovern's experiment supported the predictions based on the analyses from interference theory. Any situation involving an A–B, A–D paradigm may be expected to lead to forgetting via interference.

Extraexperimental Interference The laboratory study of interference as the cause of forgetting has depended on evidence from the retroactive and the proactive inhibition paradigms. In both cases, the list to be retained and the other assumed interfering list are laboratory tasks, and the situation is specifically designed to study the interaction in the laboratory.

Other evidence supporting interference theory comes from comparisons of studies which were primarily designed for other purposes. Underwood (1957) observed that substantial differences in the amount of forgetting occurred in a number of different experiments. As indicated in Figure 6.7, he noted that forgetting was slightest in studies where the subjects were new to verbal learning experiments, and that it was greater in studies where the subject had served in other verbal learning studies or had to learn several lists in the same study. The greater forgetting Underwood attributed to proactive inhibition effects of these past experiences. Although in these studies the investigators had not intended

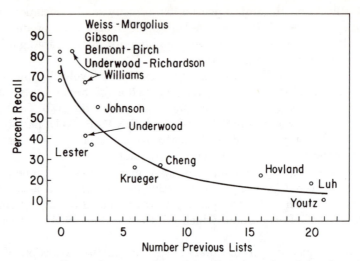

Figure 6.7. Recall as a function of number of previous lists learned as determined from a number of studies. [From B. J. Underwood: Interference and forgetting. *Psychological Review*, 1957, **64**, 49–60. Reprinted by permission of the American Psychological Association and the author.]

to assess PI experimentally, this effect still occurred because the preceding verbal tasks served to interfere with the retention of the last, or only, list they learned.

This comparison of different studies was strong circumstantial evidence for interference as a general source of forgetting. Furthermore, it suggested that whereas RI might be greater than PI in experimental situations, preexperimental habits might lead to more PI. That is, we could consider as potential sources of PI all the naturally learned habits possessed by the subject before the experiment which are similar to what he has to learn in the laboratory. Then, the possible amount of PI would far exceed the amount of RI practically possible due to habits formed during the retention interval of an experiment. Consequently, PI may be the larger factor in interference theory.

It is interesting to see the similarity between this conception and an observation noted in 1925 by the American author, Frank Harris, who wrote,

> I had no idea then that one should select with the greatest care everything that one learns by heart in youth; for whatever one learns then sticks in the memory and prevents one from recalling with ease words or passages learned later. Memory has its limitations. I hate to think now that I was fool enough to waste my time and pack some memory drawers with Demosthenes' rhetoric instead of Russian vocables.

Even in studies with naïve subjects who learned only one list of verbal materials, it could be maintained that forgetting was due to proactive inhibition of a sort. If one considered all similar preexperimental verbal habits acquired in naturalistic settings as an enormous and much over-learned first task, A–X, then the experimental task might be viewed as the second task, A–B, of a PI paradigm. Forgetting of this single experimental task could be attributed to the spontaneous recovery and interference of the lifetime habits which had been presumably extinguished during the original learning of the experimental task. The naturalistic pre-experimental habits (List 1) are much stronger than any experimentally acquired habits (List 2) could practically be made. Thus, it appears that the forgetting of laboratory tasks may be due to interference from extra-experimental sources. The assumed relationship is depicted in Table 6.4.

TABLE 6.4

HYPOTHETICAL RELATIONSHIP OF
PREEXPERIMENTAL LEARNING AND LABORATORY LEARNING CAUSING
INTERFERENCE

List 1	List 2	
A–X	A–B	A $\nearrow^{B}$ $\searrow_{X}$
Strong Preexperimental Associations	Laboratory Associations	Retention of Laboratory Task

A further analysis of forgetting based on extraexperimental interference was proposed by Underwood and Postman (1960) to account for differences in retention as a function of the meaningfulness of the material. According to this theory, the retention of nonsense syllables is subject to interference from letter-sequence habits of the subject, such as alphabetical sequences or frequently occurring linguistic sequences. These stronger prior habits are assumed to be extinguished when nonsense syllable sequences are first learned, but they eventually recover and interfere with the retention of the weaker experimentally learned habits. The extent to which extraexperimental letter-sequence habits interfere is greater for low meaningfulness syllables than for high meaningfulness syllables, which are more similar to natural letter sequences and hence more compatible. Therefore, Underwood and Postman postulated a gradient of letter-sequence interference which was maximal with low meaningfulness units and which decreased as syllables became more like words.

Word lists learned in the laboratory are subject to interference from a unit-sequence interference, such as syntactical word order in the language. A gradient of unit-sequence interference was postulated which predicted increasing interference, the more meaningful the word. It appeared that the least total amount of interference from a combination of these sources of extraexperimental interference, letter- and unit-sequence, would be present in nonsense syllables which were almost but not yet words. The theory is diagramed in Figure 6.8.

Numerous attempts to confirm the Underwood and Postman theory

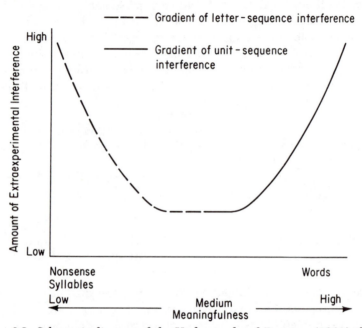

Figure 6.8. Schematic diagram of the Underwood and Postman (1960) theory of extraexperimental interference.

experimentally have failed to provide convincing support (Postman, 1961a, 1962a; Underwood and Keppel, 1963). Underwood and Keppel evaluated the letter-sequence gradient by examining the retention of lists of pairs of letters after 1 and 7 days. In one list, the letters in any pair had a high frequency of association, such as B and A, whereas in the other list the letters within a pair had a low frequency of association, such as B and J. It was predicted that retention would be more impaired with the low frequency list because the extraexperimental letter-sequence habits would interfere. In the learning of a sequence of letters, it was assumed that older and stronger associations would have to be extinguished. The extent to which this process occurs depends on how similar or dissimilar the sequence to be learned is to the extraexperimental habits. If the sequence to be learned is similar to natural habits, it is easily learned.

However, the extinguished extraexperimental habits presumably recover with the passage of time and interfere with the learned sequences. The extent of this interference is greater for sequences which are dissimilar from natural letter sequences, that is, low meaningfulness sequences. Thus, the letter-sequence gradient leads to the prediction of greater forgetting for the low meaningfulness sequences. The results obtained by Underwood and Keppel failed to support the prediction; retention was equal for both levels of meaningfulness.

Postman (1961a) tested the unit-sequence gradient of extraexperimental interference by comparing retention of words differing in frequency of occurrence. The theory proposed by Underwood and Postman (1960) predicted that retention would be poorer for high-frequency words since it would encounter more interference from language habits that involved word sequences.

Postman performed three studies, using serial word lists and taking measures of retention after 30 seconds, 2, or 7 days. Although learning was directly related to word frequency, there were no differences in retention. Thus, no support was obtained for the unit-sequence gradient. The unit-sequence gradient of interference was unsuccessfully tested again later (Postman, 1962a).

Limitations of Interference Theory The interference theory of forgetting (Postman, 1961b) has been successful in accounting for a number of experimental findings. Unlike its rival, the decay theory, which is more difficult to test, the interference theory leads to explicit and testable predictions. It has accounted for many facts of forgetting. The most notable failure has been its extension from laboratory situations to predictions about the effects of preexperimental habits on laboratory associations. It may simply be that the subject is able to isolate his laboratory learning from his prior nonlaboratory learning enough to prevent interference from occurring between the two situations.

Postman (1963a) proposed some principles of conservation of learning from interference. Theoretically, when two different responses are associated to the same stimulus there is optimal interference of associations, and consequently forgetting occurs. The theory is based on the learning of two laboratory tasks. But when such A–B, A–D situations exist between preexperimental and experimental tasks, the predicted loss in retention does not occur in as great a magnitude as predicted by interference theory.

If the subject can somehow transform the two unrelated responses associated to each stimulus into related responses, interference is eliminated. Rather than unlearning the first association to make way for the second one, the subject may form a chain linking the stimulus to the first and second responses. Thus, instead of having an A–B, A–D paradigm we have an A–B, A–B′ paradigm in which learning may proceed as a chain, A–(B)–B′, without interference.

In practical situations, the stimuli on two tasks are not identical although they may be highly similar. If the subject can recode the stimuli so that he can discriminate between the stimuli of the two lists, he effectively reduces interference. In effect, the A–B, A–D paradigm for interference would be altered to fall somewhere along the continuum of paradigms with identical sets of responses on the two lists. For example, it might be changed into an A–B, A′–D paradigm in which the stimuli between lists are similar, or into an A–B, C–D paradigm in which the stimuli between lists are dissimilar, neither of which involve interfering forward associations.

Postman also suggested that differentiation may be great enough between the stronger preexperimental habits and the laboratory associations to minimize interference between them. In this regard, Slamecka (1966a) has provided evidence. He gave several groups a word-association test to determine the strongest preexperimental associates to each stimulus. Then one group learned two additional lists with the same stimuli paired with different responses in the two lists. If we consider the association test stimuli and their responses as a list A–X, then the two added lists could be represented as A–B and A–D. A second group learned only one list, A–B, while a third group did not learn any lists.

All groups were then compared for recall of their original responses on the association test. According to interference theory, unlearning of these responses should have been greatest for the group learning two lists with the same stimuli paired with different responses, next for the group with one list, and least for the group with no lists. All groups were equivalent in recalling their preexperimental associations to the stimuli on the association test. Thus, there was no evidence that preexperimental associations are unlearned. However, a comparison of the group which learned two lists with the group which learned only one list indicated that recall of the list common to both groups was higher for the group with only one list. This comparison is a replication of the Barnes and Underwood (1959) study, and Slamecka's results confirmed their findings: that is, unlearning occurs between two laboratory tasks.

Slamecka maintained that unlearning occurs between laboratory tasks but not between preexperimental and laboratory tasks. He suggested that subjects are able to differentiate the stronger past learning from the weaker laboratory learning, so that unlearning is prevented. It is possible that such an isolation of preexperimental and experimental learning accounts for Underwood and Postman's failures to validate their notions of extraexperimental interference.

Interference theorists have been alarmed by the lack of support for the extraexperimental-interference hypothesis. The possibility that extraexperimental associations actually undergo extinction when a list is learned in the laboratory has not been supported by evidence. Underwood and Ekstrand (1966) attempted to determine why extraexperimental habits fail to affect laboratory habits in the same manner as laboratory habits affect each other. The two major differences between habits formed outside the laboratory before the experiment and those formed during the experiment are the higher degree of practice and the greater distribution of practice over time for the former habits.

If we could demonstrate that one or both of these factors reduce the amount of PI, then we might explain why tests of extraexperimental habits have failed to show interference. Underwood and Ekstrand conducted an experiment varying these two factors, using an A–B, A–D paradigm. They treated the first list as if it represented the extraexperimental habits and gave it varying degrees of practice and degrees of distribution of practice over time. Then they examined performance on the second list to assess the effects of these two factors. The study demonstrated a sharp reduction in PI under distributed practice, the condition simulating the manner in which extraexperimental habits are presumably acquired. The degree of first-list practice, within the ranges used, did not affect performance on the second list unless massed practice was employed.

Underwood and Ekstrand concluded that previous failures to confirm the extraexperimental-interference hypothesis may be due to the fact that such habits are acquired under practice that is widely distributed over time. This factor leads to a reduction of interference, possibly due to the greater differentiation between tasks that would otherwise involve competition and unlearning. Again the question of what causes the forgetting of a single laboratory task is thrown open.

The decay theorist would simply assert that forgetting occurs because the trace weakens over time. One alternative still exists for the interference theorist, and that is a return to the concept of retroactive inhibition. During the retention interval, the subject probably acquires verbal habits outside the laboratory which should be more similar in strength to the laboratory habits than would be the very strong preexperimental associations. At the time of retention, the laboratory habits might encounter interference from these extraexperimental associations formed during the retention interval rather than those formed before the experiment (over the subject's lifetime). If so, forgetting could still be attributed to extraexperimental interference. Keppel (1968) has similarly suggested that the forgetting of a single laboratory learned task may be due to interference from learning acquired during the retention interval.

Short-Term Memory (STM)

In recent years, more attention has been given to short-term memory than in the past. The distinction between short- and long-term memory can be made on operational as well as on theoretical grounds. When we look up a new telephone number, it is often forgotten almost immediately after we dial the number, if not even faster! In this case we are dealing with short-term memory. On the other hand, the retention over weeks or months of a foreign language vocabulary, which the student has spent many hours of practice in acquiring, involves long-term memory.

The operational distinction is based simply on the relative duration of the retention interval between the point in time of input and the point of retention. The example above suggests that another difference is the amount of practice involved. Theoretically, however, there is a question as to whether the same processes and laws govern short- and long-term memory (Broadbent, 1958; Hebb, 1949; Melton, 1963; Postman, 1964a).

Trace theorists assume that each stimulus received by a subject leaves a neural memory trace which decays with the passage of time. Loss of retention stems from the decay of the trace unless repetition and rehearsal occur. The human has a certain span of immediate memory, that is, he can recall a limited amount of material without error when he is tested immediately after receiving the material. He forgets material which exceeds the span of immediate memory, in amounts comparable in magnitude to that of long-term memory loss.

According to the trace theorist, *time,* and not the events that occur during the time interval, accounts for the retention loss. This position is difficult to test because it is virtually impossible to prevent some form of activity from occurring during the retention interval. One possible test is to compare short-term retention as a function of rate of presentation. Decay theorists assume that since faster presentation rates would involve shorter retention intervals, less decay should occur. Of course, if rehearsal occurs and aids retention, performance should be higher with slow rates. While some studies (for example, Conrad and Hille, 1958) have upheld the prediction of better recall with faster rates, other studies (Mackworth, 1962a,b; Pollack, Johnson, and Knaff, 1959) have found just the opposite results. More will be said on this problem shortly.

An experiment (Peterson and Peterson, 1959) with a new methodology was important in stimulating new research on the problem. Whereas most of the studies previously conducted on short-term memory involved retention after the presentation of whole lists of materials, Peterson and Peterson measured retention of each individual item *before* presenting additional items. This procedure avoids the possibility studied by Tulving and Arbuckle (1963) that different items might interact with each other and affect retention, as under the procedure of presenting entire lists of items before measuring retention of any item.

Peterson and Peterson presented trigrams and measured retention immediately after intervals from 3 to 18 seconds in which no other verbal materials were presented. Since it is imperative that rehearsal be prevented during the retention intervals, subjects were required to count backwards by 3s or 4s after each trigram was presented until they were signaled to recall the trigram.

Each subject received eight items at each of six different retention intervals in counterbalanced order. Figure 6.9 shows that substantial forgetting occurred during these very short intervals. Retention was an inverse function of the length of the retention interval. The shape of the retention curve was very similar to that usually found in long-term memory studies. Decay theorists viewed these data as support for their position.

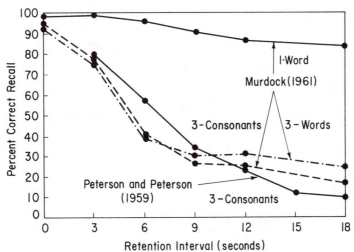

Figure 6.9. Percentage frequency of completely correct recall of 3-consonant trigrams (Peterson and Peterson, 1959; Murdock, 1961), and 1-word and 3-word units (Murdock, 1961). [From A. W. Melton: Implications of short-term memory for a general theory of memory. *Journal of Verbal Learning and Verbal Behavior*, 1963, 2, 1–21. Reprinted by permission of Academic Press, Inc., and the author.]

Two major criticisms have been leveled at this important study by Peterson and Peterson. Both attacks were aimed at demonstrating the existence of interference in the study. Keppel and Underwood (1962) argued that proactive inhibition was a strong possibility in the design of Peterson and Peterson, which required repeated measures of each subject. The retention of later individual items might be reduced by proactive inhibition from previously presented items in the test session.

Keppel and Underwood compared performance at the 3- and 18-second intervals at different stages of practice. Proactive inhibition should be low on early stages but increase with later stages. In addition, it was hypothesized that PI would be greater with the longer retention interval during which the earlier trigrams could spontaneously recover in strength and create more interference. The predictions were supported by an interaction between length of retention interval and stage of practice. Figure 6.10 shows that in early stages of practice, performance was equal for 3- and 18-second intervals, but in later stages, performance was more impaired for the longer retention interval.

Murdock (1961) conducted a series of studies using the Peterson and Peterson paradigm. First, he was able to replicate their findings successfully with consonant trigrams. However, using integrated units such as monosyllabic words as stimuli, he found virtually no drop in retention

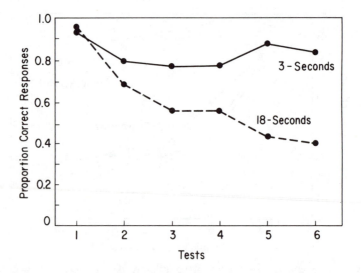

Figure 6.10. Retention as a function of number of prior syllables and length of retention interval. [From G. Keppel and B. J. Underwood: Proactive inhibition in short-term retention of single items. *Journal of Verbal Learning and Verbal Behavior,* 1962, **1**, 153–161. Reprinted by permission of Academic Press, Inc., and the authors.]

with longer intervals. On the other hand, he found that triads of unrelated words were forgotten at the same rate as the trigrams of groups of three unrelated letters. These results are presented in Figure 6.9 in conjunction with those from Peterson and Peterson. (The fact that recall of single words did not drop with longer intervals shows that a word is one unit, whereas either three unrelated letters or three unrelated words involve three units of material.)

In a second study, Murdock (1961) actually manipulated PI in STM. After reading 0, 3, 6, 9, or 12 words, the subject was presented a stimulus word which he was required to recall after either 0, 3, 6, 9, 12, or 18 seconds of a counting-backwards task designed to prevent rehearsal. If PI were operative, then retention of the stimulus words should be lowered as the number of preceding words increased. Murdock obtained PI, but it appeared to be a U-shaped function such that retention dropped as the number of preceding words increased, up to three, but then surprisingly improved with additional preceding words.

If PI were the only factor in Murdock's study, one would expect more PI, the greater the number of preceding items. One explanation for the U-shaped function is that subjects began anticipating the point at which the lists would terminate and thus set themselves for a retention test. Although subjects were not informed of the length of the series of items, it is possible that the longer the list, the more likely the subjects thought it would soon be over and tests would be given. If such strategies were devised, this might explain why PI did not continue to increase as the list length increased. Murdock considered but rejected this account of the U-shaped function.

In a later study, however, Murdock (1964) failed to find support for PI in STM. He devised a different task in which the subject received six A–B pairs in each of six lists. Within each list only one of the pairs was tested by presenting A and requiring recall of B. The particular pair tested was counterbalanced over six different lists so that all serial positions were tested equally often.

The number of correct responses did not drop as practice continued, as predicted from the concept of PI. However, retention did vary as a function of the serial position of the tested items. Retention was highest for the last presented item and lower for items presented in the first five serial positions. One interpretation of this finding of Murdock might be that RI may operate in this situation to reduce retention. Earlier items may be reduced in retention due to interference from additional input items prior to the test. However, the last presented item has no additional input prior to its test so it would not encounter RI.

The failure to find PI in this task does not rule out the possibility that it operates in the Peterson and Peterson paradigm. In that task, there are no interpolated items between a presented item and its recall test, whereas Murdock's task fills the retention interval with additional material of the same nature. Keppel (1965) suggested that both PI and RI could be present in Murdock's paradigm. We must conclude that interference in the form of PI is still tenable in the Peterson and Peterson paradigm.

Keppel (1965) and Postman (1964a) questioned the neutrality of the rehearsal prevention activity employed during the retention interval of STM studies. One question is how effectively counting backwards can prevent rehearsal. Then, if one assumes that it does prevent rehearsal, another question is whether or not it actually interferes with retention of the trigrams. Although counting backwards is highly dissimilar to learning trigrams, it still might affect performance of the verbal task by disrupting the subject's task set. In other words, the interpolation of activity between presentation and retention of material constitutes a potential source of interference; thus, there is a possibility that the Peterson and Peterson findings can also be accounted for by some form of interference.

The decay theorist is in a difficult situation. In order to study memory, it is necessary to exclude further practice during the retention interval. The very task used to prevent rehearsal is always suspect as a source of interference.

Theoretical Relationship of STM and LTM

We have pointed out earlier that the distinction between STM and LTM could simply represent differences in the relative retention intervals involved. However, theorists have disagreed as to whether the mechanisms underlying STM and LTM are the same or different. The critical distinction between STM and LTM may not be differences in the length of the retention interval.

Hebb (1949) proposed a dual-mechanism theory of memory in which STM was attributed to the effects of a single stimulation which decays rapidly. On the other hand, LTM involved the formation of a permanent structural trace by means of repeated stimulation. Interference among competing associations or structures would account for losses in LTM. Thus, a two-factor theory is involved, with decay accounting for STM and interference affecting LTM. This theory should not be confused with the Melton–Irwin two-factor theory described earlier, in which both factors involve interference.

Melton (1963) viewed interference as the process underlying retention losses in both STM and LTM. He ruled out evidence for the decay posi-

tion based on Peterson and Peterson's study on the grounds that interference is involved there in the form of proactive inhibition.

Melton based his argument for a continuum of short- and long-term
memory on additional evidence regarding the effect of repetition in short–
term memory. He noted that repetition increases the probability of recall
for material of subspan and supraspan length. Span refers to the capacity of recall on an immediate test after a single repetition. (We can assume that smaller amounts of material can be recalled perfectly on a
test immediately after one repetition, whereas greater amounts of material
should require two or more repetitions.) Melton considers the fact that
both subspan and supraspan sequences are affected in the same manner
by repetition to be evidence for the continuum position.

Evidence on the role of repetition for subspan units comes from Hellyer
(1962), who employed 1, 2, 4, or 8 repetitions of consonant trigrams
tested after intervals of 3, 9, 18, and 27 seconds. Better recall was obtained at all intervals when more repetitions were provided. Recall decreased as the interval lengthened, as in the Peterson and Peterson study.
These results are shown in Figure 6.11.

Supraspan sequences also are better recalled with more repetition
(Hebb, 1961). He presented several sequences of nine digits which the
subject had to recall in exact order. On every third trial, the same sequence was presented, whereas different sequences were given on all

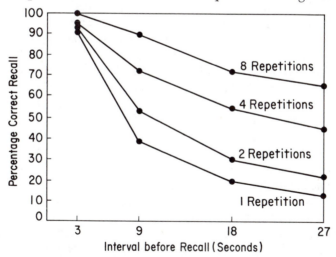

Figure 6.11. Percentage frequency of completely correct recall of 3-consonant
trigrams as a function of the frequency of 1-second presentations of the
trigram before beginning the retention interval (Hellyer, 1962). [From A. W.
Melton: Implications of short-term memory for a general theory of memory.
Journal of Verbal Learning and Verbal Behavior, 1963, **2**, 1–21. Reprinted by
permission of Academic Press, Inc., and the author.]

other trials. Hebb found recall improved over trials for the repeated sequence whereas it did not for the nonrepeated sequences. Similar results were obtained in a replication by Melton. In addition, he found that the benefits of repetition were weakened as a function of the number of different sequences that intervened between repetitions of the critical sequence.

Repetition produces its effect by leading to the formation of bigger units or "chunks." The original units are integrated into larger, and therefore fewer discrete, units so that, in a sense, there is less to remember. Thus, in Murdock's (1961) study reported earlier, short-term forgetting occurred for trigrams but not for three-letter words.

Melton's evidence does not prove beyond all doubt that STM and LTM vary along the same continuum. However, a theorist who maintained an STM–LTM dichotomy certainly might reconsider in the face of such evidence. First, interference has been demonstrated to occur in both situations. Second, repetition operates in similar fashion in STM and LTM. If there is a real dichotomy, it is necessary to find evidence of different processes operating in the two situations.

One such instance of a variable which differentially affects STM and LTM has been reported by Baddeley and Dale (1966). They examined RI as a function of semantic or meaningful similarity. Whereas substantial RI was obtained for LTM, there was no impairment of STM due to RI. Thus, semantic similarity affects LTM but not STM. On the other hand, variations in acoustic similarity are effective in reducing STM (Wickelgren, 1965). The latter study did not examine LTM.

Baddeley and Dale suggest that items in LTM are probably encoded by meaning, whereas Conrad (1964) and Wickelgren hypothesize that encoding of items in STM is on the auditory dimension. The over-all pattern of results is consistent with the view of STM and LTM as different processes, since similarity has different effects on the two situations.

The other major argument for a dichotomy has been the substantial amount of forgetting in STM situations where presumably no interference was operative. Therefore, it is argued, the memory trace must have undergone rapid decay.

However, Keppel (1965) and Postman (1964a) have emphasized the fact that original degrees of learning in STM and LTM situations are difficult to equate. If anything, the level of learning is lower in such paradigms as that of Peterson and Peterson since only one presentation is made in most STM studies. As a result, substantial forgetting could occur even though there was little interference and very brief retention intervals.

On the other hand, most long-term memory studies involve many trials of practice on whole lists of items. Thus, comparisons of short- and long-term memory assume that the retention interval is the major variable, whereas in fact the situations also vary with respect to the level of original practice. Table 6.5 illustrates these differences between STM and LTM situations which prevent sound quantitative comparisons. Arguments for a dichotomy based primarily on comparisons of the relative rates of forgetting in STM and LTM are misleading.

TABLE 6.5

SOME PROCEDURAL DIFFERENCES BETWEEN STM AND LTM STUDIES

		Retention Interval	
		SHORT Less than 1 minute	LONG More than 1 minute
Number of Repetitions	One	Most STM studies	
	More than one		Most LTM studies

Other Evidence

Waugh and Norman (1965) restricted themselves to aspects of short-term memory. They adopted a distinction made earlier (1890) by William James between primary memory (PM) and secondary memory (SM) as components of STM. According to James, events that are still in consciousness represent PM, while events that can be recalled but which had not been conscious at the time of the recall test constitute SM. There is a limited capacity to the size of PM, just as our primary senses are restricted in the range and number of stimuli which they can process. All events must pass through PM initially, according to Waugh and Norman; but since PM has a limited capacity, old items may be displaced when new items are presented. These older items are forgotten in a permanent sense. However, if items are rehearsed, they can hold on to their positions in PM and also become more permanent by moving into SM. Forgetting, under this formulation, shown in Figure 6.12, would not be due to decay. Instead, earlier items in the sequence would be lost because later items displaced them from the limited capacity PM.

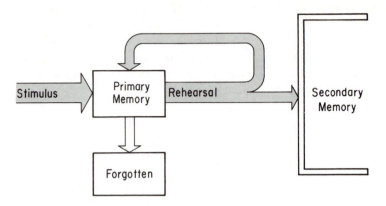

Figure 6.12. The primary and secondary memory system. (All verbal items enter PM, where they are either rehearsed or forgotten. Rehearsed items may enter SM.) [From N. C. Waugh and D. A. Norman: Primary memory. *Psychological Review*, 1965, **72**, 89–104. Reprinted by permission of the American Psychological Association and the authors.]

The situation employed by Waugh and Norman differs from that used by Peterson and Peterson. The latter investigators presented only one item before each retention test and did not strain the PM capacity. Insofar as their rehearsal-prevention task was effective, no items were transferred into SM either. Although both studies dealt with short-term memory, the situations are totally different. The distinction between PM and SM is unnecessary for the task used by Peterson and Peterson.

It is possible to compare the Waugh and Norman situation with long-term memory situations more readily than with the Peterson and Peterson paradigm. The PM–SM distinction would be just as applicable if the retention intervals were 24 hours or more as if they were 24 seconds or less. Regardless of the length of the retention interval, rehearsal should increase the permanence of the material involved. During rehearsal an item would be in PM, but eventually it would also become part of SM.

The Peterson and Peterson situation, on the other hand, does not consider the role of repetition through possible rehearsal during the retention interval. It deals with retention of items which receive only one trial after short intervals, whereas long-term memory situations examine retention of items that receive repeated exposure.

Waugh and Norman used a probe technique to study memory of a series of sixteen single digits. The term *probe* refers to the last number in the series, which is actually a repetition of an earlier item. The task is to recall the item which followed the original occurrence of the probe item. The location of the first occurrence of probe digits was varied over the serial positions of the list on successive tests. Only nine of the fifteen different serial positions were tested, but each locus was involved in ten tests so that each subject received a total of ninety lists.

The major variable was the rate of presentation of the list. According to decay theory, forgetting of an item at a given locus should be greater with a slower presentation rate, since more time elapses between presentation and test. On the other hand, an interference theory would not predict differences as a function of presentation rate. The amount of forgetting attributable to interference should be a direct function of the number of items that come between the presentation of an item and its recall test.

Waugh and Norman found no differences in recall as a function of presentation rate. As predicted on the basis of interference theory, the amount of forgetting was a direct function of the number of items occurring after the item to be recalled. They concluded that their evidence supports a distinction between PM and SM as independent memory mechanisms. However, they do not insist on a formulation of two nonoverlapping processes. An item may be in both PM and SM at the same time. The likelihood that it is in PM depends on the number of items presented after the item in question is presented. However, items in SM are a function of other factors, such as the number of repetitions they received.

Perceptual versus Memory Trace

The present evidence appears to support the view that loss of retention over intervals as short as 3 seconds, such as those used by Peterson and Peterson, can be accounted for by interference theory. Their results cannot be regarded as strong evidence for the decay position.

In general, direct empirical support for the decay theory is weak except when very short retention intervals are employed. For example, in the study cited earlier, Conrad and Hille (1958) found support for the decay position. They tested immediate recall of strings of digits which were presented at a fast or a slow rate. Recall was higher with the fast rate, so they concluded that less decay occurred because there was a shorter time lag between input and test.

On the other hand, Mackworth (1962a,b) has consistently found just the opposite results. Immediate serial recall of digit strings was higher when the presentation rates were slower. She attributed her findings to the occurrence of rehearsal under slower presentation rates.

In a review article, Aaronson (1967) suggests that one factor responsible for the confusing pattern of findings may be perceptual in nature. With very fast presentation rates, performance may be impaired due to errors in the perception of the items. If items are misperceived initially, they will be incorrect on recall even if subjects accurately reported what they thought was presented.

The findings regarding the effects of presentation rate are unclear. Furthermore, the relevance of immediate memory studies to those using the Peterson and Peterson paradigm is questionable. In the latter situation the shortest retention intervals have been 3 seconds, whereas in the former case the retention test is immediate. Even if decay were demonstrated to occur in immediate memory situations, it would not prove that decay operated in situations with retention intervals of 3 seconds or more. Actually, there is some support for the view that decay processes are involved in immediate memory tasks. However, this decay appears to involve the perceptual rather than the memory trace.

Sperling (1960) presented a matrix display of single letters forming three rows of four letters each, for a very brief period of 50 milliseconds. After the visual stimulus had terminated, one condition received a tone that, on the basis of a prearranged code, served to indicate which one row was to be recalled. A comparison of results revealed that subjects required to recall part of the matrix had two to three times as much recall, on a percentage basis, than those in the total recall condition. However, this superiority occurred only if recall was measured within a few tenths of a second after the stimulus input, and vanished if recall was delayed over 1 second.

Sperling assumed that the visual afterimage of the stimulus matrix persists for about 1 second after the stimulus is terminated. This afterimage decays by the time total recall is completed but is still present for the duration of partial recall. When recall is measured immediately, the partial recall condition can make use of this rapidly decaying trace and increase its performance whereas the total recall condition cannot. When recall is delayed more than 1 second following the stimulus input, there is not such an advantage for the partial recall condition, and performance is equal under the two conditions.

The results of immediate memory studies are compatible with the decay theory. However, it is the perceptual trace rather than the memory, or postperceptual, trace which appears to decay. When the amount of input is exceedingly large, the subject may still recall some items from perceptual afterimages for a short period before they decay. Once the input has been transferred from the perceptual stage into the memory stage, it seems that losses are due to interference rather than to decay.

SUMMARY

Retention refers to the stability of learned material over time. The converse of retention, forgetting, is a process over which theorists have disagreed. The trace or decay theory views forgetting as a weakening of memory traces simply due to the passage of time, whereas the interference theory assumes that competition among different associations leads to the losses of retention.

Interference theory has been tested using the retroactive and proactive inhibition paradigms. Two tasks are learned, and then either the first or the second one is tested for retention. If the retention is poorer than that of a control condition which learns only one task, it is assumed that the other task involved (for the conditions learning two tasks) led to interference.

The interference theory assumes that proactive inhibition is the more powerful source of forgetting. That is, a learned task is forgotten primarily because earlier learning interferes at the time of retention. It is further assumed that this earlier learning was unlearned, or extinguished, when the task to be tested for retention was itself originally acquired. However, the unlearned first task is assumed to be capable of spontaneous recovery eventually, so that by the time the second task is tested for retention, there is interference between the two tasks. When only one task is learned in the laboratory, it is assumed that preexperimental associations are unlearned. When this "first list" recovers, it produces interference with the laboratory list, thus causing forgetting.

These assumptions have received numerous experimental tests. There is substantial evidence in favor of the notion of unlearning of the first task, but the evidence is mixed regarding the spontaneous recovery of the first task. Finally, there has been negative support for the formulation that preexperimental associations interfere with the retention of laboratory produced associations.

Despite these limitations, the interference theory has been highly useful in generating testable predictions. As more evidence becomes available, perhaps some revision of the theory will be made to enable it to be compatible with the findings. It may be unnecessary to assume that unlearned associations undergo spontaneous recovery. The role of PI on forgetting may have been overemphasized, and a reemphasis on RI may be forthcoming.

In recent years, substantial interest has been shown in the area of short-term memory. Decay theorists see the large amount of forgetting that occurs over very brief intervals as contrary to interference theory,

since there does not appear to be opportunity for competing associations
to operate.

However, interference theorists have demonstrated that proactive
and retroactive inhibition do occur in these situations, and that there
may be no basic discontinuity in the nature of long- and short-term memory. One difficulty in arriving at any firm conclusions regarding the
relationship of the two phenomena is the fact that they differ not only
with respect to the length of the retention intervals involved but also
with respect to the frequency of repetition received.

If there is any strong evidence for decay of traces, it appears to be
limited to the perceptual level. Stimuli leave a rapidly decaying perceptual trace following their presentation. However, once the stimulus
has been perceived, the memory trace appears to be subject to interference rather than to decay.

A schematic diagram of the processes assumed to be involved in the
retention of a hypothetical single list of items is shown in Figure 6.13.
The diagram is based on the work of many different investigators and
is a tentative proposal, rather than a definitive analysis, of retention.

A list of thirteen trigrams presented at a 1-second rate pass through immediate memory; because the immediate memory span has a limited
capacity of about seven items, some of the thirteen items are immediately
forgotten due to decay of the perceptual trace. On the basis of some

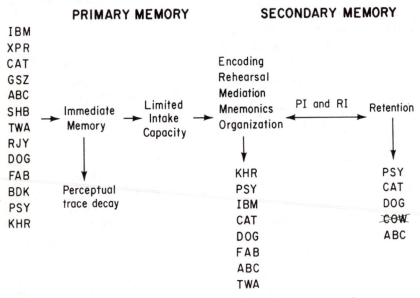

Figure 6.13. A hypothetical example of the processes involved in memory
of a single list as measured by the method of recall.

selective process, some items are retained, such as those with high meaningfulness, interassociations, or idiosyncratic properties. Items presented at the end or beginning of the list are also favored by some selective process.

These remaining items are rehearsed and encoded. The subject attempts to relate them to previous associations and find ways of organizing the input. In terms of Waugh and Norman's (1965) theory, the material he can recall at this point represents the primary memory, whereas secondary memory refers to the material retained on a test after an interval without additional practice.

During the retention interval, the preexperimental associations—which are assumed by interference theory to have been unlearned—may spontaneously recover to produce PI. In addition, during the retention interval the subject may learn other material that produces RI at the time of retention. As a result, the amount he retains will show a decrement or forgetting. Furthermore, items that were not originally presented may occur as intrusions on the retention test.

CHAPTER 7

Free Recall: Organizational Processes

A paradigm which has received increasing study in recent years has been that of *free recall*. This task is also referred to as *free learning*.

The recall test is immediate when learning is being studied, rather than delayed, as it is in studies of retention that use the recall method. It involves a very simple procedure but affords the examination of some rather complicated processes. Typically, free recall studies present, in a single trial, a list of items and follow it with an immediate recall test on which the subject may recall items in any order. This latter feature of the paradigm, recall in any order, allows the subject freedom to utilize past associations, mnemonic devices, and organizational techniques. In serial and paired-associate tasks, subjects must recall items or respond to stimuli which are relatively specific. In contrast, a distinction between the stimulus and the response in free recall is not feasible since all items may serve as both stimuli and responses. Item availability appears to be the main goal; that is, the task is to produce the items of the list, but subjects are not required to give each item as a response to any specific stimulus.

The distinction between response and associative learning, which was found to be useful in serial and paired-associate tasks, is less readily made for free recall. Earlier we pointed out that, in the serial anticipation paradigm, response terms not only had to be available in recall but also had to be produced in a specified serial order. Similarly, in recall, response terms had to be available for paired-associate tasks as well as to be associated to specific stimulus terms. On the other hand, in free recall tasks it is not easy to make a distinction between response and associative learning since they are interwoven. Response learning is not independent of interassociations among the response terms; in fact, perhaps the associative relationships are important in facilitating the availability of response terms. Furthermore, because most free recall studies use words rather than nonsense syllables, there is often no response learning required.

Our treatment of free recall will involve, first, an examination of variables producing quantitative and qualitative differences in performance in situations involving only one trial; then, a consideration of some aspect of free recall under multiple trials.

Amount of Recall

Murdock (1960) performed several studies of some factors involved in free recall. One of the main conclusions concerned the relationship between amount of recall and length of list. His results showed a linear increase in amount of recall with increases in list length. However, when rate of presentation was equal for all list lengths, necessarily the total presentation time was unequal, being proportionately longer for longer lists. This fact suggests that the basis for greater recall with longer lists may simply be the greater presentation time they receive.

In one study dealing with this problem, Murdock gave lists of varying length to different groups but maintained the same total exposure time. He was able to do this by using faster rates of presentation for the longer lists. When total time was equated by this procedure, it was found that amount of recall did not differ as a function of list length.

In a later study, Murdock (1962) compared several different combinations of list length and presentation rate. The total presentation time was equated for all conditions by presenting shorter lists at a slower rate and longer lists at a faster rate. Murdock found no differences in amount of free recall as a function of list length when the total time was equated.

Amount of recall appears to vary with the type of material employed. If nonsense syllables are used, amount of recall is greater with units of higher association value (Postman, Adams, and Phillips, 1955). Twenty nonsense syllables consisting of five items at each of four levels of association value were presented at a 4-second rate. The subjects were allowed five minutes for recall. They recalled significantly more nonsense syllables for the two higher association value levels than for the two lower association value levels. These results indicate that availability of nonsense syllables in recall varies with their association strength.

Postman and Phillips (1961) compared free recall of nonsense syllables and words. Lists of forty-eight nonsense syllables or words were presented at a 10-second rate to two groups. The long inter-item interval was necessary in order to provide a distractor task for one group which was tested for incidental learning. Regardless of whether intentional or incidental learning was involved, more adjectives were recalled than nonsense syllables.

These two studies by Postman and his associates suggest that free recall is similar to other learning situations insofar as performance improves as one goes from low to high association nonsense syllables to meaningful words.

Perhaps a greater factor affecting amount of recall than the characteristics of individual items is the interrelationship among items of the list. In the case of nonsense syllables, the evidence seems conflicting. Horowitz (1961) demonstrated that free recall was higher for lists of trigrams of high formal intralist similarity whereas Underwood, Ekstrand, and Keppel (1964) found just the opposite effect. They pointed out that Horowitz' materials favored correct responses by guessing for the high similarity condition.

Underwood, Runquist, and Schulz (1959) employed a paired-associate task but had some groups tested for free recall of the response terms, which were adjectives of either high or low meaningful similarity. They found higher recall with responses of high intralist similarity using words as responses.

When words are employed for free recall, it is possible that interassociations among the items affect recall. For example, Deese (1960) has compared free recall of high and low frequency word lists of differing length. He used all combinations of Thorndike–Lorge (1944) words, from six levels of frequency of occurrence, and four list lengths (12, 25, 50, and 100 items).

The results indicated that recall was greater with high frequency lists and this superiority was greater with longer lists. Deese reasoned that the interassociations among items in high frequency lists were greater than those in low frequency lists. He computed an index of inter-item associative strength (IIAS) based on the mean number of times each item in the list was given as a response to other items in the list on a word-association test administered to independent groups. Values of IIAS were greater with high frequency lists; furthermore, they increased as list length increased for high frequency lists. This relationship between frequency and list length on IIAS parallels the interaction of these variables on amount of recall. Deese concluded that greater recall with high frequency words is not due to frequency, per se. Instead, the greater interassociative strength in lists of high frequency items accounts for the greater recall.

Deese (1959) conducted another test of the hypothesis that the free recall of unrelated words is aided by associations among the items comprising the list. He obtained lists of fifteen words which were responses to particular stimuli on the Kent–Rosanoff test in the Minnesota norms compiled by Russell and Jenkins (1954). Some lists consisted of words which were high frequency associates while other lists contained words of low or zero frequency of association. All lists contained words matched in Thorndike–Lorge word frequency. In order to relate the amount of recall to the number of interassociations among members of each list, Deese employed his index of inter-item associative strength (IIAS) to measure the tendency of each item in a list to elicit other list items as free associates. Each of the lists used for free recall was given to independent groups in the manner of a word-association test. The values of IIAS were highest for lists containing associates of high frequency, followed by low frequency, and finally by zero frequency.

A high correlation of 0.88 was obtained between IIAS and amount of recall. Thus, the stronger the interassociations within a list, the better the recall. Furthermore, lists with high IIAS also led to fewer extralist errors or intrusions. These findings imply that free recall could be viewed as a selective guessing situation. Although the subject may be able to recall only a portion of the total list, he can add to his total recall by guessing additional items. His chances of guessing correctly are higher if the list has a high IIAS value, since the guesses are restricted to strong associates of those words already recalled correctly.

Additional evidence that interassociations are involved in free recall was obtained by Rothkopf and Coke (1961). To three subjects they presented 99 of the 100 Kent–Rosanoff stimulus words, in different order, for 5 seconds each. After 15 minutes of rest, they measured free recall. The probability that a word was recalled was correlated with the number of other words in the list to which it had occurred as an associate in the Kent–Rosanoff word-association test norms. Rothkopf and Coke reasoned that the associatively related words serve as cues for recall so that the probability that a given word would be recalled was directly related to its number of cues in the list.

Once again, it is interesting to note the views of the philosopher, James

Mill. In 1829, he suggested the same mechanism in his *Analysis of the Phenomena of the Human Mind.*

> If we have not the idea itself, we have certain ideas connected with it. We run over those ideas, one after another, in hopes that some one of them will suggest the idea we are in quest of; and if any one of them does, it is always so connected with it as to call it up in the way of association.

An alternative view of free recall offered by Asch and Ebenholtz (1962b) rejects the role of interassociations as a factor influencing recall. They tested subjects for free recall of lists of eight nonsense syllables of low similarity for several study-test trials. Since different serial orders were employed on each trial, Asch and Ebenholtz maintained that interassociations among the items were ruled out or minimized. However, this procedure only prevents the same association being formed between two items on all trials but does not rule out the formation of multiple associations between an item and the remaining items. One trial may be sufficient for the formation of numerous associations.

In any case, Asch and Ebenholtz took issue with Deese's explanation of free recall. According to these investigators, free recall is a situation that measures item availability and not associations among items. One factor affecting availability is frequency of experience, since higher frequency improves recall by strengthening the availability of the memory trace of each individual item. No recourse to increased associations between items with higher frequency is made by these investigators. On the other hand, Deese (1959) accounted for the higher recall of lists with high frequency items in terms of the greater degree of interassociation in such lists.

The difficulty with Asch and Ebenholtz' position is the lack of a satisfactory means of preventing the presence of interassociations. Merely using different serial orders on each trial is inadequate. Unless interassociations can be ruled out, one cannot test their hypothesis adequately. On the other hand, Deese's hypothesis that interassociations aid free recall can be directly evaluated by varying the associative properties of the material. As Rothkopf and Coke (1961) showed, items which had more interassociations with other items in a list were better recalled.

Units of Analysis Tulving (1968) has questioned the validity of the units of analysis specified by the experimenter in measuring the amount recalled. He distinguished between experimenter-defined units (E units) and subject-defined units (S units). Thus, in a 20-word list there are 20 E units. However, from the subject's standpoint, there may be fewer S units, especially if he employs some grouping or organizing of the material so that several *E* units comprise a single *S* unit. For example, *North, South, East,* and *West* may be viewed as four *E* units in a list but as only one *S* unit since they comprise one exhaustive category.

Because of this discrepancy between nominal and functional units of measurement, it is difficult to compare *amount* of recall as a function of certain variables. Tulving cites the example of a comparison of free recall of nonsense syllable lists with word lists. Although more *E* units may be recalled with word lists, it may not mean that more *S* units are also recalled with this material than with the nonsense syllables. Tulving suggested that the number of *S* units may be smaller than the number of *E* units recalled for lists of words.

Serial Position Effects

We will first examine relationships between the input order in which items are presented and the probability with which different serial positions are recalled. Since the items in a list are generally selected to be homogeneous and are also presented in random order for each subject, any differences in recall for different serial positions must reflect properties of the positions, per se, rather than of the items employed in each position.

Deese and Kaufman (1957) examined the relationship between the input order and the amount of free recall. In one study, one group learned lists of 10 unrelated words and another group learned lists of 32 unrelated words. A third group received a passage of approximately 100 words containing 10 simple statements about one of three topics.

For unrelated words, the items at the end of the input order were recalled best (recency effect), followed by the initial items (primacy effect), and the middle terms were recalled poorest. This serial position curve for free recall, shown in Figure 7.1, is the reverse of that typically obtained in serial anticipation studies. The temporal order in which items were given during output was correlated with the probability of recall. Figure 7.2 indicates that the temporal order of recall corresponded with the amount of recall for the different serial positions of input. Items from the end of the list are given first, those from the beginning are next, and items from the middle occur last. Thus, there are primacy and recency effects in free recall, with the latter being stronger.

However, the group receiving connected discourse did not produce the same results. With sentences, the relationships between input order and probability of recall showed that early sections were best recalled, followed by final sections, with recall of middle sections being poorest. Thus,

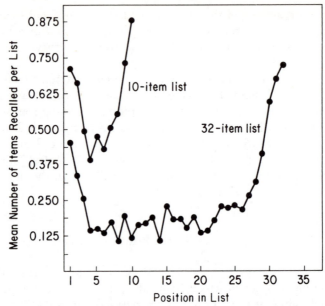

Figure 7.1. Mean frequency of recall per list per subject for lists of randomly arranged words as a function of position of items in original lists. [From J. Deese and R. A. Kaufman: Serial effects in recall of unorganized and sequentially organized verbal material. *Journal of Experimental Psychology*, 1957, 54, 180–187. Reprinted by permission of the American Psychological Association and the authors.]

serial position curves for sequential material resemble those obtained for serial anticipation learning. In addition, the temporal order of recall of words in sentences tends to correspond directly with the order of input. That is, the earlier a word was presented in a sentence, the earlier it was produced in recall.

As described earlier, Murdock (1962) compared free recall under several combinations of list length and presentation rate. An idealized serial position curve of free recall based on a composite of his findings is presented in Figure 7.3. He accounted for the shape of the serial position curve in terms of a combination of short-term proactive and retroactive inhibition. Items occupying early positions in the list are subject to little proactive but much retroactive inhibition. Later items in the list may encounter much proactive inhibition but little retroactive inhibition. However, items in the middle of the list should undergo both proactive and retroactive inhibition, since they are both preceded and followed by a number of other items. Consequently, performance is poorest for the middle portions of the list.

The pronounced recency effect in free recall may also be due to the

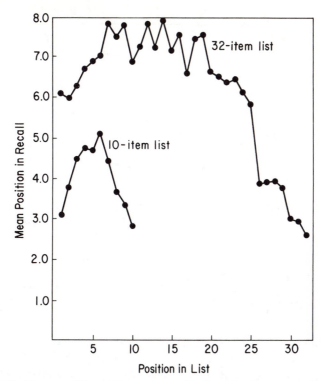

Figure 7.2. Mean position of items in recall of randomly arranged words as a function of items in original lists. [From J. Deese and R. A. Kaufman: Serial effects in recall of unorganized and sequentially organized verbal material. *Journal of Experimental Psychology*, 1957, **54**, 180–187. Reprinted by permission of the American Psychological Association and the authors.]

fact that items presented at the end of the list are nearest in time to the recall test. A common recall strategy may be to recall the most recently presented items while they are still strong. Imposing a delay between the input and time for output of 30 seconds has been found to eliminate the recency effect (Postman and Phillips, 1965), although it did not affect the primacy effect.

A similar finding by Glanzer and Cunitz (1966) led them to conclude that the recency effect reflects short-term memory, which has also been found to be impaired by delayed recall. On the other hand, slower presentation rates which improve long-term memory also increased the primacy effect without influencing the recency effect. Glanzer and Cunitz attributed the primacy effect to long-term memory. Thus, they attribute the serial position curve of free recall to the joint effects of short- and long-term memory.

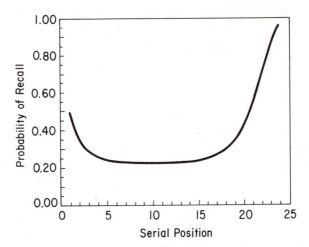

Figure 7.3. Idealized serial position curve for 24-word list. [From B. B. Murdock, Jr.: The retention of individual items. *Journal of Experimental Psychology,* 1961, **62**, 618–625. Reprinted by permission of the American Psychological Association and the author.]

The primacy effect typically found in free recall has been attributed to two factors by Tulving (1968). First, in agreement with Murdock (1962), Tulving noted that there is less intraserial proactive interference for earlier items in the list. In addition, subjects may rehearse earlier items during the entire course of input and hence pay less attention to the middle items.

Associative Clustering

In the preceding section, we attempted to account for the differential probability of recall for different serial positions of input. We also examined the order in which the items successfully recalled are given in output, and saw that the order of output is consistently related to the input order. Are there any other factors affecting the order of output in free recall?

Preexperimental associations among list items have been found to affect the order of recalled items. Jenkins and Russell (1952) presented, in random order, a list composed of Kent–Rosanoff stimulus words and their primary responses from word-association norms. The recall order revealed a tendency for the associated members of each pair which had been separated during input to be recalled contiguously.

Jenkins, Mink, and Russell (1958) performed a further study of associative clustering. Four groups were given different lists of Kent–Rosanoff stimuli and their primary responses from word-association norms. The mean frequency with which the primaries occurred in the norms differed in each condition. The pairs of Kent–Rosanoff stimuli and primary responses were randomly arranged in each list and were presented at a 1-second rate. The mean number of words recalled varied directly with the associative strength between the Kent–Rosanoff stimuli and their primaries comprising each list. Associative clustering, the tendency to recall the two members of each pair in succession, also increased with higher interpair associative strength.

Clustering represents a pattern in the output phase of free recall which is possible because recall in any order is allowed. This effect occurs despite the influences of the input order on recall, such as primacy and recency. Associative clustering suggests that strong preexperimental habits, such as word associations, tend to recombine during output even though the members of each pair are separated during input.

Category Clustering

Another situation involving clustering employs lists of logically related or categorized sets of words. It may be recalled from Chapter 1 that Bousfield (1953) studied category clustering with a list of sixty nouns composed of fifteen words from each of four taxonomic categories: animals, names, vegetables, and professions (ANVP). This basic list has been used in a number of the studies by Bousfield and his associates. The items are presented in random order on slides at a 3-second rate of presentation, followed immediately by a 10-minute recall trial.

Clustering occurs if more items from the same category are recalled contiguously than expected by chance. Several objective measures have been devised to index the extent of clustering. Perhaps the simplest measure is the repetition ratio (RR), which is the fraction derived by dividing the number of consecutive items recalled from the same category by the total number of items recalled minus one. Thus, if clustering were complete such that every item recalled was adjacent to another item from the same category, an RR of 1.0 would be obtained. Since the first item recalled cannot count as a "repetition," Bousfield's index subtracts one item in specifying the denominator of the RR index.

Bousfield (1953) found that the RR obtained in the recall of his categorized list exceeded that expected by chance. His subjects tended to cluster by category during recall. Bousfield and Cohen (1953, 1955) hypothesized that the recall of any item belonging to a given category tended to activate the recall of the superordinate or category itself, which in turn aided the recall of other members of that category. Each item in the list should aid the recall of the category of which it is a member. Categories were viewed as superordinate structures operating much in the manner of Hebb's (1949) hypothetical cell assemblies. If the subject could not recall a particular instance, the activation of the superordinate by recall of another instance of the same category might aid in recovering unavailable instances of that category. Thus, suppose the subject had forgotten the item *dog*. However, assume he recalls *cat* correctly and thereby activates the category ANIMAL, which in turn leads him to remember *dog*.

The fact that intrusions in these studies of clustering are generally limited to instances of the same categories as those comprising the list is consistent with the view that category clustering proceeds by a mediational process, such as that suggested by Bousfield and Cohen (1953). Yet, it is also possible that an explanation based on simple direct association may account for category clustering as well as associative clustering. The words belonging to a given category are probably more strongly interassociated than are noncategorized groups of words. Recall of *cat* may lead to recall of *dog* by direct association without recourse to mediation via activation of ANIMAL.

Different amounts of reinforcement were provided on the ANVP list by Bousfield and Cohen (1953). Groups received from one to five study trials before being tested for recall. Both the degree of clustering and the amount of recall increased with higher amounts of practice.

Bousfield and Cohen (1955) examined clustering in lists of words differing in frequency of occurrence (Thorndike and Lorge, 1944). They compared performances on high and low frequency lists of ANVP words, and found that greater clustering and recall occurred with the high frequency list. The investigators attributed the superior performance to the greater past reinforcement which high frequency words have received preexperimentally.

Early studies of category clustering relied entirely on the investigator's judgment for classifying words into categories. It is possible that the classifications which subjects might use would differ from that of the experimenter, thus producing misleading expectations. A direct assessment of the words which subjects consider to be members of various categories was made by Cohen, Bousfield, and Whitmarsh (1957), who instructed 200 subjects each to give four examples for each of eight categories.

Using these taxonomic norms, Bousfield, Cohen, and Whitmarsh (1958) obtained lists of words with high and low frequencies of taxonomic occurrence. Some groups were given lists containing ten high frequency instances of each of four categories, while other groups were presented lists with ten low frequency instances of each of four categories. For example, the instance *doctor* is an example of a strong associate and *ditchdigger* is a weak associate in the norms to the category, PROFESSION. More clustering and more recall was obtained with lists containing words of high taxonomic frequency. Thus, using instances known to belong to various categories as perceived by subjects themselves, Bousfield *et al.* have not only provided further evidence of clustering but demonstrated that it varies with the extent to which the instances "belong" in their categories.

Cofer, Bruce, and Reicher (1966) also varied the frequency with which instances occurred as associates to category names. In addition, they manipulated the degree of contiguity among instances of the same category, the time between presentation and recall, and the presentation rate. Using the Cohen *et al.* (1957) taxonomic norms as a base, these investigators selected high and low frequency words to form categorized lists. Presentation of the lists was either blocked so that all instances of a category occurred consecutively or nonblocked so that the instances of all categories were in a mixed order. Items were presented at a 1-, 2-, or 4-second rate. Finally, a test of free recall was given either immediately or following a delay of about 10 minutes. The results indicated that clustering was higher with blocked presentation for both high and low frequency lists. The investigators assumed that blocking enhanced the activation of the relevant category name for each set of instances. Clustering was slightly higher for high frequency items. Furthermore, immediate recall and slower presentation rates produced more clustering.

Cofer *et al.* also obtained evidence on the amount of recall. Higher recall occurred under blocked presentation, but only for the high frequency list. Recall was also better if followed by an immediate test, and if the presentation rates were slower. The results on clustering and amount of recall agreed with those obtained by Bousfield *et al.*

Another factor which should affect both clustering and the amount of recall is the number of categories. If the size of the list is held constant, will the amount and pattern of recall be affected by the number of categories within the list? At one extreme, where there are as many different categories as there are words in the list, the list is one of unrelated words. At the other extreme, all words in the list belong to the same (one) category. In either case, clustering is logically impossible. However, for situations between these extremes, clustering and amount of recall should be influenced by the number of categories in the list.

The presence of categories in a list is assumed to aid recall via clustering. But if the number of categories is high, then for a list of a given size, there will be relatively few items per category. In addition, the more categories involved, the more difficult it may be to recall all of the category names to aid recall. On the other hand, if there are few categories in the list, then, for a list of a given size, there will be more items per category. Even though it may be easier to recall all of the category names to aid recall, there may be too many items in each category to recall. Perhaps there is some optimal number of categories for a list of a given length.

Several studies varying the number of categories were made by Bousfield and Cohen (1956). They used lists of forty nouns composed of items from two, four, or eight categories. They hypothesized that less reinforcement of each category would result if they employed larger numbers of categories, since this would provide fewer instances of each category in a list of a given length. Recall was found to be highest for the lists with the smallest number of categories, provided the subjects had previously served in similar experiments. On the other hand, with naïve subjects, higher recall was obtained for lists with more categories. One possible reason for the opposed results is that subjects who had learned prior categorized lists might not remember which categories were involved on the latest list. In that situation, the fewer categories used, the easier it would be to remember the categories involved in the most recent list.

Dallett (1964b) performed five studies of the effects of number of categories on amount of recall. The findings differed depending on whether he used short lists (12 items) with one to six categories or long lists (24 items) with two to twelve categories. In studies with short lists he found a curvilinear relationship, with best recall occurring for an intermediate number of categories, whereas with long lists he found that recall dropped with more categories in the list. More categories mean less items per category, and hence fewer interassociations among the items of a category to aid recall. Furthermore, it becomes more difficult to remember the categories, per se, as their number increases. This limitation would especially exist for longer lists and may account for Dallett's findings, which showed impairment of recall as the number of categories increased under long lists.

In contrast to Dallett's findings, Mathews (1954) found that free recall of 24-item lists improved as she increased the number of categories from two to three to six. Thus, the number of categories is not excessively large compared to those used by Dallett for the same list length. We should also note that Mathews provided subjects with a list of the category names at the time of recall, since pretesting had indicated low recall in the absence of such cues. Subjects did not have to recall the category names; therefore the increased number of categories did not impair performance.

The materials Mathews used were names of famous persons which had been sorted in several categories, such as artists, musicians, and the like, by subjects prior to recall. Lists with many categories were formed by including the instances which were most frequently sorted into each category, whereas lists with few categories were composed of all of the instances sorted into each category. Thus, the instances in lists with many categories were more strongly associated to those categories than were the instances in lists with few categories. This may be another reason why Mathews found higher recall for lists containing more categories.

The speculation that the critical difference between the Dallett and Mathews studies was the presence or absence of category names as cues is supported by the findings of Tulving and Pearlstone (1966). Although the length of list was also varied in this study, our attention will be directed at only two other variables: the number of items per category (which is inversely related to the number of categories for a list of a given length), and the presence or absence of category names as cues at time of recall.

There were either 1, 2, or, 4 items for each category represented in lists of 12, 24, or 48 items. As Figure 7.4 indicates, the relationship between the number of items per category and the amount of recall differed, depending on whether or not cues were provided. For all list lengths,

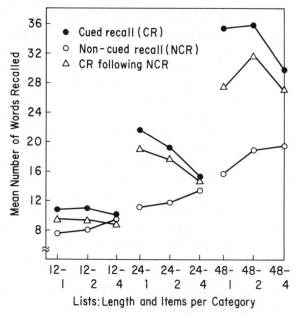

Figure 7.4. Mean number of words recalled in the first recall test (circles) and the second recall test (triangles) as a function of list length and number of items per category. [From E. Tulving and Z. Pearlstone: Availability versus accessibility of information in memory for words. *Journal of Verbal Learning and Verbal Behavior*, 1966, **5**, 381–391. Reprinted by permission of Academic Press Inc., and the authors.]

there was a tendency for recall to improve with fewer items per category (more categories) when cues were provided, but the opposite held when there were no cues provided. When there were fewer items per category (more categories), the subject could not make use of such categorical organization in the list because he could not remember so many category names. Unless the cues were provided, his recall was impaired as the number of categories increased, as in Dallett's study.

Tulving and Pearlstone also gave a second test under cued conditions to all groups. The noncued conditions were able to increase their scores when retested under cued conditions, as shown in Figure 7.4. However, they still did not reach the level achieved by the cued conditions, which did equally well on both tests. The results of only the first test are shown for cued conditions.

Theoretical Aspects of Clustering

What mechanisms are involved in the free recall of a list of related or categorized items? Bousfield (1953), in his early work, suggested that clustering involved the activation and recall of superordinates, that is, the category names, which themselves were not explicitly presented in the list. For example, the presentation of names of animals interspersed through a categorized list would activate the superordinate, ANIMAL, which could be employed by the subject during recall so that clustering of the items in that category would result. A similar process would occur for each of the other categories in the list.

On the other hand, Jenkins and Russell (1952), using noncategorized lists of strongly associated pairs of words presented in scrambled unpaired arrangements, found that the associatively related members of each pair tended to be given consecutively in recall. In this situation the clustering that occurred was accounted for in terms of associative relationships.

Thus, we have two types of situations, one involving category clustering and the other showing associative clustering. Because the materials employed in the two situations are different, we need not necessarily consider the two explanations of clustering opposed.

One approach is to consider category clustering as a special case of associative clustering involving two stages of association. First, there may have been previous associations among the items within each category. Then, there may have been associations formed between each of the instances of the category and the category name itself. Thus, category clustering in free recall can still be considered as involving associative factors without recourse to explanations based on the use of the category name as a recall cue.

Evidence consistent with this interpretation was found in the studies described earlier by Bousfield *et al.* (1958) and Cofer *et al.* (1966), which used lists of categorized words that differed in the degree to which the instances were associated to the category names. In both experiments, conditions that received categorized lists with strongly associated instances showed high clustering compared with conditions that received lists of categorized words which happened to be weakly associated instances. Since categories were involved in both lists, one would predict equal clustering if categories, per se, were responsible for clustering. But findings support the view that associative factors are involved in category clustering, perhaps in conjunction with mediational mechanisms.

Cofer (1965) accepted the existence of both associative and category clustering, although he did not consider the distinction to be useful. His conclusion is that the learner employs both types of mechanisms, depending on the nature of the test conditions. If associative relationships in the items are prevalent, the subject will utilize these; if categorical relationships are dominant in the list, he will employ them.

It is likely, as Cofer *et al.* suggested, that categorized lists contain items which contain stronger interassociations than those items comprising noncategorized lists. If so, the higher recall and greater clustering of categorized lists would not necessarily mean that subjects used the category name as a cue for recall. Recall could simply be higher because the associative properties of the categorized list were stronger.

On the other hand, Cofer (1966) noted that lists of categorized pairs are better recalled than noncategorized ones, even when precautions have been taken to equate the associative characteristics of the two types of items. In such a situation, it may be necessary to employ explanations based on category cues for recall. Cofer cited some unpublished research by Marshall (1963), who compared recall of categorized pairs such as *spider–beetle* and noncategorized pairs such as *mountain–high*. He selected pairs such as these in which the number of associates common to the members of each type of pair were equal, so that the only difference between the lists was the presence or absence of categorization.

He presented members of such pairs in a scrambled order and tested for free recall. More clustering and higher recall occurred for categorized pairs in the list. In an attempt to determine how subjects coded items, Marshall then gave a word-association test, using the single members of the pairs as stimuli. Common responses were elicited by the members of categorized pairs more frequently than by members of noncategorized pairs. However, the associative responses given to the categorized pairs were not always the category names themselves. For example, the pair *hammer–chisel* elicited the category name TOOL as an associate only 20 percent of the time.

The results of the word-association test suggest that the categorized pairs are easier to code, as reflected by the fact that members of such pairs frequently elicited a common response. This difference, rather than the fact that some pairs are categorized and others are not, may be the critical factor leading to higher recall and clustering in categorized pairs. Cofer concluded that the use of category names as recall cues may operate in Marshall's situation but that it is only one of many possible ways of coding.

Storage or Retrieval?

There are questions as to what is represented by recalled items. Does the amount of recall reflect the amount stored in memory, or does it indicate the limits of memory retrieval? Some theorists view recall as an underestimate of what is stored in memory inasmuch as subjects may not always efficiently retrieve what has been stored.

Suppose a subject recalls 60 percent of the original input. Does this mean that he has only 60 percent of the original material left in storage, or that he may have more but can retrieve only that amount? Of course, in order to retrieve material, one must have it in storage, but there is always the possibility that what is retrieved and produced on the test is less than what is still in memory storage. For example, if retrieval requires certain cues but they are absent, retrieval will be impaired. One alternative view is to equate storage and retrieval on the assumption that the subject can retrieve all that is stored. Either interpretation is consistent with the fact of less-than-perfect recall.

Miller, Galanter, and Pribram (1960) consider the problem of retrieval to be the major one in memory. Subjects who devise better retrieval plans and strategies can recall better than less efficient subjects. Miller *et al.* draw an analogy between a subject in a memory experiment and a librarian. Books are stored in the library, and the efficiency of retrieval by the librarian depends on the use of a systematic code for storing the books. Failure to find a book does not mean it is not in the library but that it may be misshelved and therefore cannot be retrieved. Similarly, items "forgotten" by the subject may still be in storage but the memorizer simply cannot retrieve them.

The Tulving and Pearlstone study described earlier has implications on this issue. The fact that amount of recall can be augmented by the inclusion of cues at the time of recall supports the distinction that one can make between what is stored in memory and what can be retrieved from it. Many items may be stored in memory that may not be accessible at the time of recall unless appropriate retrieval cues are present.

Bilodeau, Fox, and Blick (1963) have also investigated the effects of retrieval cues or, in their terms, reminders, on recall. Using a list of Kent–Rosanoff stimuli, they determined the second most frequent responses for these stimuli in the Minnesota norms (Russell and Jenkins, 1954). The subjects studied a list of these secondary responses. Two minutes later, one group was tested for free recall without external cues, while another test group was provided with the appropriate Kent–Rosanoff stimuli as reminders. Better recall occurred for the latter group. The results of Bilodeau *et al.* are consistent with the view that more material may be in storage than is usually retrievable unless appropriate cues are present.

On the other hand, the evidence provided by Tulving and Pearlstone and by Bilodeau *et al.* could simply reflect reconstruction rather than recall. That is, the items "recalled" with the aid of cues may have been permanently lost from storage; instead, it is possible that the subject merely free-associates to the cues provided at the time of recall. Since the cues are associated with the items, this process would produce higher performance even if the items were no longer in storage.

Tulving (1968) also favored the view that the amount of recall is a function of the limits of retrieval ability. The extent of the retrieval capacity is considered to be fixed at a certain *number* of S units, which are similar to Miller's (1956) concept of chunks. However, the *size* of the S units or chunks is not assumed to be invariant but may increase with practice, mnemonic strategies, and opportunities for rehearsal. In this way, we may increase the number of units presented by the experimenter that we can store, although the number of S units or chunks we can handle is limited biologically.

Multiple-Trial Free Recall

Studies of clustering clearly illustrate the organized nature of free recall. These studies employ materials which are classifiable into various common categories. However, it seems that free recall is also organized with materials which are associatively unrelated and noncategorizable.

Tulving (1962) assumed that organization is reflected by the occurrences of the same sequences of items in recall on successive trials. An analysis of how sequential dependencies among items develop and change

over repeated learning (input) and recall (output) trials can be used
to study the operation of organization. Insofar as the organization imposed on the material comes from the subject himself, Tulving refers to
this as *subjective organization*. Apparently, transfer of past learning to
the new material can aid in its organization even if there is no inherent
pattern in the material.

A list of sixteen words was presented at a 1-second rate in different
serial orders on each of sixteen trials. After each trial, a 90-second recall
period was given the subject in which to write down as many words as he
could recall in any order. The mean number of items recalled increased
over trials, as one would expect; furthermore, the amount of subjective
organization, as measured by an index based on the repetition of sequences from trial to trial, also increased over trials. For the set of words
used, it appeared that the subject was imposing his own organization to
aid recall. The particular organization adopted by different subjects
seemed to be similar; thus, the organization was inherent in the materials,
and the subjects discovered rather than created the subjective organization.

Studies of multiple-trial free recall usually employ varied orders of
input on each trial so that any organization imposed upon the material
by the subject will lead to consistent recall patterns. If, on the other hand,
the items are presented in the same order on each trial, there is one form
of organization already present. The task becomes similar to a serial
learning task except that the anticipation method is not employed. Although the subject is instructed for free recall, he might learn the list
as a serial task. It is possible for the subject to anticipate successive
items during the presentation of the list if input orders are constant,
whereas this is not possible if the input orders are varied on each trial.
In effect, this difference between the situations may allow the subject to
obtain more practice under the constant order method.

A comparison of multiple-trial free recall under constant and varied
input orders was made by Waugh (1961). She gave six study-test trials
on lists of 48 common words; she did not find any differences in the
amount of recall as a function of type of input order.

On the other hand, whereas Waugh used college students, Jung and
Skeebo (1967) used eighth-grade students. Using lists of 24 items, they
found more recall under the constant input order. When they used only
12-item lists, the results agreed with those of Waugh, showing no difference. Furthermore, there was a tendency for the typical output pattern
of free recall to shift in opposite directions as more trials were given
under the two input orders. Usually items from the end of the list are
recalled first, then those from the beginning, and finally those from the

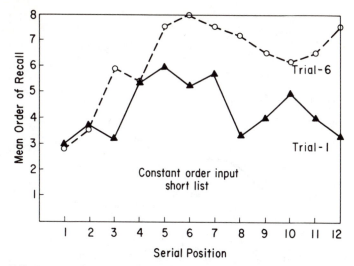

Figure 7.5. Mean order of recall for constant order condition on Trials 1 and 6 for short list. [From J. Jung and S. Skeebo: Multi-trial recall as a function of constant versus varied input orders and list length. *Canadian Journal of Psychology*, 1967, **21**, 329–336. Reprinted by permission of the *Journal* and the authors.]

middle, as shown in Figure 7.2. By the sixth trial, in the Jung and Skeebo study, the constant order conditions began recalling items from the beginning of the list first, whereas the tendency to recall items from the end first was enhanced in the varied order conditions. These shifts are shown in Figures 7.5 and 7.6 for the short lists. In other words, whereas the output order under varied input order was typical of those obtained under free recall, the one for the constant input order became more like those obtained with serial learning. The use of constant input orders leads the subject to employ a serial learning approach even though the instructions allow free recall.

One other finding about multiple-trial free recall with varied input order deserves mention. Several investigators working on different problems (Battig, Allen, and Jensen, 1965) each obtained evidence on the nature of the order of output on each successive trial with college students. These experimenters, using a variety of test conditions, discovered that on each trial the subject tends to recall earliest those items learned correctly for the first time on that trial. He later recalls items learned on previous trials. It is *as if* the subject decides to unload the newly acquired items before they are forgotten and to save the well-learned items (from previous trials) for later stages of each output trial. On the other hand,

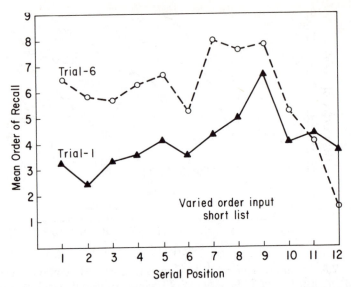

Figure 7.6. Mean order of recall for varied order condition on Trials 1 and 6 for short list. [From J. Jung and S. Skeebo: Multi-trial recall as a function of constant versus varied input orders and list length. *Canadian Journal of Psychology*, 1967, **21**, 329–336. Reprinted by permission of the *Journal* and the authors.]

the recency effect became stronger on successive trials in the Jung and Skeebo study. This difference may be due to the use of different learning techniques in eighth graders and college students.

The phenomenon reported by Battig *et al.* occurs under a wide range of test conditions since the individual studies made by these investigators varied in procedural details. If their results reflect the use of a strategy of recall devised by subjects, it is another example of organizational tendencies on the part of the learner. Possibly, this particular strategy may accompany the development of subjective organization of the form studied by Tulving. Thus, the subject recalls the newer items first, and then recalls the well-learned items in their organized pattern.

SUMMARY

The free recall or free learning paradigm and its multiple-trial variant are well suited for the study of the role of past habits and organizational strategies with respect to memory. The basic technique has much to recommend its expanded use inasmuch as it involves a simple procedure but allows the examination of some complex memory processes.

As with other paradigms, the amount of recall has been found to be constant when the total presentation time is equated. Lists containing words of higher frequency are better recalled, suggesting that the greater number of interassociations among such items is the basis for free recall.

The recall pattern typically shows a recency and a primacy effect. Items from the end of the list are recalled best, then those from the beginning, and finally those from the middle. The temporal order of recall also corresponds closely to this pattern.

When lists containing related items, such as instances from logical or associative categories, are used instead of unrelated words, recall is clustered; that is, related items occur closely together in the order of recall, and serial position of presentation has less influence on recall. This organized responding has been explained both in terms of associations among items and in cognitive terms. Items from the same category may be clustered in recall because they are associated to each other, or because the subject remembers the category name and employs it as a cue for recall.

When multiple-trial free recall of unrelated words is involved, two processes affect the pattern of recall. Newly learned items on each successive trial are recalled prior to already learned items. In addition, certain sequences of items tend to repeat on successive trials, presumably reflecting the development of subjective organization among the items by the subject.

CHAPTER 8

Mediation and Concept Learning

W e have mentioned the role of mediation in several earlier contexts. As subjects only too often report after serving in a learning experiment, they have utilized many pre-experimental associations with the material to be learned to facilitate the learning of the laboratory task. For example, suppose the subject is required to associate the pair of nonsense syllables, MON and SEL. It is possible that the subject may encode MON as MONey and SEL as SELl. Furthermore, both MONey and SELl may independently elicit previous associations. Some of these past associations may be identical, such as BUY. The formation of an association between MON and SEL may be facilitated by the common preexperimental association BUY to each item. By employing some third item which is an association common to both of the items to be associated, the subject may learn faster. Such processes are examples of mediation or mediated generalization.

Undoubtedly mediation occurs in many learning experiments, often without the experimenter's awareness. In fact, because the experimenter may not be interested in these central processes, he may not bother to interrogate the subject after the experiment about the latter's technique for learning. Several reasons account for this lack of interest. The investigator may be interested in comparing the relative effects of different levels of a variable, or the effects of different factors, on performance rather than in evaluating the learning process itself. Verbal report is often unreliable, and interrogation may suggest interpretations to the subject which did not exist originally. Furthermore, the factors responsible for the occurrence of reported mediation cannot be determined in such situations. Granted that mediation is an important process, we must point out that there is usually no control over the process by the experimenter. Perhaps the subject will mediate on one occasion but not on another; some subjects will mediate and others will not under identical test conditions.

As a consequence of these and other limitations of *ad hoc* examinations of mediation, investigators have attempted to devise tasks and conditions that manipulate the extent to which mediation is possible. Variables hypothesized to have some effect on the operation of mediation can be tested experimentally.

The tasks employed involve the formation of mediational sequences in the laboratory and do not rely on the operation of preexperimental associations whose nature can only be assumed. In the example above, it was assumed that BUY might act implicitly as a mediator between MON and SEL because BUY might be a preexperimental association to both MONey and SELl. Rather than rely on such assumptions, we could experimentally ensure that BUY was associated with both MON and SEL. First, we could have the subject learn the associations MON–BUY and BUY–SEL. Finally, we could test for mediation by requiring the learning of MON–SEL. If the laboratory-formed associations between each trigram and BUY provide mediating properties to BUY, the acquisition of an association between MON and SEL will be facilitated.

Basic Paradigms

There are three basic laboratory situations in which the formation of associations between two items may be influenced by a third item serving as a mediator. In all situations, we will employ the terms A, B, and C to represent the three items, with B constituting the assumed mediator between A and C. Paradigms involving three elements may be grouped into three basic paradigms: *chaining, stimulus equivalence,* and *response equivalence.*

Chaining   Suppose the subject is required to form associations between A and B on a first paired-associate list. Then he is given a second list, B–C, in which the first-list responses, B, are re-used as stimulus terms for new responses, C. After both lists are learned, we can assume that two sets of associations exist, A–B and B–C. Note that B terms are in both lists, serving as responses in the first list and as stimuli in the second list. Theoretically, because B represents a mediating association between A and C, a chain is assumed to exist from A to B to C.

What would happen if the subject was now required to learn a third list, A–C? Although he has had prior acquaintaince with both A and C terms, separately, he has not encountered these items in conjunction with each other. From the standpoint of mediation, his learning of A–C should be facilitated because both A and C have been previously associated with a common term, B. When A is presented on the third list, it implicitly elicits the B term acquired on the first list, which, in turn, evokes the C term linked with the B term on the second list. This process, known as chaining, is assumed to facilitate the learning of the third list, A–C.

One could object that faster A–C learning might occur simply because the subject has greater familiarity with the A and C terms through their presence on the first two lists. The fact that B was involved directly with both A and C might not be essential for the facilitation. Warm-up and practice effects might also favor the learning of the third list.

To meet with these cogent criticisms, a control condition can be, and usually is, employed. One procedure has been to have all subjects learn A–B and B–C pairs on their first two lists, but to have some learn A–C and others learn A–D (where D represents words shown for the first time) pairs on their third list. The A–C test pairs permit the operation of B as a mediator, but the learning of A–D pairs cannot be facilitated by B as a mediator since D was never associated with B. With this procedure, it is necessary to check on the equality of the difficulty of the A–C mediation test pairs and the A–D control test pairs. For example, if the A–D pairs happen to be more difficult than the A–C pairs, the results cannot be attributed to the facilitation by mediation. A related procedure using a mixed-list design employs only one group by having half of the test-list pairs formed in an A–C arrangement and the other half in an A–D manner. A shortcoming of the above control procedures is that the C items will be more familiar to subjects than the D items encountered for the first time at the test stage.

A more common procedure employs the same list, A–C, as the test list for both experimental and control conditions, thus avoiding the possibility of test lists of unequal difficulty. Whereas the experimental condition receives A–B, B–C, as its first two lists, the control condition receives A–B, D–C. Thus, both conditions receive equal familiarity with

A and C terms prior to the test list as well as equal amounts of warm-up and practice. However, unlike the experimental condition, the control condition does not permit the formation of a common B association to A and C terms during the first two lists.

Stimulus Equivalence Stimulus equivalence paradigms involve the formation of associations to a common response term with different stimuli in two different paired-associate lists. For example, a first list, A–B, is followed by a second list, C–B, containing the response terms of the first list but re-paired with new stimuli. It is assumed that the A and C stimuli of the two lists acquire equivalence due to their independent association with the same term, B. If the subject is then confronted with a list composed of A–C pairs, it is assumed that B will be implicitly activated by both A and C, which will serve to facilitate the formation of the A–C associations required at the test stage.

An example of stimulus equivalence may be found in the everyday situation in which the learning of synonyms occurs. Imagine a young child trying to learn the meaning of the stimulus words *evil* and *wicked*. Assume that he already knows the meaning of the word *bad*. We may tell him that *evil* means *bad* and that *wicked* means *bad*. This is analogous to the formation of the A–B and C–B associations. According to mediation, it may also be assumed that the child can readily learn the association between *evil* and *wicked* via the mediator *bad*, which has been independently associated with each new word.

As in the chaining paradigm, we need a control condition which receives A terms as part of its first list and C terms as part of its second list, but not in conjunction with B terms on both lists. One possible control might be the arrangement A–B, C–D, A–C, which permits the subject to become acquainted with A and C terms before the test stage but does not allow formation of associations with a common term.

Response Equivalence The third class of mediation paradigms we shall consider here is response equivalence paradigms. In this situation, the subject learns two different sets of responses on his first two lists although the stimulus terms are identical on the two lists. Then he is given a test for mediation that involves the learning of a list of pairs consisting of responses from the two lists. This paradigm may be diagramed as B–A, B–C, A–C. It is assumed that the response terms, A and C, from the first two lists will be easily associated in the test stage, due to the fact that a common term, B, was associated to each of the response terms separately.

Response equivalence situations exist in the learning of several foreign languages. If we learn that *house* is *maison* in French and *haus* in German, we have a situation where two different responses are associated with the same stimulus. According to mediation, if we are required to form an association between *maison* and *haus*, learning will be facilitated by the implicit occurrence of the mediator, *house*, which was associated independently with each term.

As in the other types of paradigms, a control condition is necessary for response equivalence paradigms. One possible arrangement might be the sequence B–A, D–C, A–C. Equal familiarity with the test-stage elements, A and C, is possible for the experimental and control conditions, but for the control condition no mediating link for A and C is formed during the first two lists.

Although we have described only one example from each of the three types of mediation paradigms involving three elements, it is actually possible to devise eight such three-stage paradigms (see Table 8.1), as

TABLE 8.1
EIGHT THREE-STAGE MEDIATION PARADIGMS

	Forward Chaining		Reverse Chaining		Stimulus Equivalence		Response Equivalence	
	I	II	III	IV	V	VI	VII	VIII
List 1	A–B	B–C	B–A	C–B	A–B	C–B	B–A	B–C
List 2	B–C	A–B	C–B	B–A	C–B	A–B	B–C	B–A
Test List	A–C	A–C	A–C	A–C	A–C	A–C	A–C	A–C

Source: After D. L. Horton and P. M. Kjeldergaard. An experimental analysis of associative factors in mediated generalization. *Psychological Monographs,* 1961, **75** (11, Whole No. 515). Modified by adding and changing labels. Reprinted by permission of the American Psychological Association and the authors.

did Horton and Kjeldergaard (1961), four of which involve chaining (I–IV), two stimulus equivalence (V–VI), and two response equivalence (VII–VIII). The differences between the several paradigms within each basic type are based on the directional order of the stimulus and response terms within some of the lists, or on the temporal order of the first two lists. Although such differences may affect the extent to which mediation effects are obtained theoretically (Horton and Kjeldergaard), the paradigms within each basic type will be treated as equivalent for our purposes.

Experimental Findings

One early successful demonstration of mediation by chaining of associations formed in the laboratory was made by Bugelski and Scharlock (1952).

Each subject received three paired-associate lists of nonsense syllables, one in each of three sessions spaced 48 hours apart. A chaining paradigm was involved such that the response terms of the first list (A–B) served as stimulus terms for the second list (B–C). In the third and test list, half of the first–list stimuli were paired with second–list responses to form test pairs for mediation (A–C). The other half of the third list served as a control condition consisting of pairs constructed from first–list stimuli and new responses to form A–D pairs.

Performance was better for the mediated test pairs, which were learned not only better but faster. Although postexperimental interrogations can be ambiguous, Bugelski and Scharlock found no indication of awareness on the part of subjects that mediators were being used for the mediation pairs.

One large scale investigation (Horton and Kjeldergaard, 1961) compared mediation in several paradigms from each basic class—chaining, stimulus equivalence, and response equivalence as shown in Table 8.1.

The investigators hypothesized that mediated facilitation of learning would occur in all eight paradigms. This prediction was based simply on the analysis presented above, showing that the test or third list, A–C, for all paradigms involves two terms, each of which had been independently associated with a common term, B, during one of the two earlier lists. In addition, by analyzing the relationship between the first and second lists, these investigators arrived at some differential predictions among the eight mediation paradigms. We cannot attempt to go into their assumptions and predictions concerning the differences among paradigms, especially since their results did not yield clear-cut support.

Eight groups were tested, one for each three-stage mediation paradigm. Rather than employ eight additional control groups, Horton and Kjeldergaard had each subject serve as his own control, since half of the pairs on the test list involved mediation effects. Because the same individuals were learning experimental and control pairs, there is no question about the equality of learning ability under the two conditions. Three paired-associate lists containing eight pairs of very infrequent words in the Thorndike–Lorge (1944) word count were used. The list for the third or test list was identical for all paradigms in order that any differences in performance could be attributed to the different arrangements of the first two lists rather than to any differential difficulty of the third list. The first two lists were so devised as to form the appropriate mediation paradigm when considered in combination with the common test list, A–C. Significantly more correct responses occurred for the mediation test pairs than for the control test pairs in seven of the eight paradigms. As mentioned earlier, the differences among the eight paradigms themselves were not reliable. Thus, mediation was obtained but in equal amounts in seven of the paradigms.

With the exception of Paradigm III, which failed to show mediation, approximately 25 percent of the subjects in each paradigm failed to show mediation (more correct responses on the mediation than on the control test pairs). The evidence obtained indicated that these nonmediator subjects were unaware of the relationship among the lists. Independent measures also suggested that nonmediators were slower learners than subjects who mediated.

An evaluation of mediation under the same eight paradigms was also made by Peterson, Colavita, Sheahan, and Blattner (1964) under markedly different procedures. Consider the chaining paradigm as an example. The usual procedure has been to present all of the pairs of each list before requiring the subject to learn the next list in the sequence, A–B, B–C, A–C. On the other hand, Peterson *et al.* presented three pairs in succession, such as A_1–B_1, B_1–C_1, A_1–C_1, which formed a mediation paradigm. Then a second set of three pairs with this mediational arrangement would be shown, and so on, until the equivalent of three lists had been presented. The investigators assumed that this procedure might enhance mediation effects by presenting three related pairs of a mediation paradigm in greater contiguity than possible when all pairs of a list are learned before the next list is presented.

A second innovation in procedure aimed at facilitating mediation was the use of a recognition test instead of a test that required the subject to recall the correct response. For example, in the test for chaining the subject would be presented the stimulus A_1 and the three alternatives, C_1, D_1, E_1, in random order. The two incorrect alternatives on each test were items which were correct for earlier items; thus, all alternatives were familiar to subjects. This method provides a more sensitive measure, since the subject who cannot *recall* the correct response may be able to *recognize* it. One shortcoming of this procedure is the fact that the correct alternative is more recently encountered than the two wrong alternatives. Thus, correct responses at the test stage may not necessarily stem from mediational processes but merely reflect the fact that the most recently seen alternative is the correct one. The test procedures used by Peterson *et al.* are diagramed in Table 8.2.

In Experiment I, Peterson *et al.* employed consonant trigram pairs in a mixed-list design to assess mediational effects in the eight three-stage paradigms. Significant mediation effects were limited to the two response equivalence and one of the stimulus equivalence paradigms.

In Experiment II, Peterson *et al.* used more meaningful CVC trigrams. Greater mediation effects were obtained in the paradigms which led to mediation in Experiment I (which used consonant trigrams), as well as in two of the chaining paradigms. In the Horton and Kjeldergaard (1961) study in which mediation was obtained in seven paradigms, low frequency words were employed. The over-all pattern of results in these

TABLE 8.2
THE EIGHT PARADIGMS

Stage		Paradigms			
		CHAINING MODELS			
		I	II	III	IV
Acquisition	1	A–B	B–C	B–A	C–B
	Cue	A	B	B	C
	2	B–C	A–B	C–B	B–A
	Cue	B	A	C	B
Test		A–CDE	A–CDE	A–CDE	A–CDE

Stage		STIMULUS-EQUIVALENCE MODELS		RESPONSE-EQUIVALENCE MODELS	
		V	VI	VII	VIII
Acquisition	1	A–B	C–B	B–A	B–C
	Cue	A	C	B	B
	2	C–B	A–B	B–C	B–A
	Cue	C	A	B	B
Test		A–DCE	A–CDE	A–CDE	A–CDE

Source: From M. J. Peterson, F. B. Colavita, D. B. Sheahan, III, and K. C. Blattner. Verbal mediating chains and response availability as a function of the acquisition paradigm. *Journal of Verbal Learning and Verbal Behavior,* 1964, 3, 11–18. By permission of Academic Press, Inc., and the authors.

studies suggests that the amount of mediation increases as one proceeds from consonant trigrams to CVCs to words.

Similar evidence regarding the beneficial effects of meaningfulness on mediation was reported by Horton (1964), who compared a chaining and a response equivalence paradigm. Horton hypothesized that the more meaningful the mediator, the better the mediation, since stronger associations would be formed in the learning of both the first and second lists. Higher meaningfulness mediators might also be more available during the test stage.

The items comprising the test list pairs were Glaze (1928) nonsense syllables of moderately high association value, and the common terms assumed to mediate between these nonsense syllables were dissyllables selected from the extremes of Noble's (1952a) scale. A high meaningfulness dissyllable might be DINNER whereas DAVIT is an example of a low meaningfulness item.

In Experiment I, there was better performance on the test list in both paradigms for high meaningfulness mediators. The absolute extent to which mediation occurred is not clear, since a control condition for nonspecific effects was omitted; but to the extent that mediation took place, it was better with high meaningfulness mediators.

Half of the pairs of the test list in Experiment II were mediation pairs, and the other half were control pairs. Because control pairs were employed in this study, it is possible to determine whether net positive mediation occurred. More mediation pairs were learned than control pairs, demonstrating mediation, and this superiority was larger for conditions with high meaningfulness mediators.

The finding of better mediation with high meaningfulness mediators is consistent with the associative probability hypothesis of Underwood and Schulz (1960). According to this view, more meaningful units possess more associations. Consequently, in Horton's study stronger associations may have been formed with the mediator when it was of high meaningfulness.

Rather than assume that more associations exist for high meaningfulness mediators, it is possible, as Houston (1964a) has done, to actually manipulate the number of mediating associations between the members of the pairs of the test stage. Houston employed stimulus equivalence paradigms in which the subject associated the same response to different stimuli. One group received only one mediator, B, learning the sequence A–B, C–B. A second condition learned two mediators by learning two pairs of lists, A–B, C–B, followed by A–D, C–D. In the latter condition, both B and D may serve as mediators between A and C on the test list. Appropriate control conditions were included for warm-up and learning-to-learn. Higher performance occurred in both mediation conditions, and to a greater extent when there were two mediators rather than one.

Some comparisons were made by Horton (1964) of his two studies described above, one of which used an unmixed-list design while the other employed a mixed-list design. An unmixed list is homogeneous in the arrangements between pairs across the lists. In such a design, all the test-list pairs either involve mediational relationships with earlier lists, or they do not (and serve as control pairs). This procedure requires separate groups for experimental and control conditions. On the other hand, the mixed-list design allows the same group to learn both experimental and control pairs. Half of the items on the test list bear mediational relationships with earlier lists, whereas the other half of the items do not.

Although the unmixed-list design is less economical in the number of subjects needed and may thus be subject to greater sampling error in the equality of groups formed by random sampling, it does possess the advantage that mediational responding is appropriate for every pair in the test list. On the other hand, with a mixed-list design, subjects are reinforced for mediation on only half of the test list. Such conditions may impair the tendency for mediation to occur, since there is no consistent rule for responding within the whole list.

A comparison between Experiments I and II of Horton's study is *ad hoc* since the type of design was not an independent variable. However, some suggestions about the effect of type of design on the magnitude of mediation may be obtained. Horton found better performance on mediation pairs (the entire list) in the unmixed design than in the mixed-list design (he doubled the score obtained here, since mediation was possible with only half of the mixed list). It appears that greater mediation will occur in an unmixed list because subjects are reinforced for mediation on all pairs in the list.

After the experimental session, each subject was interviewed in an attempt to determine his level of awareness. Although such procedures are not always sound, an examination of the results should be made. Higher awareness was obtained with high meaningfulness mediators, unmixed lists, and higher learning ability as defined by a test of verbal aptitude. Greater awareness was correlated with amount of mediation.

It is tempting to conclude that greater awareness caused the increased mediation, but, as Horton realized, it is possible to argue from the other direction that better mediation caused the greater awareness. Horton's findings appear to question earlier observations that mediation seems to occur without awareness, as judged by postexperimental inquiry. Furthermore, in agreement with Horton, results in the area of verbal conditioning have accumulated which demonstrate that awareness is positively correlated with degree of verbal conditioning (Spielberger, 1965).

One possible resolution offered by Horton is that the correlation between awareness and mediation depends on the test conditions. If, in the experimental setting, cues exist which favor awareness, such as high meaningfulness mediators, then awareness will be directly correlated with mediation performance. On the other hand, if few cues are available to enhance awareness, performance will be uniformly lower for both aware and unaware subjects.

Preexperimental Associations An alternative method of studying mediation is to infer the nature of the existing preexperimental associations rather than to create such associations in the laboratory. This approach, used by Russell and Storms (1955), anticipated a later observation by Jenkins (1963) that substantial mediation cannot be demonstrated in many investigations because it is difficult to provide enough reinforced practice in laboratory settings to create associations which are sufficiently strong for mediational effects. The use of preexperimental associations which are substantially stronger than any laboratory associations avoids this difficulty and may enhance the occurrence of mediation.

Russell and Storms treated ten Kent–Rosanoff stimulus words as the first links of ten different associative chains. They considered as the second links the primary responses to these stimuli in the Minnesota norms (Russell and Jenkins, 1954). Then, they used the second links as stimuli on a word-association test to determine the third links of each chain. As an example, one chain consisted of a Kent–Rosanoff stimulus word, *stem,* its primary associate, *flower,* and the primary response to *flower, smell.*

In their experiment, they employed different subjects who learned two lists in which the same set of nonsense syllable stimuli were paired with the first and third links of each associative chain. For example, *cef* was paired with the first link, *stem,* on the first list, and *cef* was re-paired with the third link of that chain, *smell,* on the second list.

It should be noted that this A–B, A–D arrangement of same stimulus, different response, on two lists has been found to produce negative transfer when the responses paired with same stimulus are unrelated. However, in this situation, the two responses paired with a given stimulus are associatively related. Russell and Storms assumed that the learning of the second list would be facilitated by mediation, since the responses on the two lists paired with the same stimulus were from the same associative chain. Because *cef* was paired with *stem* on the first list, the learning of the corresponding pair on the second list, *cef–smell,* might be facilitated. On the second list, the investigators assumed that *cef* would implicitly elicit its first-list response, *stem,* which in turn would trigger the rest of the chain, *flower–smell.* Thus, the learning of *cef–smell* on the second list would be facilitated by mediation, *cef·· ·* (*stem–flower*) · · *·smell.*

As a control for warm-up between the two lists, half of the second-list pairs involved response terms which were not related associatively to the first–list response terms. In the case of the first–list pair *cef–stem,* the control pairing on the second list was *cef–joy,* since *stem* and *joy* are not in the same associative chain.

The results obtained by Russell and Storms indicated better learning of the half of the list in which there were preexperimental associations between the response terms of the two lists. In addition, they found no evidence to indicate any awareness on the part of the subjects that mediation had occurred.

Pseudomediation The findings of the preceding studies support the predictions made from mediation theory. However, alternative explanations for these results have been offered

(Earhard and Mandler, 1965; Mandler and Earhard, 1964). Their major attack involves interpretations of the results obtained under chaining paradigms, although these critics also question the role of mediation in the other paradigms. In all paradigms, better performance on the test list for experimental pairs over the control pairs has been attributed to the facilitory effects of mediated associations. Earhard and Mandler offered an alternative explanation for these findings, based on the assumption that there is less interlist interference in the mediation condition. The superior performance of the latter condition, therefore, is an artifact referred to by Earhard and Mandler as *pseudomediation.*

According to these investigators, the first (A–B) and third (A–C) lists in the chaining paradigm constitute a transfer paradigm in which the same stimuli are paired with different responses on the two lists. We should recall that this situation is considered a negative transfer paradigm. Learning of the A–C associations on the third list is interfered with by incompatible A–B associations from the first list. However, if A–B associations were unlearned or extinguished by the time learning of the third list (A–C) began, performance would be better on the test list.

The core of the Earhard–Mandler position is that such extinction of A–B associations does occur during the learning of the second list, B–C, of the experimental condition, but not during the learning of the second list, D–C, of the control condition. For the "mediation" condition, they assumed that backward associations, B–A, are formed during the first list, which are weakened during the learning of the second list, B–C, since this relationship is basically a "same stimulus, different response" negative transfer paradigm. Notice that no such arrangement exists between first–list backward associations B–A and second–list D–C associations for the control condition. Thus, more extinction of the first list occurs during second–list learning for the experimental condition. The significance of this difference lies in the relationship between the first and third, or test, list. Both the experimental and control conditions contain the "same stimulus, different response" arrangement between their first and third tests, but due to the processes just described A–B is weaker for the experimental condition by the time the third list is presented. Consequently, better performance is expected from the mediation condition on the test list. However, Earhard and Mandler maintain this is not what is meant by mediation, and that is why they term it pseudomediation. Pseudomediation is actually due to the lower interlist interference for the mediation condition.

In one test of their hypothesis, Mandler and Earhard (1964) compared performance in a condition involving the learning of A–B, B–C, A–E with that of a control condition, A–B, D–C, A–E. Although a mediational view would predict that the learning of the first two lists in the experimental condition would lead to the development of a mediator, B, it could not predict faster learning of the third list, A–E. The learning of the first two lists would theoretically aid the learning on the test list, via B as a mediator if it involved A–C associations. However, since the test list is A–E, no mediated facilitation is predicted although one can assume that a mediating tendency is formed between A and C. Actually, a mediational view might even predict poorer performance, since the A–C tendencies formed during the first two lists through mediation might interfere with the A–E test list. Such interference is assumed due to the fact that an A–C, A–E arrangement corresponds to the now familiar negative transfer paradigm.

On the other hand, the interlist interference view would hold that the backward associations formed in the first list, B–A, would be extinguished during the learning of the second list, B–C, since an unlearning paradigm, B–A, B–C, would exist. When the test list, A–E, is presented, there would be less interference with it from the first list, A–B. In short, the mediation view would predict performance worse than, or no better than, that of the control condition. However, the interlist interference, or pseudomediation, position would predict better learning for the condition receiving A–B, B–C, A–E.

The results supported Mandler and Earhard's prediction. They concluded that pseudomediation was involved since "true" mediation could not predict the better performance obtained. Furthermore, they generalized their findings to other mediation paradigms where it is theoretically possible for mediation to facilitate test-stage learning. Even in these situations, they concluded, pseudomediation is operative.

One criticism of Mandler and Earhard's study made by Jenkins (1965) was that no "true" mediation condition was included in the experimental design. The same point was emphasized in an investigation by Schulz, Weaver, and Ginsberg (1965), who replicated the Mandler–Earhard study and added a "true" mediation, and corresponding control condition. They did not question the possibility that interlist interference of the sort postulated by Mandler and Earhard might occur and aid performance in the chaining paradigm. However, they did question whether all of the mediation effect found in previous studies could be attributed to interlist interference; they maintained that some "true" as well as "pseudo" mediation could be operative, but that Mandler and Earhard's failure to include necessary conditions did not allow this conclusion to be reached. Accordingly, they tested the following conditions: pseudomediation (A–B, B–C, A–E), pseudomediation control (A–B, D–C, A–E), mediation (A–B, B–E, A–E), and mediation control (A–B, D–E, A–E).

We should not be confused by the difference between the notation used for the mediation condition and its control in the Schulz *et al.* study and that used by other investigators such as Horton and Kjeldergaard (1961), as presented earlier. In the Schulz *et al.* study, the test list was designated as A–E rather than A–C (as usually done) so that the test list could be identical across the four conditions of the study. We should recall from the chapter on transfer that use of identical test lists avoids the possibility that differences in performance attributed to transfer actually stem from test lists of unequal difficulty. Although A–E is designated as the test list in the Schulz *et al.* study, corresponding changes were made among the other lists to ensure that tests for mediation and pseudomediation could be made. The notation may differ from study to study, if necessary, as long as it is internally consistent.

The results obtained by Schulz *et al.* showed significantly higher scores for the mediation condition over its control, but not between the pseudomediation condition and its control. They concluded that if pseudomediation occurred it was small relative to "true" mediation under their test situation. They acknowledged that their procedures favored mediational effects but that other test situations might favor pseudomediation effects.

Thus, the experimental status of pseudomediation is undecided. There is also theoretical controversy over the nature of mediation. On one hand, associationists view mediation as a form of higher-order classical conditioning. They considered that certain stimuli are conditioned to certain responses. And they assume that implicit chains or mediational bonds formed by conditioning exist among items which share common associations. Mandler (1963) and Earhard and Mandler (1965) criticized this formulation. They view mediation paradigms of the variety used by Horton and Kjeldergaard as concept formation, or quasi-logical tasks, in which the subject's performance depends on whether or not he discovers the rule or pattern governing the structure within the material to be learned.

Thus, in the chaining paradigm, the successful learner discovers eventually that As go with Bs, and that Bs go with Cs. Furthermore, the particular A term and C term that were linked with a given B term go together on the test list. Thus, mediation is a cognitive operation of perceiving relationships or structures. It is a conscious process, not an automatic running-off of conditioned bonds.

Which view is the correct one? Is mediation in the paradigms discussed above accountable for by associationistic or cognitive formulations? Can an experimental test be made? One approach to the theoretical debate is to insist on differential predictions. If the different conceptions of mediation do not lead to different predictions, perhaps both associationistic and cognitive formulations are equally acceptable.

Concept Learning

The preceding discussion of mediation has centered around situations in which only one stimulus was associated with a given response within a given list. For example, in the A–B, C–B, A–C paradigm, two different stimuli were paired with a given response, B, over the first two lists. Then a third list tested the extent to which the common response term facilitated the learning of the two stimuli from the first two lists, A and C, as a pair.

Mediational processes may also be examined in situations which differ from the above in that two or more stimuli are associated with a given response within the *same* list. In one type of situation, stimuli assigned to a particular response are selected which have some similar properties. For example, names of different trees might serve as the stimuli for one response, whereas names of different birds would be paired with another response, and so on. There would be high conceptual similarity within groups of stimuli assigned to one response, and low similarity between the groups of stimuli assigned to different responses. Because the specific instances of each group belong to a common category they share many associations. All birds elicit such responses as *fly, sky, nest, wing*. Of course, all birds are not alike; thus, *hawk* might arouse different responses from those elicited by *sparrow* or *robin*. Still, all birds might be considered to elicit the common mediator of BIRD as a response. This common mediator should facilitate the learning and retention of the response term which is assigned to each instance of the category of BIRDS in the concept learning task.

Concepts represent learning that involves both associationistic and cognitive aspects. A young child learns a number of pairings—that a *hawk* is a bird, a *sparrow* is a bird, and a *robin* is a bird, and soon he also notices similarities and differences among the exemplars of the category. Eventually he determines the relevant criteria for classifying birds and can ignore irrelevant criteria, such as size, color, or shape. Later the child is able to classify as a bird or nonbird an animal which he has never encountered previously by comparing its characteristics with those common to all examples of birds known to him.

Thus, the learning of specific instances involves rote learning. From this associationistic learning develops the capacity for such cognitive behavior as concept learning. The question is not one of whether the learning of concepts is associationistic or cognitive, but one of what are the relative roles of both types of learning in acquiring concepts.

Concepts are classes of objects, attributes, or relationships among objects. They differ in degree of concreteness or abstractness. Although we may argue that objects *possess* attributes and that relationships *exist* among objects, it is important to note that concepts are inventions devised by the user. When users notice certain groupings of objects or attributes, they have "discovered" a particular concept. This emphasis on the functional significance of concepts can be illustrated by a consideration of a relatively new abstract concept, *serendipity,* which has become popular in recent years. It refers to the happy accident which occurs when a person unintentionally discovers something of great importance. Usually, he is engaged in some search for solutions to other problems when he arrives at the more significant discovery. Such serendipitous events have occasionally happened in history, but until someone noticed this class of situations there was really no need for such a concept. The availability of such a term makes communication easier; otherwise, a lengthier description of situations to which the term applies would be necessary.

Experimental Studies The experimental investigation of concepts generally employs concrete concepts. One common procedure employs stimuli consisting of geometrical forms, such as circles, triangles, squares, and the like. These vary in such attributes or dimensions as size, number, and color. All instances representing a given concept—large circles, for example—would be considered positive instances, and all remaining instances would be considered negative instances. The subject's task is to discover the correct concept which is defined by the pattern of positive and negative instances. Another situation requires the subject to learn several concepts in the same task. Each set of stimuli is paired with a different common response. The subject's task would be to learn the correct response for each stimulus. The set of stimuli paired with a common response would be analogous to a set of instances of a concept. Suppose a list involves names of four birds, four trees, and four fish as stimuli. All bird stimuli are paired with the response PQ, all tree stimuli with AG, and all fish stimuli with RW. If the subject learns each pairing by mediational processes, he would know that *eagle* is paired with PQ, even if he had not seen that particular pair, if he remembered that PQ was paired with *sparrow, hawk,* and *dove* but never with any fish or tree stimuli. It is assumed that learning of conceptual pairings such as these would be easier than the learning of rote pairings where there would be no systematic rule governing the pairings or where each stimuli was paired with a unique response.

The present discussion can consider only a few selected examples of such concepts as those described above. Our primary purpose is not to analyze concept learning, per se, but to examine its relationship to the question of whether learning is associationistic or cognitive.

First, we should make a distinction between concept learning and concept identification. The learning or formation of such concepts as circles, squares, and triangles has already occurred for most subjects who participate in concept experiments. The problem confronting the subject is not the learning but the *identification* of the concept defined by the pattern of positive and negative instances encountered in this type of situation. Terms used interchangeably with identification have been *attainment* and *utilization*. In all these cases, we assume that the concepts involved have already been formed.

Rote versus Concept Learning Several experiments have attempted to demonstrate the relationship between rote learning and concept learning with paired associates. Metzger (1958) compared rote, systematic concept, and random concept learning. Geometrical forms served as stimuli and single digits were responses. The rote condition received pairs in which each stimulus was paired with a different response. The systematic concept condition had two similar stimuli paired with each response. The random concept condition also had two stimuli paired with each response but they were dissimilar or unsystematic. Systematic and random concept conditions were also studied with four stimuli for each response.

Metzger was unable to find any differences between the rote and the systematic concept conditions, and the latter condition was no better than the random concept condition when there were only two stimuli per response. Increasing the number of stimuli to four per response led to higher performance for the systematic concept condition.

Several factors may have prevented concept conditions from doing better than the rote condition. A rapid 2-second rate of presentation may have restricted mediational processes. Similarly the presence of only two stimuli per response may have been too few to permit the subject to identify them as a conceptual grouping. The pairing of several stimuli to a given response does not constitute a concept situation unless there is some perceivable similarity among those stimuli. Thus, the systematic concept condition may have been a random concept condition as far as the subjects were concerned.

Some evidence to support this conclusion comes from Fallon and Battig (1964), who replicated and extended the Metzger study. They compared rote learning, Metzger's systematic concept learning, and a third condition which we might term *functional* concept learning. They used either single- or double-digit responses, and assumed that double digits would make the task more difficult and widen the predicted superiority of the concept condition. For each response, the functional concept condition received two stimuli which had been judged similar by subjects in the rote and systematic concept conditions. Thus, the assignment of stimuli to responses was not done arbitrarily, as in the systematic concept condition, but it was based on ratings of similarity by other subjects.

Fallon and Battig found that both concept conditions were better than the rote condition when double-digit responses were used. Furthermore, the functional concept condition was better than the systematic concept condition, thus supporting the view that Metzger's subjects may have been unable to detect any similarity among the group of stimuli paired with each response in his systematic concept condition.

It is important for the stimuli which are attached to the same response to be functionally similar. Such stimuli are interchangeable or equivalent, since the subject can ignore differences among them and utilize their common features. If dissimilar stimuli from unrelated categories are paired with the same response, interference may develop. Returning to our earlier example of BIRDS and TREES, suppose that two stimuli are paired with each response but that one stimulus is a bird name and one is a tree name. Then each response will be associated with one bird and one tree name so that the category names, per se, would not be distinctive cues for any response. Interference would exist because different members of each category are paired equally often with different responses. In a functional concept situation, all bird names would be paired with one response whereas all tree names would be attached to a second response. The category to which a stimulus belonged would then be able to act as a distinctive cue for its response.

Another comparison of rote and concept learning was made by Smith, Jones, and Thomas (1963), who employed color patches as stimuli and nonsense syllables as responses. The circular color caps or patches came from a series which differed only with respect to hue. A high similarity set was composed of consecutive caps in the series, whereas a low similarity set was composed of every fifth cap in the series. One, two, or four different caps were paired with each response; the responses were medium-difficulty CVC nonsense syllables.

Smith et al. maintained that concept learning is involved if the several items paired with a given response are adjacent caps on the scale. On the other hand, rote learning is involved if the caps paired with a given response are nonadjacent on the hue scale. In the case where only one stimulus is paired with each response, there is no distinction between rote and concept learning. However, when more than one stimulus is paired with a given response, the type of learning involved is considered rote if the stimuli are nonadjacent, and conceptual if they are adjacent, on the hue scale.

The investigators gave 100 trials, at the subject's own pace. Concept learning was significantly superior to rote learning, as shown in Figure 8.1.

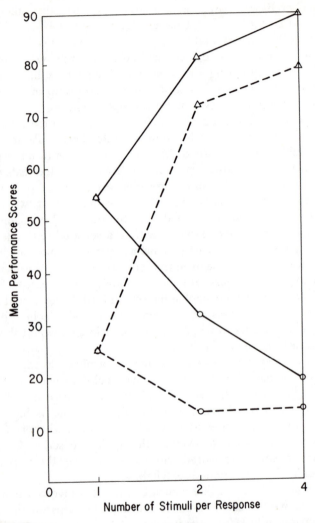

Figure 8.1. Mean performance scores (number of correct responses minus a correction for guessing) for rote learning (circles) versus concept learning (triangles), contrasting similar-stimulus conditions (dashed lines) with dissimilar-stimulus conditions (solid lines) for varying numbers of stimuli per response (Experiment 1). [From T. A. Smith, L. V. Jones, and S. Thomas: Effects upon verbal learning of stimulus similarity, number of stimuli per response, and concept formation. *Journal of Verbal Learning and Verbal Behavior,* 1963, **1**, 470–476. Reprinted by permission of Academic Press Inc., and the authors.]

This advantage increased as more stimuli were attached to each response. We can note that increasing the number of stimuli per response actually impeded rote learning whereas it facilitated concept learning. Finally, findings indicated that low similarity led to better learning under both rote and concept conditions.

Smith *et al.* suggested that a rote learning component is involved in all concept learning situations. However, as more stimuli from the same category or region on the hue scale are paired with the same response, it is unnecessary for each pair to be learned by rote. The same response would be appropriate for any stimulus within the category, even if it had not been previously encountered in the experiment. On the other hand, rote learning requires that each pairing be learned independently of the others, since the several stimuli which are paired with a particular response come from nonadjacent regions or categories.

Verbal Concepts The preceding studies have employed geometrical and nonverbal stimuli. An alternative approach by Underwood and Richardson (1956a) uses words as stimuli. Obviously, words differ in considerably more numerous and more subtle dimensions than do such geometrical stimuli as those used in many concept studies.

Words which elicit common associates may be considered members of the same associative category; that is, a verbal concept is defined by the particular associate which a number of words share in common. For example, *barrel, doughnut, knob,* and *balloon* refer to objects which vary in many dimensions. This conclusion might be supported by the variety of word associates these words would elicit on a word-association test. Nonetheless, such words would also elicit a common response, ROUND. We may think of ROUND as a verbal concept and regard *barrel, doughnut, knob,* and *balloon* as specific instances of the concept.

In their approach, Underwood and Richardson conducted a word-association test with 213 words. Responses were restricted to words referring to sensory impressions aroused by each word. The various attributes occurring as associates were considered as verbal concepts, while the stimulus words themselves were treated as instances of such concepts. Thus, *barrel* elicits ROUND while *pillow* elicits SOFT. ROUND and SOFT would be concepts, with *barrel* being an instance of the first concept and *pillow* being an instance of the second concept.

It should be apparent that some instances are more frequently given as examples of a specific category. Both *barrel* and *grapefruit* are instances of the concept ROUND, but the former is a more frequent instance than the latter. Underwood and Richardson used the term

TABLE 8.3
CONCEPT-LEARNING LISTS WITH CONCEPT
AND AVERAGE DOMINANCE LEVEL INDICATED

List 1		List 2		List 3	
NOUN	CONCEPT AND DOMINANCE LEVEL	NOUN	CONCEPT AND DOMINANCE LEVEL	NOUN	CONCEPT AND DOMINANCE LEVEL
Barrel Doughnut Knob Balloon	"round" high (66%)	Bracelet Derby Platter Pill	"round" medium (31%)	Snail Cherry Grapefruit Skull	"round" low (13%)
Village Minnow Crumb Germ	"small" high (75%)	Bungalow Capsule Mouse Pollen	"small" medium (45%)	Earthworm Closet Freckle Tack	"small" low (16%)
Bone Collar Frost Lint	"white" medium (37.5%)	Baseball Fang Paste Sugar	"white" low (12%)	Milk Chalk Snow Teeth	"white" high (76.5%)
Garlic Gasoline Pine Sulphur	"smelly" medium (51%)	Daffodil Goat Gym Sauerkraut	"smelly" low (19%)	Ether Garbage Gardenia Manure	"smelly" high (74.5%)
Custard Lips Moss Sheep	"soft" low (21.5%)	Bed Chamois Fur Pillow	"soft" high (76.5%)	Bread Flannel Jellyfish Moccasin	"soft" medium (42%)
Camel Forest Hospital Limousine	"big" low (15%)	Auditorium City Elephant Mansion	"big" high (80.5%)	Boulder Gorilla Ocean Zoo	"big" medium (38%)

Source: From B. J. Underwood and J. Richardson. Verbal concept learning as a function of instructions and dominance level. *Journal of Experimental Psychology,* 1956, **51**, 229–238. Reprinted by permission of the American Psychological Association and the authors.

dominance level in referring to the strength between a response and its concept.

Underwood and Richardson (1956*b*) devised a concept identification task in the form of a word-association test. They selected four instances from each of six concepts. There were two concepts in the list at each of the three dominance levels, low, medium, and high (see Table 8.3).

Association trials were continued until the subject could give the concept name as his response to each of the four instances of each concept. The ease of concept identification was directly related to the level of dominance for the instances of each concept. Thus, if the words of a given category have a strong association with the concept name, it is easier to identify that concept or attribute.

The purpose of the Underwood and Richardson study was to show that words which share a common associate constitute a concept. The investigators also demonstrated that some groups of words are more strongly related to certain concepts than other groups of words. However, the task they employed did not require the subject to learn new associations or form new concepts. What their study did was to show that subjects could identify the common associates or concepts shared by different groups of words. Thus, this study provides us with an associative explanation of verbal concepts although it does not examine the learning of new concepts.

Reception versus Selection Situations

Most studies of concept learning have employed what might be called a *reception* situation, since the occurrence of positive and negative instances is beyond the control of the subject. The instances presented are determined by the experimenter. The subject's task is to identify the concept embodied by the pattern of positive and negative instances, or to identify the set of stimuli associated with different common responses.

An analogy may be drawn between the situation confronting the subject in reception situations and that faced by an observer of natural phenomena, such as an astronomer. Astronomers, like other scientists, attempt to formulate concepts and determine laws regarding their discipline. Unlike such experimental sciences as physics or chemistry, in astronomy one cannot control the occurrence of events for laboratory observation but must await the natural occurrence of events. Thus, a reception situation is involved for the astronomer, who attempts to formulate laws and principles from observing events which are beyond his own control. On the other hand, the physicist or chemist can experimentally study events in the laboratory. Depending on his own hypotheses, he selects the particular observations he wants to observe which might test his views.

In psychology, it might be hypothesized that forgetting is due to interference from similar tasks acquired during the retention interval. The investigator then performs an experiment in which he selects the conditions for his observations so that his question can be answered. He might, during the retention interval, provide different groups with learning material which varied in degree of similarity to the original task. He could then analyze the amount of retention loss as a function of this variable to test his hypothesis.

Also, it is possible to study concept learning under conditions in which the subject is allowed to select his own instances on the basis of his own hypotheses. The experimenter provides appropriate feedback so that the subject can confirm, reject, or modify his original hypothesis. The subject selects the instances to be evaluated in view of whatever hypothesis he is attempting to validate. The subject is analogous to the scientist who performs controlled observations and is not dependent on natural occurrences of phenomena.

A study by Hunt (1965) compared concept learning under reception and selection situations. In one experiment, the subject had to form four-letter nonsense words by choosing one of four alternative letters for each spatial position in the word. Legitimate words or positive instances were defined by Hunt as those starting with the letter T *and* ending with the letter H. All other words were illegitimate words or negative instances. Each subject in the selection condition created and classified ten nonsense words, and was provided with feedback. On the other hand, each subject in the reception condition was presented with the items created by one of the selection subjects. Thus, the over-all difficulty of the items was equal for the two conditions.

In the test phase, each subject was presented with fifteen positive and fifteen negative instances in random order and required to sort them into legitimate and illegitimate categories. Performance was significantly better in the selection condition.

Hunt suggested that reception subjects performed poorly because it is unlikely that they would start out with the same hypotheses as those employed by the selection subjects whose items they were attempting to classify. Selection subjects adopt one hypothesis and then form nonsense words to test the validity of their hypotheses; if they are wrong, they may alter their hypotheses and form other items. The reception subject who receives the items made up by a selection subject is more likely than not to start out with a different hypothesis. Consequently, the instances which he receives are less likely to aid him in testing his hypothesis, since they were formed to test the hypothesis of the selection subject. As a result, lower performance occurs under reception conditions.

Mandler and Pearlstone (1966) performed a similar study. They used four types of materials: high frequency words, low frequency words, patterns containing 2 Xs randomly placed on a 10 x 10 matrix, and patterns containing 8 Xs randomly placed on a 10 x 10 matrix. Each set contained 52 stimuli.

The free condition corresponds to Hunt's selection condition, whereas the constrained condition resembles his reception condition. Free subjects were given one of the sets of materials and instructed to sort them into from two to seven categories on any basis. They continued to do this task until they could sort the 52 items consistently on two successive trials. Unlike Hunt's task, where subjects had to discover a rule, in this study the subjects had to form their own categorization.

The categorization formed by a free subject was used as the basis for the task for a constrained subject, who was required to sort the 52 items until he attained one perfect trial as judge by the categorization used by the free subject. If he sorted a given item in the wrong category, corrective feedback was provided.

After sorting the items, both types of subjects who received word sets were tested for free recall.

The results indicated that free subjects were substantially lower in the number of trials-to-criterion, the time per trial, and the number of errors. In fact, almost half of the free subjects were able to employ a consistent categorization before they had actually examined all of the items. Most subjects in either group employed about four different categories.

Word recall was expectedly higher for the high frequency words, but no difference in recall occurred between the free and constrained conditions. Mandler and Pearlstone pointed out that the constrained group actually used more trials in sorting the items and might be expected to recall more items. However, equal recall occurred. Mandler and Pearlstone attributed this finding to the fact that the degree of organization, as measured by the number of categories used for sorting, was equal in the two conditions. On the assumption that recall is a function of the degree of organization, recall should be equal even if one condition had more study time than the other.

Their explanation for the higher performance by the free condition on the sorting task is similar to Hunt's account of superior performance in his selection condition. With a large number of alternative hypotheses, it is unlikely that the one selected by a free subject would coincide with the one adopted by a constrained subject. Support for this argument can be found in the fact that the 8–X condition led to the fastest performance for the free condition and the slowest performance for the constrained condition. When there were 8 Xs, more concepts or categorizations were possible. This factor serves to aid the free condition in forming clear-cut categorizations. On the other hand, the greater the number of possible categories, the less likely it is that the hypothesis selected by a free subject will coincide with that used by the constrained subject who receives his categorization.

Although mediational processes led to higher performance in concept than in rote learning, the level of concept learning depends on whether a selection or reception situation is employed. Perhaps the greater control the subject has over the sequence of stimulus events under the selection procedure leads to higher performance, since there is more opportunity for mediational processes to occur.

SUMMARY

Mediation refers to the processes which intervene between the presentation of a stimulus and the production of a response. The type of mediator that occurs to a given stimulus is determined by past associations. The mediator or implicit response which does occur to a given stimulus, in turn serves as an implicit stimulus that determines the type of overt response which will occur to it.

Although we have limited ourselves to verbal mediation, generally speaking, mediation is any process assumed to intervene between stimuli and responses. It could occur at any of several different levels, ranging from peripheral autonomic reactions, to imagery, to thinking. Mediational responses can be viewed as fractions of the responses originally made to the same stimulus at an earlier time. Their occurrence in the present situation may aid the formation of new associations between the stimulus and new responses.

In natural learning situations where connections must be formed between stimuli and responses, it may be assumed that mediational processes occur. However, they may vary from one person to another in kind and amount. Furthermore, there is no control over their occurrence or absence. The experimental investigation of mediation employs situations in which specific mediational responses can be predicted to lead to certain effects, if they occur. The parameters of mediation can be determined under standard test conditions.

The situation in the laboratory involves the formation of investigator-determined mediators, whereas natural learning situations involve the operation of mediators formed from past learning. In all likelihood, the latter variety are of greater strength.

The laboratory studies of mediation described in this section have been primarily concerned with the creation of mediational bonds in the laboratory. Other laboratory investigations concerned with mediation make use of preexperimentally established associations and mediators. The concern there is not with the formation of mediators, but with the use of mediators.

Controversy exists regarding the factors responsible for better performance in conditions where mediation is assumed to operate. Some investigators regard mediation effects as examples of associationistic conditioned responses, whereas others suggest that they involve cognitive concept learning.

In the final section, we examined mediational situations where two or more related stimuli have been associated with a common response. Although the ability to use concepts appears to be more complex than associative learning, evidence was found that suggested that rote learning is an integral component of cognitive behavior, especially during early stages of learning.

Concept behavior might also be considered as a situation in which there is positive transfer from previous learning to new learning. Whereas forgetting has been assumed to stem from interference between pre-experimental associations and new associations, concept behavior reflects the facilitation of performance on new material by preexperimental associations.

The learner plays an active role in applying his past learning to new situations so that he may identify concepts. He selects aspects of the stimuli to attend or ignore, notices similarities and differences among the stimuli and the responses to which they are paired, and formulates and tests hypotheses regarding the correct concept. However, behind this cognitive and organized behavior is a background of prior rote and associationistic learning acquired by the laws of frequency, similarity, and contiguity.

In our earlier analysis of rote learning, we included an examination of such cognitive factors as encoding, stimulus selection, and mediation. Here, the situation is reversed and our treatment of cognitive behavior includes consideration of associative factors. We arrive at a conclusion that both types of processes operate in so-called rote learning as well as in so-called concept learning. Rather than debate whether learning is associationistic or cognitive, we might more productively consider both types of mechanisms as aspects of learning.

References

Aaronson, D. Temporal factors in perception and short-term memory. *Psychological Bulletin*, 1967, **67**, 130–144.

Archer, E. J. A re-evaluation of the meaningfulness of all possible CVC trigrams. *Psychological Monographs*, 1960, **74** (10, Whole No. 497).

Arnoult, M. D. Stimulus predifferentiation: Some generalizations and hypotheses. *Psychological Bulletin*, 1957, **54**, 339–350.

Asch, S. E., and S. M. Ebenholtz. The principle of associative symmetry. *Proceedings of the American Philosophical Society*, 1962a, **106**, 135–163.

————, and ————. The process of free recall: Evidence for nonassociative factors in acquisition and retention. *Journal of Psychology*, 1962b, **54**, 3–31.

Atwater, S. K. Proactive inhibition and associative facilitation as affected by degree of prior learning. *Journal of Experimental Psychology*, 1953, **46**, 400–404.

Baddeley, A. D., and H. C. A. Dale. The effect of semantic similarity on retroactive interference in long- and short-term memory. *Journal of Verbal Learning and Verbal Behavior*, 1966, **5**, 417–420.

Bahrick, H. P. Retention curves: Facts or artifacts. *Psychological Bulletin*, 1964, **61**, 188–194.

Barnes, J. M., and B. J. Underwood. "Fate" of first-list associations in transfer theory. *Journal of Experimental Psychology*, 1959, **58**, 97–105.

Battig, W. F., M. Allen, and A. R. Jensen. Priority of free recall of newly learned items. *Journal of Verbal Learning and Verbal Behavior*, 1965, **4**, 175–179.

————, and H. R. Brackett. Comparison of anticipation and recall methods in paired-associate learning. *Psychological Reports*, 1961, **9**, 59–65.

————, S. C. Brown, and D. Nelson. Constant vs. varied serial order in paired-associate learning. *Psychological Reports*, 1963, **12**, 695–721.

Besch, N. F., and W. F. Reynolds. Associative interference in verbal paired-associative learning. *Journal of Experimental Psychology*, 1958, **55**, 554–558.

Bilodeau, E. A., P. W. Fox, and K. A. Blick. Stimulated verbal recall and analysis of sources of recall. *Journal of Verbal Learning and Verbal Behavior*, 1963, **2**, 422–428.

Bilodeau, I. McD., and H. Schlosberg. Similarity in stimulating conditions as a variable in retroactive inhibition. *Journal of Experimental Psychology*, 1951, **41**, 199–204.

Birnbaum, I. Long term retention of first-list associations in the A–B, A–C paradigm. *Journal of Verbal Learning and Verbal Behavior*, 1965, **4**, 515–520.

Bousfield, W. A. The occurrence of clustering in the recall of randomly arranged associates. *Journal of General Psychology*, 1953, **49**, 229–240.

————, and B. H. Cohen. The effects of reinforcement on the occurrence of clustering in the recall of randomly arranged associates. *Journal of Psychology*, 1953, **36**, 67–81.

————, and ————. The occurrence of clustering in the recall of randomly arranged words of different frequencies-of-usage. *Journal of General Psychology*, 1955, **52**, 83–95.

————, and ————. Clustering in recall as a function of the number of word-categories in stimulus-word lists. *Journal of General Psychology*, 1956, **54**, 95–106.

————, ————, and G. A. Whitmarsh. Associative clustering in the recall of words of different taxonomic frequencies of occurrence. *Psychological Reports*, 1958, **4**, 39–44.

Braun, H. W., and S. P. Heymann. Meaningfulness of material, distribution of practice, and serial position curves. *Journal of Experimental Psychology*, 1958, **56**, 146–150.

Briggs, G. E. Acquisition, extinction, and recovery functions in retroactive inhibition. *Journal of Experimental Psychology*, 1954, **47**, 285–293.

————. Retroactive inhibition as a function of the degree of original and interpolated learning. *Journal of Experimental Psychology*, 1957, **53**, 60–67.

Broadbent, D. E. *Perception and communication*. New York: Pergamon Press, 1958.

Bruce, R. W. Conditions of transfer of training. *Journal of Experimental Psychology*, 1933, **16**, 343–361.

Bugelski, B. R. Presentation time, total time, and mediation in paired-associate learning. *Journal of Experimental Psychology*, 1962, **63**, 409–412.

————, and T. G. Cadwallader. A reappraisal of the transfer and retroaction surface. *Journal of Experimental Psychology*, 1956, **52**, 360–366.

————, and D. P. Scharlock. An experimental demonstration of unconscious mediated association. *Journal of Experimental Psychology*, 1952, **44**, 334–338.

Cieutat, V. J., F. E. Stockwell, and C. E. Noble. The interaction of ability and amount of practice with stimulus and response meaningfulness (m, m') in paired-associate learning. *Journal of Experimental Psychology*, 1958, **56**, 193–202.

Cofer, C. N. On some factors in the organizational characteristics of free recall. *American Psychologist*, 1965, **20**, 261–272.

————. Some evidence for coding processes derived from clustering in free recall. *Journal of Verbal Learning and Verbal Behavior*, 1966, **5**, 188–192.

————, D. R. Bruce, and G. M. Reicher. Clustering in free recall as a function of certain methodological variations. *Journal of Experimental Psychology*, 1966, **71**, 858–866.

Cohen, B. H., W. A. Bousfield, and G. A. Whitmarsh. Cultural norms for verbal items in 43 categories. Technical Report No. 22 (1957), University of Connecticut, Contract Nonr 631 (00), Office of Naval Research.

Coleman, E. B. The association hierarchy as a measure of extraexperimental transfer. *Journal of Psychology*, 1964, **57**, 403–417.

Conrad, R. Acoustic confusions in immediate memory. *British Journal of Psychology*, 1964, **55**, 75–84.

————, and B. A. Hille. The decay theory of immediate memory. *Canadian Journal of Psychology*, 1958, **12**, 1–6.

Cook, J. O., and M. E. Spitzer. Supplementary report: Prompting versus confirmation in paired-associate learning. *Journal of Experimental Psychology*, 1960, **59**, 275–276.

Dallett, K. M. The transfer surface re-examined. *Journal of Verbal Learning and Verbal Behavior*, 1962, **1**, 91–94.

————. Implicit mediators in paired-associate learning. *Journal of Verbal Learning and Verbal Behavior*, 1964a, **3**, 209–214.

————. Number of categories and category information in free recall. *Journal of Experimental Psychology*, 1964b, **68**, 1–12.

Deese, J. Influence of inter-item associative strength upon immediate free recall. *Psychological Reports*, 1959, **5**, 305–312.

————. Frequency of usage and number of words in free recall: The role of association. *Psychological Reports*, 1960, **7**, 337–344.

————. From the isolated verbal unit to connected discourse. In C. N. Cofer (ed.), *Verbal learning and verbal behavior*. New York: McGraw-Hill, 1961.

————, and R. A. Kaufman. Serial effects in recall of unorganized and sequentially organized verbal material. *Journal of Experimental Psychology*, 1957, **54**, 180–187.

Earhard, B., and G. Mandler. Mediated associations: Paradigms, controls, and mechanisms. *Canadian Journal of Psychology*, 1965, **19**, 346–378.

Ebbinghaus, H. *Memory: A contribution to experimental psychology*. Tr. by Henry A. Roger and Clara E. Bussenius. New York: Dover, 1964.

Ebenholtz, S. M. Serial learning: Position learning and sequential associations. *Journal of Experimental Psychology*, 1963, **66**, 353–362.

Ekstrand, B. R. Backward associations. *Psychological Bulletin*, 1966, **65**, 50–64.

Epstein, W., and J. R. Platt. Free recall of paired associates as a function of meaningfulness. *Journal of Verbal Learning and Verbal Behavior*, 1964, **3**, 269–273.

————, and R. Streib. The effect of stimulus meaningfulness and response meaningfulness in the absence of response learning. *Journal of Verbal Learning and Verbal Behavior,* 1962, **1,** 105–108.

Estes, W. K. Learning theory and the new mental chemistry. *Psychological Review,* 1960, **67,** 207–223.

————, B. L. Hopkins, and E. J. Crothers. All-or-none and conservation effects in the learning and retention of paired associates. *Journal of Experimental Psychology,* 1960, **60,** 329–339.

Fallon, D., and W. F. Battig. Role of difficulty in rote and concept learning. *Journal of Experimental Psychology,* 1964, **68,** 85–88.

Gagné, R. M., H. Foster, and M. E. Crowley. The measurement of transfer of training. *Psychological Bulletin,* 1948, **45,** 97–130.

Gannon, D. R., and C. E. Noble. Familiarization (n) as a stimulus factor in paired-associate verbal learning. *Journal of Experimental Psychology,* 1961, **62,** 14–23.

Gibson, E. J. A systematic application of the concepts of generalization and differentiation to verbal learning. *Psychological Review,* 1940, **47,** 196–229.

————. Retroactive inhibition as a function of degree of generalization between tasks. *Journal of Experimental Psychology,* 1941, **28,** 93–115.

————. Intra-list generalization as a factor in verbal learning. *Journal of Experimental Psychology,* 1942, **30,** 185–200.

Glanzer, M., and A. R. Cunitz. Two storage mechanisms in free recall. *Journal of Verbal Learning and Verbal Behavior,* 1966, **5,** 351–360.

————, and S. C. Peters. Re-examination of the serial position effect. *Journal of Experimental Psychology,* 1962, **64,** 258–266.

Glaze, J. A. The association value of nonsense syllables. *Journal of Genetic Psychology,* 1928, **35,** 255–267.

Hamilton, R. J. Retroactive facilitation as a function of degree of generalization between tasks. *Journal of Experimental Psychology,* 1943, **32,** 363–376.

Hawker, J. R. The influence of training procedure and other task variables in paired-associate learning. *Journal of Verbal Learning and Verbal Behavior,* 1964, **3,** 70–76.

Hebb, D. O. *The organization of behavior.* New York: Wiley, 1949.

————. Distinctive features of learning in the higher animal. In J. F. Delafresnaye (ed.), *Brain mechanisms and learning.* London and New York: Oxford University Press, 1961, pp. 37–46.

Hellyer, S. Supplementary report: Frequency of stimulus presentation and short-term decrement in recall. *Journal of Experimental Psychology,* 1962, **64,** 650.

Horowitz, L. M. Free recall and ordering of trigrams. *Journal of Experimental Psychology,* 1961, **62,** 51–57.

Horton, D. L. The effects of meaningfulness, awareness, and type of design in verbal mediation. *Journal of Verbal Learning and Verbal Behavior,* 1964, **3,** 187–194.

————, and P. M. Kjeldergaard. An experimental analysis of associative factors in mediated generalization. *Psychological Monographs,* 1961, **75** (11, Whole No. 515).

————, D. Marlowe, and D. P. Crowne. The effect of instructional set and need for social approval on commonality of word association responses. *Journal of Abnormal and Social Psychology,* 1963, **66,** 67–72.

Houston, J. P. Ease of verbal S–R learning as a function of the number of mediating associations. *Journal of Verbal Learning and Verbal Behavior,* 1964a, **3**, 326–329.

———. S–R stimulus selection and strength of R–S associations. *Journal of Experimental Psychology,* 1964b, **68**, 563–566.

———. First-list retention and time and method of recall. *Journal of Experimental Psychology,* 1966, **71**, 839–843.

Hovland, C. I. Experimental studies in rote-learning theory: III. Distribution of practice with varying speeds of syllable presentation. *Journal of Experimental Psychology,* 1938, **23**, 172–190.

Hull, C. L. The meaningfulness of 320 selected nonsense syllables. *American Journal of Psychology,* 1933, **45**, 730–734.

———. The conflicting psychologies of learning—a way out. *Psychological Review,* 1935, **42**, 491–516.

Hunt, E. Selection and reception conditions in grammar and concept learning. *Journal of Verbal Learning and Verbal Behavior,* 1965, **4**, 211–215.

Hunt, R. G. Meaningfulness and articulation of stimulus and response in paired-associate learning and stimulus recall. *Journal of Experimental Psychology,* 1959, **57**, 262–267.

Irion, A. L. Rote learning. In S. Koch (ed.), *Psychology: A study of a science.* Vol. 2. New York: McGraw-Hill, 1959.

James, W. *The principles of psychology.* Vol. 1. New York: Henry Holt and Company, 1890.

Jantz, E. M., and B. J. Underwood. R–S learning as a function of meaningfulness and degree of S–R learning. *Journal of Experimental Psychology,* 1958, **56**, 174–179.

Jenkins, J. J. Comments on pseudomediation. *Psychonomic Science,* 1965, **2**, 97–98.

———. Mediated associations: Paradigms and situations. In C. N. Cofer and B. S. Musgrave (eds.), *Verbal behavior and learning.* New York: McGraw-Hill, 1963.

———, W. D. Mink, and W. A. Russell. Associative clustering as a function of verbal association strength. *Psychological Reports,* 1958, **4**, 127–136.

———, and W. A. Russell. Associative clustering during recall. *Journal of Abnormal and Social Psychology,* 1952, **47**, 818–821.

Jensen, A. R. An empirical theory of the serial-position effect. *Journal of Psychology,* 1962, **53**, 127–142.

Johnson, G. J., and R. K. Penney. The effect of mixed vs. unmixed list designs in paired-associate learning. *Journal of Verbal Learning and Verbal Behavior,* 1966, **5**, 234–239.

Jung, J. Transfer of training as a function of degree of first list learning. *Journal of Verbal Learning and Verbal Behavior,* 1962, **1**, 197–199.

———. Effects of response meaningfulness (m) on transfer of training under two different paradigms. *Journal of Experimental Psychology,* 1963, **65**, 377–384.

———. A cumulative method of paired-associate and serial learning. *Journal of Verbal Learning and Verbal Behavior,* 1964, **3**, 290–299.

———. Comments on Mandler's "From association to structure." *Psychological Review,* 1965a, **72**, 318–322.

———. Two stages of paired-associate learning as a function of intralist response similarity (IRS) and response meaningfulness (M). *Journal of Experimental Psychology,* 1965b, **70**, 371–378.

Jung, J. Experimental studies of factors affecting word associations. *Psychological Bulletin*, 1966, **66**, 125–133.

————, and S. Skeebo. Multi-trial free recall as a function of constant vs. varied input orders and list length. *Canadian Journal of Psychology*, 1967, **21**, 329–336.

Kausler, D. H., and E. P. Trapp. Motivation and cue utilization in intentional and incidental learning. *Psychological Review*, 1960, **67**, 373–379.

————, ————, and C. L. Brewer. Intentional and incidental learning under high and low emotional drive levels. *Journal of Experimental Psychology*, 1959, **58**, 452–455.

Kent, G. H., and A. J. Rosanoff. A study of association in insanity. *American Journal of Insanity*, 1910, **67**, 37–96, 317–390.

Keppel, G. Problems of method in the study of short-term memory. *Psychological Bulletin*, 1965, **63**, 1–13.

————. Retroactive and proactive inhibition. In T. S. Dixon and D. L. Horton (eds.), *Verbal behavior and general behavior theory*. Englewood Cliffs, N.J.: Prentice Hall, 1968.

————, and L. Postman. Studies of learning to learn: III. Conditions of improvement in successive transfer tasks. *Journal of Verbal Learning and Verbal Behavior*, 1966, **5**, 260–267.

————, and B. J. Underwood. Proactive inhibition in short-term retention of single items. *Journal of Verbal Learning and Verbal Behavior*, 1962, **1**, 153–161.

Kleinsmith, L. J., and S. Kaplan. Interaction of arousal and recall interval in nonsense syllable paired-associate learning. *Journal of Experimental Psychology*, 1964, **67**, 124–126.

Koppenaal, R. J. Time changes in the strengths of A–B, A–C lists: Spontaneous recovery? *Journal of Verbal Learning and Verbal Behavior*, 1963, **2**, 310–319.

Krueger, W. C. F. The relative difficulty of nonsense syllables. *Journal of Experimental Psychology*, 1934, **17**, 145–153.

L'Abate, L. Manifest anxiety and the learning of syllables with different associative values. *American Journal of Psychology*, 1959, **72**, 107–110.

Lepley, W. M. Serial reactions considered as conditioned reactions. *Psychological Monographs*, 1934, **46** (1, Whole No. 205).

Lippman, L. G., and M. R. Denny. Serial position effect as a function of intertrial interval. *Journal of Verbal Learning and Verbal Behavior*, 1964, **3**, 496–501.

Lockhead, G. R. Methods of presenting paired associates. *Journal of Verbal Learning and Verbal Behavior*, 1962, **1**, 62–65.

Luh, C. W. The conditions of retention. *Psychological Monographs*, 1922, **31** (Whole No. 142).

Mackworth, J. F. Presentation rate and memory. *Canadian Journal of Psychology*, 1962a, **16**, 42–47.

————.The visual image and the memory trace. *Canadian Journal of Psychology*, 1962b, **16**, 55–59.

Mandler, G. From association to structure. *Psychological Review*, 1962, **69**, 415–427.

————. Comments on Professor Jenkin's paper. In C. N. Cofer and B. S. Musgrave (eds.), *Verbal behavior and learning*. New York: McGraw-Hill, 1963.

Mandler, G. Subjects do think: A reply to Jung's comments. *Psychological Review*, 1965, **72**, 323–326.

———, and B. Earhard. Pseudomediation: Is chaining an artifact? *Psychonomic Science*, 1964, **1**, 247–248.

———, and Z. Pearlstone. Free and constrained concept learning and subsequent recall. *Journal of Verbal Learning and Verbal Behavior*, 1966, **5**, 126–131.

Marshall, G. R. The organization of verbal material in free recall: The effects of patterns of associative overlap on clustering. Unpublished Ph.D. dissertation. New York University, 1963.

———, and C. N. Cofer. Associative indices as measures of word relatedness: A summary and comparison of ten methods. *Journal of Verbal Learning and Verbal Behavior*, 1963, **1**, 408–421.

Martin, C. J., and E. Saltz. Serial versus random presentation of paired associates. *Journal of Experimental Psychology*, 1963, **65**, 609–615.

Martin, E. Transfer of verbal paired associates. *Psychological Review*, 1965, **72**, 327–343.

Mathews, R. Recall as a function of number of classificatory categories. *Journal of Experimental Psychology*, 1954, **47**, 241–247.

McCrary, J. W., Jr., and W. S. Hunter. Serial position curves in verbal learning. *Science*, 1953, **117**, 131–134.

McGeoch, J. A., and A. L. Irion. *The psychology of human learning*. Sec. Edit. New York: Longmans, Green, 1952.

———, and B. J. Underwood. Tests of the two-factor theory of retroactive inhibition. *Journal of Experimental Psychology*, 1943, **32**, 1–16.

McGovern, J. B. Extinction of associations in four transfer paradigms. *Psychological Monographs*, 1964, **78** (16, Whole No. 593).

McGuire, W. J. A multiprocess model for paired-associate learning. *Journal of Experimental Psychology*, 1961, **62**, 335–347.

McLaughlin, B. "Intentional" and "incidental" learning in human subjects. *Psychological Bulletin*, 1965, **63**, 359–376.

McNulty, J. A. An analysis of recall and recognition process in verbal learning. *Journal of Verbal Learning and Verbal Behavior*, 1965, **4**, 430–436.

Mechanic, A. The responses involved in the rote learning of verbal materials. *Journal of Verbal Learning and Verbal Behavior*, 1964, **3**, 30–36.

Melton, A. W. Implications of short-term memory for a general theory of memory. *Journal of Verbal Learning and Verbal Behavior*, 1963, **2**, 1–21.

———, and J. M. Irwin. The influence of degree of interpolated learning on retroactive inhibition and the overt transfer of specific responses. *American Journal of Psychology*, 1940, **53**, 173–203.

Merikle, P. M., and W. F. Battig. Transfer of training as a function of experimental paradigm and meaningfulness. *Journal of Verbal Learning and Verbal Behavior*, 1963, **2**, 485–488.

Metzger, R. A comparison between rote learning and concept formation. *Journal of Experimental Psychology*, 1958, **56**, 226–231.

Miller, G. A. The magical number seven plus or minus two: Some limits on our capacity for processing information. *Psychological Review*, 1956, **63**, 81–97.

———, E. Galanter, and K. H. Pribram. *Plans and the structure of behavior*. New York: Holt, Rinehart and Winston, 1960.

Miller, G. A., and J. A. Selfridge. Verbal context and the recall of meaningful material. *American Journal of Psychology*, 1950, **63**, 176–185.

Montague, W. E., J. A. Adams, and H. O. Kiess. Forgetting and natural language mediation. *Journal of Experimental Psychology*, 1966, **72**, 829–833.

Murdock, B. B., Jr. Transfer designs and formulas. *Psychological Bulletin*, 1957, **54**, 313–326.

————. The immediate retention of unrelated words. *Journal of Experimental Psychology*, 1960, **60**, 222–234.

————. The retention of individual items. *Journal of Experimental Psychology*, 1961, **62**, 618–625.

————. The serial position effect of free recall. *Journal of Experimental Psychology*, 1962, **64**, 482–488.

————. Proactive inhibition in short-term memory. *Journal of Experimental Psychology*, 1964, **68**, 184–189.

Newman, S. E., and E. Saltz. Serial position as a cue in learning. *American Journal of Psychology*, 1962, **75**, 102–108.

Noble, C. E. An analysis of meaning. *Psychological Review*, 1952a, **59**, 421–430.

————. The role of stimulus meaning (m) in serial verbal learning. *Journal of Experimental Psychology*, 1952b, **43**, 437–446.

————, and D. A. McNeely. The role of meaningfulness (m) in paired-associate verbal learning. *Journal of Experimental Psychology*, 1957, **53**, 16–22.

Osgood, C. E. The similarity paradox in human learning: A resolution. *Psychological Review*, 1949, **56**, 132–143.

Palermo, D. S., and J. J. Jenkins. *Word association norms: Grade school through college.* Minneapolis: University of Minnesota Press, 1964.

Peterson, L. R., and M. J. Peterson. Short-term retention of individual verbal items. *Journal of Experimental Psychology*, 1959, **58**, 193–198.

Peterson, M. J., F. B. Colavita, D. B. Sheahan, III, and K. C. Blattner. Verbal mediating chains and response availability as a function of the acquisition paradigm. *Journal of Verbal Learning and Verbal Behavior*, 1964, **3**, 11–18.

Pollack, I., L. B. Johnson, and P. R. Knaff. Running memory span. *Journal of Experimental Psychology*, 1959, **57**, 137–146.

Porter, L. W., and C. P. Duncan. Negative transfer in verbal learning. *Journal of Experimental Psychology*, 1953, **46**, 61–64.

Postman, L. Extra-experimental interference and the retention of words. *Journal of Experimental Psychology*, 1961a, **61**, 97–110.

————. The present status of interference theory. In C. N. Cofer (ed.), *Verbal learning and verbal behavior.* New York: McGraw-Hill, 1961b.

————. The effects of language habits on the acquisition and retention of verbal associations. *Journal of Experimental Psychology*, 1962a, **64**, 7–19.

————. Repetition and paired-associate learning. *American Journal of Psychology*, 1962b, **75**, 372–389.

————. Transfer of training as a function of experimental paradigm and degree of first-list learning. *Journal of Verbal Learning and Verbal Behavior*, 1962c, **1**, 109–118.

————. Does interference theory predict too much forgetting? *Journal of Verbal Learning and Verbal Behavior*, 1963a, **2**, 40–48.

Postman, L. One-trial learning. In C. N. Cofer and B. S. Musgrave (eds.), *Verbal behavior and learning.* New York: McGraw-Hill, 1963*b*.

———, Short-term memory and incidental learning. In A. W. Melton (ed.), *Categories of human learning.* New York: Academic Press, 1964*a*.

———. Studies of learning to learn: II. Changes in transfer as a function of practice. *Journal of Verbal Learning and Verbal Behavior,* 1964*b*, **3**, 437–447.

———, P. A. Adams, and L. W. Phillips. Studies in incidental learning: II. The effect of association value and of the method of testing. *Journal of Experimental Psychology,* 1955, **49**, 1–10.

———, and J. Goggin. Whole versus part learning of serial lists as a function of meaningfulness and intralist similarity. *Journal of Experimental Psychology,* 1964, **68**, 140–150.

———, and ———. Whole versus part learning of paired-associate lists. *Journal of Experimental Psychology,* 1966, **71**, 867–877.

———, W. O. Jenkins, and D. L. Postman. An experimental comparison of active recall and recognition. *American Journal of Psychology,* 1948, **61**, 511–519.

———, and L. W. Phillips. Studies in incidental learning: IX. A comparison of the methods of successive and single recall. *Journal of Experimental Psychology,* 1961, **61**, 236–241.

———, and ———. Short-term temporal changes in free recall. *Quarterly Journal of Experimental Psychology,* 1965, **17**, 132–138.

———, and L. Rau. Retention as a function of the method of measurement. *University of California Publications in Psychology,* 1957, **8**, 217–270.

———, and M. Schwartz. Studies of learning to learn: I. Transfer as a function of method of practice and class of verbal materials. *Journal of Verbal Learning and Verbal Behavior,* 1964, **3**, 37–49.

———, and V. L. Senders. Incidental learning and generality of set. *Journal of Experimental Psychology,* 1946, **36**, 153–165.

Rock, I. The role of repetition in associative learning. *American Journal of Psychology,* 1957, **70**, 186–193.

Rothkopf, E. Z., and E. U. Coke. The prediction of free recall from word association measures. *Journal of Experimental Psychology,* 1961, **62**, 433–438.

Russell, W. A., and J. J. Jenkins. The complete Minnesota norms for responses to 100 words from the Kent–Rosanoff Word Association Test. Technical Report No. 11 Contract N8 ONR-66216 (1954).

———, and L. H. Storms. Implicit verbal chaining in paired-associate learning. *Journal of Experimental Psychology,* 1955, **49**, 287–293.

Saltz, E. Spontaneous recovery of letter-sequence habits. *Journal of Experimental Psychology,* 1965, **69**, 304–307.

Schulz, R. W., and I. F. Tucker. Supplementary report: Stimulus familiarization in paired-associate learning. *Journal of Experimental Psychology,* 1962, **64**, 549–550.

———, G. E. Weaver, and S. Ginsberg. Mediation with pseudomediation controlled: Chaining is not an artifact! *Psychonomic Science,* 1965, **2**, 169–170.

Schwartz, H. A. Influence of instructional set and response frequency on retroactive interference. *Journal of Experimental Psychology,* 1963, **66**, 127–132.

Sheffield, F. D. The role of meaningfulness of stimulus and response in verbal learning. Unpublished doctoral dissertation, Yale University, 1946.

Siipola, E., W. N. Walker, and D. Kolb. Task attitudes in word association, projective and nonprojective. *Journal of Personality*, 1955, **23**, 441–459.

Silverstein, A. Unlearning, spontaneous recovery, and the partial reinforcement effect in paired-associate learning. *Journal of Experimental Psychology*, 1967, **73**, 15–21.

Slamecka, N. J. Differentiation versus unlearning of verbal associations. *Journal of Experimental Psychology*, 1966a, **71**, 822–828.

————. Supplementary report: A search for spontaneous recovery of verbal associations. *Journal of Verbal Learning and Verbal Behavior*, 1966b, **5**, 205–207.

Smith, T. A., L. V. Jones, and S. Thomas. Effects upon verbal learning of stimulus similarity, number of stimuli per response, and concept formation. *Journal of Verbal Learning and Verbal Behavior*, 1963, **1**, 470–476.

Spear, N. E., B. R. Ekstrand, and B. J. Underwood. Association by contiguity. *Journal of Experimental Psychology*, 1964, **67**, 151–161.

Spence, J. T., and R. W. Schulz. Negative transfer in paired-associate learning as a function of first-list trials. *Journal of Verbal Learning and Verbal Behavior*, 1965, **4**, 397–400.

Spence, K. W. A theory of emotionally based drive (D) and its relations to performance in simple learning situations. *American Psychologist*, 1958, **13**, 131–141.

————, I. E. Farber, and H. H. McFann. The relation of anxiety (drive) level to performance in competitional and non-competitional paired-associate learning. *Journal of Experimental Psychology*, 1956, **52**, 296–305.

Sperling, G. The information available in brief visual presentations. *Psychological Monographs*, 1960, **74** (11, Whole No. 498).

Spielberger, C. D. Theoretical and epistemological issues in verbal conditioning. In S. Rosenberg (ed.), *Directions in psycholinguistics*. New York: Macmillan, 1965, pp. 149–200.

Standish, R. L., and R. A. Champion. Task difficulty and drive in verbal learning. *Journal of Experimental Psychology*, 1960, **59**, 361–365.

Thorndike, E. L., and I. Lorge. *The teacher's word book of 30,000 words*. New York: Columbia University Press, 1944.

————, and R. S. Woodworth. The influence of improvement in one mental function upon the efficiency of other functions. (I) II. The estimation of magnitudes; III. Functions involving attention, observation, and discrimination. *Psychological Review*, 1901, **8**, 247–261, 384–395, 553–564.

Thune, L. E. Warm-up effect as a function of level of practice in verbal learning. *Journal of Experimental Psychology*, 1951, **42**, 250–256.

Tulving, E. Subjective organization in free recall of "unrelated" words. *Psychological Review*, 1962, **69**, 344–354.

————. Theoretical issues in free recall. In T. R. Dixon and D. L. Horton (eds.), *Verbal behavior and general behavior theory*. Englewood Cliffs, N.J.: Prentice-Hall, 1968.

————, and T. Y. Arbuckle. Sources of intratrial interference in immediate recall of paired associates. *Journal of Verbal Learning and Verbal Behavior*, 1963, **1**, 321–334.

————, and Z. Pearlstone. Availability versus accessibility of information in memory for words. *Journal of Verbal Learning and Verbal Behavior,* 1966, **5,** 381–391.

Twedt, H. M., and B. J. Underwood. Mixed vs. unmixed lists in transfer studies. *Journal of Experimental Psychology,* 1959, **58,** 111–116.

Underwood, B. J. Retroactive and proactive inhibition after five and forty-eight hours. *Journal of Experimental Psychology,* 1948, **38,** 29–38.

————. Associative transfer in verbal learning as a function of response similarity and degree of first-list learning. *Journal of Experimental Psychology,* 1951, **42,** 44–53.

————. Studies of distributed practice: VII. Learning and retention of serial nonsense lists as a function of intralist similarity. *Journal of Experimental Psychology,* 1952, **44,** 80–87.

————. Speed of learning and amount retained: A consideration of methodology. *Psychological Bulletin,* 1954, **51,** 276–282.

————. Interference and forgetting. *Psychological Review,* 1957, **64,** 49–60.

————. An evaluation of the Gibson theory of verbal learning. In C. N. Cofer (ed.), *Verbal learning and verbal behavior.* New York: McGraw-Hill, 1961.

————. Degree of learning and the measurement of forgetting. *Journal of Verbal Learning and Verbal Behavior,* 1964a, **3,** 112–129.

————. The representativeness of rote verbal learning. In A. W. Melton (ed.), *Categories of human learning.* New York: Academic Press, 1964b.

————, and B. R. Ekstrand. An analysis of some shortcomings in the interference theory of forgetting. *Psychological Review,* 1966, **73,** 540–549.

————, ————, and G. Keppel. Studies of distributed practice: XXIII. Variations in response-term interference. *Journal of Experimental Psychology,* 1964, **68,** 201–212.

————, and A. H. Erlebacher. Studies of coding in verbal learning. *Psychological Monographs,* 1965, **79** (13, Whole No. 606).

————, M. Ham, and B. R. Ekstrand. Cue selection in paired-associate learning. *Journal of Experimental Psychology,* 1962, **64,** 405–409.

————, and G. Keppel. Coding processes in verbal learning. *Journal of Verbal Learning and Verbal Behavior,* 1962a, **1,** 250–257.

————, and ————. One trial learning? *Journal of Verbal Learning and Verbal Behavior,* 1962b, **1,** 1–13.

————, and ————. Retention as a function of degree of learning and letter-sequence interference. *Psychological Monographs,* 1963, **77** (4, Whole No. 567).

————, and L. Postman. Extra-experimental sources of interference in forgetting. *Psychological Review,* 1960, **67,** 73–95.

————, R. Rehula, and G. Keppel. Item selection in paired-associate learning. *American Journal of Psychology,* 1962, **75,** 353–371.

————, and J. Richardson. Some verbal materials for the study of concept formation. *Psychological Bulletin,* 1956a, **53,** 84–95.

————, and ————. Verbal concept learning as a function of instructions and dominance level. *Journal of Experimental Psychology,* 1956b, **51,** 229–238.

————, W. N. Runquist, and R. W. Schulz. Response learning in paired-associate lists as a function of intralist similarity. *Journal of Experimental Psychology,* 1959, **58,** 70–78.

————, and R. W. Schulz. *Meaningfulness and verbal learning.* Philadelphia: Lippincott, 1960.

Walker, E. L., and R. D. Tarte. Memory storage as a function of arousal and time with homogeneous and heterogeneous lists. *Journal of Verbal Learning and Verbal Behavior,* 1963, **2,** 113–119.

Waugh, N. C. Free versus serial recall. *Journal of Experimental Psychology,* 1961, **62,,** 496–502.

———, and D. A. Norman. Primary memory. *Psychological Review,* 1965, **72,** 89–104.

Weiner, B., and E. L. Walker. Motivational factors in short-term memory. *Journal of Experimental Psychology,* 1966, **71,** 190–193.

Weiss, W., and G. Margolius. The effect of context stimuli on learning and retention. *Journal of Experimental Psychology,* 1954, **48,** 318–322.

Wickelgren, W. A. Acoustic similarity and retroactive interference in short-term memory. *Journal of Verbal Learning and Verbal Behavior,* 1965, **4,** 53–61.

Wimer, R. Osgood's transfer surface: Extension and test. *Journal of Verbal Learning and Verbal Behavior,* 1964, **3,** 274–279.

Witmer, L. R. The association value of three-place consonant syllables. *Journal of Genetic Psychology,* 1935, **47,** 337–360.

Wynne, R. D., H. Gerjuoy, and H. Schiffman. Association test antonym-response set. *Journal of Verbal Learning and Verbal Behavior,* 1965, **4,** 354–359.

Young, R. K. Tests of three hypotheses about the effective stimulus in serial learning. *Journal of Experimental Psychology,* 1962, **63,** 307–313.

———, and B. J. Underwood. Transfer in verbal materials with dissimilar stimuli and response similarity varied. *Journal of Experimental Psychology,* 1954, **47,** 153–159.

Yum, K. S. An experimental test of the law of assimilation. *Journal of Experimental Psychology,* 1931, **14,** 68–82.

Author Index

205

Subject Index